lop

Gender Relations in Early Modern England

2 JAN 2024

Gender Relations in Early Modern England

Laura Gowing

PEARSON

Harlow, England • London • New York • Boston • San Francisco • Toronto • Sydney • Auckland • Singapore • Hong Kong
Tokyo • Seoul • Taipei • New Delhi • Cape Town • São Paulo • Mexico City • Madrid • Amsterdam • Munich • Paris • Milan

PEARSON EDUCATION LIMITED

Edinburgh Gate
Harlow CM20 2JE
United Kingdom
Tel: +44 (0)1279 623623
Fax: +44 (0)1279 431059
Website: www.pearson.com/uk

First edition published in Great Britain in 2012

The right of Laura Gowing to be identified as author of this work has been asserted
by her in accordance with the Copyright, Designs and Patents Act 1988.

Pearson Education is not responsible for the content of third-party internet sites.

ISBN: 978-1-4082-2568-4

British Library Cataloguing in Publication Data
A CIP catalogue record for this book can be obtained from the British Library

Library of Congress Cataloging in Publication Data
Gowing, Laura.
   Gender relations in early modern England / Laura Gowing.
      p. cm.
   Includes bibliographical references and index.
   ISBN: 978-1-4082-2568-4 (pbk.)
      1. Women--England--Social conditions--16th century.   2. Women--England--
Social conditions--17th century.   3. Sex role--England--History--16th century.
4. Sex role--England--History--17th century.   I. Title.
      HQ1149.G7G69 2012
      305.4094209′031--dc23

                                                                              2011050349

10 9 8 7 6 5 4 3 2 1
16 15 14 13 12

Set in 10/13.5pt Berkeley Book by 35
Printed and bound in Malaysia, CTP-KHL

Introduction to the series

History is narrative constructed by historians from traces left by the past. Historical enquiry is often driven by contemporary issues and, in consequence, historical narratives are constantly reconsidered, reconstructed and reshaped. The fact that different historians have different perspectives on issues means that there is also often controversy and no universally agreed version of past events. *Seminar Studies* was designed to bridge the gap between current research and debate, and the broad, popular general surveys that often date rapidly.

The volumes in the series are written by historians who are not only familiar with the latest research and current debates concerning their topic, but who have themselves contributed to our understanding of the subject. The books are intended to provide the reader with a clear introduction to a major topic in history. They provide both a narrative of events and a critical analysis of contemporary interpretations. They include the kinds of tools generally omitted from specialist monographs: a chronology of events, a glossary of terms and brief biographies of 'who's who'. They also include bibliographical essays in order to guide students to the literature on various aspects of the subject. Students and teachers alike will find that the selection of documents will stimulate discussion and offer insight into the raw materials used by historians in their attempt to understand the past.

Clive Emsley and Gordon Martel
Series Editors

Contents

Publisher's acknowledgements

We are grateful to the following for permission to reproduce copyright material:

Plates
Plate 1 © Hatfield House, Hertfordshire, UK/The Bridgeman Art Library; Plate 2 © Lebrecht Music and Arts Photo Library/Alamy; Plate 3 © NTPL/ W H Rendell; Plate 4 © Abbot Hall Art Gallery, Kendal, Cumbria, UK/The Bridgeman Art Library; Plate 5 © National Maritime Museum, Greenwich, UK; Plates 6, 7 and 8 © The Trustees of The British Museum. All rights reserved; Plate 9 © The British Library Board. Shelfmark 669.f.23(36); Plate 10 © The Pepys Library, Magdalene College, Cambridge.

Text
Documents 1, 29 and 67 from *The King James Bible*. The Authorized Version of the Bible (*The King James Bible*), the rights in which are vested in the Crown, are reproduced with permission of the Crown's Patentee, Cambridge University Press; Document 4 from the Midwives Book by Jane Sharp, Edited by Elaine Hobby (1999): Extract totalling 466 words from Book 1, Chptr XII and Book II By Permission of Oxford University Press, Inc.; Document 24 from *The Diary of Ralph Josselin 1616–1683*, Oxford University Press (McFarlane, A. (ed.) 1976). © The British Academy 1976, reproduced with permission; Document 39 from *The Remembrances of Elizabeth Freke, 1671–1714* (Anselment, R.A. (ed.) 2001), Camden Fifth Series, Volume 18, © Royal Historical Society 2001, published by Cambridge University Press, reproduced with permission of Cambridge University Press and R.A. Anselment.

In some instances we have been unable to trace the owners of copyright material, and we would appreciate any information that would enable us to do so.

Chronology

1509   Accession of Henry VIII

1527   Divorce crisis begins

1533   Act against Buggery

1536   Dissolution of Monasteries

1538   Registration of Births, Deaths and Marriages begins

1547   Accession of Edward VI

1553   Accession of Mary I

1563   Statute of Artificers

1569   Northern Rebellion

1576   Poor Law, including provisions for punishing bastard bearers

1585   Accession of Elizabeth I

1587   Execution of Mary Queen of Scots

1588   Spanish Armada defeated

1594   Bad harvests begin

1598   First edition of Robert Cleaver's *Godly Form of Household Government*

1601   Elizabethan Poor Law

1603   Accession of James VI of Scotland and I of England, married to Anne of Denmark

1611   Publication of King James Bible

1617–29   Buckingham's ascendancy

1623   Infanticide Act

1625   Accession of Charles I, married to Henrietta Maria

1629–40   Charles I's personal rule

1640   Long Parliament starts

1641   Rebellion of Ulster Catholics

1642   Civil War breaks out; disestablishment of Church of England and abolition of church courts

1642–6 First Civil War

1648–9 Second Civil War; execution of Charles I

1650   Adultery made capital offence

1651   Parliamentary Victory

1653   Commonwealth: Oliver Cromwell Lord Protector, married to Elizabeth Cromwell

1658   Death of Oliver Cromwell

1660   Restoration of Charles II, married to Catherine of Braganza

1679–81 Exclusion Crisis

1685   Accession of James II, married to 1. Anne Hyde 2. Mary of Modena

1688   Warming Pan Scandal

1688   Glorious Revolution

1689   Coronation of William III and Mary II

1694   Death of Mary II; William ruled alone

1702   Accession of Anne

Who's who

Mary Astell (1666–1731): writer of feminist and other tracts, Anglican and Tory, single, educated at home, daughter of a Newcastle coal merchant.

Elizabeth Barton (c.1506–34): called the 'Nun of Kent'; Benedictine nun and visionary, previously a farm servant; prophesied that Henry VIII's proposed divorce from Katherine of Aragon would be the end of his reign; eventually executed.

Margaret Cavendish (1623–73): aristocrat writer and scientist; royalist; married William Cavendish; wrote poetry, natural philosophy, science fiction and memoir.

Elizabeth Cellier (fl. 1668–88): known as the Popish Midwife, she was implicated in 1679 in the 'Meal Tub Plot' against the future James II and acquitted on trial for treason. Her published self-defence led to another trial and the pillory. She later published a plan for a corporation of midwives.

Sarah Churchill, née Jenyns, Duchess of Marlborough (1660–1744): Lady of the Bedchamber to Queen Anne; married Edward Churchill; Whig.

Lady Anne Clifford (1590–1676): Baroness, diarist, involved in extensive lawsuit over her inheritance; educated by tutor; married Richard Sackville and Edward Herbert.

Sir Edward Coke (1552–1634): Lord Chief Justice under James I; jurist, MP, defender of the common law; married Bridget Paston.

Nicholas Culpeper (1616–54): herbalist and astrologer; radical, parliamentarian; married Alice Field.

Moll Cutpurse (Mary Frith) (1584–1659): infamous thief, the subject of plays and stories.

Sir Simonds D'Ewes (1602–50): diarist, antiquary, high sheriff of Suffolk; married Anne Clopton.

Joyce Jeffries (c.1570–1650): moneylender, diarist; single.

William Laud (1573–1645): Archbishop of Canterbury 1633–45, architect and enforcer of Charles I's religious policies.

Abigail Masham, née Hill, Lady Masham (1670–1734): favourite of Queen Anne, whose household she joined in 1700; Tory; married Samuel Masham.

Samuel Pepys (1633–1703): diarist, naval administrator and MP; married Elizabeth de St Michel.

John Pym (1584–1643): leader of the Long Parliament; married Anne Hooke.

Glossary

£, s., d.: Pounds, shillings, pence. 12 d. = 1 shilling; 20 shillings = £1.

Assizes: Periodic criminal courts for the most serious offences.

Bridewell: London: Converted from a palace to a prison and poorhouse in 1566.

Benefit of clergy: A legal fiction by which, after 1575, a felon capable of reading a verse from the Bible could be excused hanging.

Charivari: Ritual of community censure, often involving 'rough music' with pots and pans.

Church courts: Courts enforcing canon law via litigation or disciplinary prosecutions, overseen by bishop.

Churchwardens: Elected unpaid lay officials of each parish, responsible for law and order in the church, poor relief and church maintenance.

Constable: Unpaid parish official, working at the orders of justices of the peace.

Coverture: The common law doctrine whereby a married woman's legal identity was subsumed under that of her husband.

Curse of Ham: Noah's curse on Ham's sons after Ham 'saw his father's nakedness'; used as a justification for slavery, with Black Africans interpreted as Ham's descendants.

Feme sole: Legal status of single woman.

Groat: Four pence.

Hearth tax: Imposed in 1662, at a rate of 2s. per hearth per year.

Homily: Printed sermons provided to be read to congregations.

Jury of matrons: Women appointed to search female felons for the proof of pregnancy, in which case execution would be delayed.

Mosaic law: Laws attributed to Moses, set out in the first five books of the Old Testament.

Proper goods of a wife: Paraphernalia.

Protestation Oaths: Oaths of allegiance to the Commonwealth.

Puritans: Protestants advocating greater purity of doctrine and worship.

Quakers: The Religious Society of Friends, founded late 1640s by George Fox, in the conviction that individual relationships with Christ could bypass the mediation of church and clergy.

Quarter sessions: Criminal courts held quarterly for lesser offences.

Ranters: Heretical sect of the Revolutionary period, seen as a threat to social order.

Recusancy: Refusal to attend church services.

Savin: Also known as pennyroyal, a herbal abortifacient.

Societies for the Reformation of Manners: Began in London in 1691, mobilising associations of gentlemen, tradesmen, constables and informers to prosecute vice.

Terms: Menstrual periods.

Tories: Opponents of Exclusion; monarchists; supporters of the Church of England.

Whigs: Originally those supporting the Exclusion of the Duke of York, eventually James II, from the throne in 1679–81.

Part 1

ANALYSIS

Introduction

Gender relations

What did it mean to be a woman or a man in early modern England?

It is a founding principle of gender studies that the gender order is not fixed: it is historical and local. In different places, at different times, the relationships between women and men, the ideals that gender roles are measured against and the assumptions of daily social relations are variable. The temporality of gender offers up the knowledge of a past and the promise of change.

The period 1500–1700 was a time of transformations: politically, culturally, economically and socially, a series of seismic shifts and subtler readjustments laid the foundations for the modern world. One of the abiding questions for early modern gender historians is that of narratives of change: the question first asked in 1977 by Joan Kelly as 'Did women have a Renaissance?' has been reformulated to consider the impact of the Reformation, the Civil War and the Revolution of 1688 on gender relations (Kelly-Gadol, 1977). Most recently Merry Wiesner-Hanks has argued that gender is central to the concept 'early modern' and the narrative of modernity which, sometimes problematically, it presupposes. To take three exemplary factors: social discipline, military change and global interactions were all gendered in their nature and impact (Wiesner-Hanks, 2008).

To reframe the subjects of history is one endeavour. A further step is to realise the force of gender at every level of historical interpretation. Gender differentiated the impact of political and social changes, and; as a cultural category, it was also subject to change itself. As rhetoric and symbol, it permeated discourses and social rituals.

By their very nature, the codes of gender relations seem implicit and unconscious: that is their power. They are hard to historicise; familiar patterns always stand out more clearly. Behind the recognisable outlines of sexual relations and marriage, a different apparatus can be discerned. Sexual difference was understood through a body shaped by humours. Marriage was based on the economic and social configurations of a pre-industrial world. Morality took biblical texts as its basis. The contours of the self were formed around collectivity and embeddedness. And yet, before modern understandings about sexual difference had been established, some of the conditions of modern gender relations were already in place. Determining what supported them is one of the tasks for historians of gender.

Gender is always relational. The last hundred years have seen a series of waves of history concerned with interested in women, sex and gender: the interest in how women and men were defined, how they related to each other and how the status and experience of women as the subordinate party in a patriarchal order changed over time have been common to most. The terminology and methodology of gender history offers its practitioners now a range of useful ways forward. The term 'gender' is itself a modern and contested one. It depends on a distinction between biological sex and cultural gender which was crucial to feminism, but which was not made by historians of a hundred years ago, and which does not necessarily describe the way sexual difference was understood before about 1750. Patriarchy is another essential term to feminist analysis, describing the system of power relations that subordinates women to men; but it is useful to separate its generic feminist usage from the specific meaning of patriarchalism as a political theory in the early modern period. As a social, political and economic system, patriarchy has dividends for those cast as winners – generally, men; but it also binds everyone caught in its net. Within that system, individual men can of course be subordinate to particular women: the relations between sons and mothers, apprentices and mistresses are as significant as those between husbands and wives. So are those between women and between men, in which gendered power was further differentiated by rank, age and marital status. Our subjects are understood in terms of gendered norms. Masculinity and femininity are modern terms to describe these; the nearest early modern equivalents are manhood and womanhood, which have specific associations of adulthood. Yet a current critical language is essential to historicise the often implicit codes of gender.

The history of gender relations draws on uneven sets of evidence, narratives and arguments. The recovery of women's history is still underway. Most early modern sources require careful reading to elicit from them the history of women, as well as the history of non-elites. The history of men, by contrast, is ubiquitous, but it has rarely been written with an eye to gender. The history of early modern masculinity is presently composed of a more social history of the pre-1660 period, and a more cultural history of the later period: comparisons and long narratives are still problematic (Harvey and Shepard, 2005).

Part of the code of gender is that women carry it and men do not: men are the norm against which everything else is measured. Compared to the often blindingly clear rules of femininity, those of masculinity are often less immediately apparent. The sociological concept of hegemonic masculinity has been useful in delineating the way particular qualities and achievements support men's authority: in early modern England, self-sufficiency and successful householding would be the most identifiable aspects. The economic and social pressures of the late sixteenth century left many men unable to attain those ends and the result seems to have been a wider set of masculinities, sometimes in tension with each other. Early modern popular culture often makes men's power look absurdly vulnerable, at risk from the promiscuity of women, impotence and cuckoldry. Mark Breitenberg has suggested masculinity is 'inherently anxious'; beneath the abstractions of order that laid down the laws of early modern gender relations seethed a cauldron of chaotic fears and vulnerabilities (Breitenberg, 1996: 2). Masculinity and femininity were both, in their different ways, unattainable ideals. Perhaps men's power was not founded on a successful achievement of manhood, but forged in the struggle to get there. Women's subordination, too, was produced and mediated through the interaction between precept and practice. The gender history of recent years has established both the power of a restrictive system, and the enterprise with which women, in particular, established agency within it.

This book deals with gender relations in England between c.1500 and 1700. Neither the period nor the place should be viewed in isolation. England's gender structure was hardly unique: much of it was recognisable across Europe, and common to other parts of Britain and Ireland, though the legal, economic, religious and social structures through which gender relations were manifested varied widely between regions and kingdoms. The border interactions between England, Scotland and Wales, and the colonial relationship with Ireland were themselves constitutive of gender relations. England itself is not a cohesive subject for the history of gender, with agricultural regions and urban/rural differences making a visible impact on how gender rules were enforced. The chapters that follow are organised around spaces. The history of space and place demands the dimension of gender. While early modern England was characteristically a heterosocial world, a legion of prescriptions about how women and men occupied space helped frame gender codes. The principle that women's world was indoors, men's outdoors was unrealistic but powerful; the enclosure of women's bodies had an impact beyond the rhetorical. The related distinction between a male public sphere and a female private world has been traced to the late seventeenth century, though it remains rightly contested. Gender history demands a dialogue between prescription and practice: both the recreation of the cultural landscape, and the reconstruction of how structures and figures moved within that landscape, changing its features as they did so, are essential to reconstruct the nuances of gender relations.

1

Bodies and minds

One of the first insights of gender studies was that sex and gender were different things. Simone de Beauvoir's formulation – 'One is not born a woman, one becomes one' – sundered the social roles ascribed to femininity from the biological nature of womanhood (de Beauvoir, 1972: 301). But this crucial distinction is not necessarily the best way to approach the gender relations of early modern society. To a considerable degree, understandings of genital, physiological and mental differences between women and men were not so much the foundations of gender roles, as the result of them. Men's power over women was an absolute social truth, embodied in the prescribed order of households: bodies exemplified that, and they did not always do so perfectly; it is possible to see the relationship between masculinity and femininity as a spectrum of difference, rather than incompatible opposites.

The collective, social nature of early modern communities also makes the early modern body markedly different from the modern one. This was a world where, for many, identity was primarily familial and social; privacy was infrequent, and the boundaries around the personal body likely to be less secure than in a more atomised society.

SEXUAL DIFFERENCE

Despite divides of scholarship and religion, Renaissance Europeans shared an understanding of sexual difference that derived from both biblical and classical sources, and that changed little between 1500 and 1700. The physiological differences between women and men demonstrated a divine design in which the female completed the male, and was naturally inferior and subject to him.

Before the Enlightenment, sexual difference was more likely to be explained with reference to the Bible, than to biology. The creation story, as told in

Genesis, underpinned female subjection by tying it not just to ethics, but to the making of male and female bodies [**Doc. 1, p. 86**]. Early modern biblical commentators and preachers noted that Eve was made *after* Adam; *from* Adam (and from his rib, not his head); and *for* Adam. The biblical narrative contained truths that applied to all humanity: all women were made for their husbands. Some of the earliest proto-feminist texts engaged with this basic argument and attempted to invert it. Jane Anger's *Protection for Women* defended women against male slanders by redefining the creation story as one of purification: the second creation was the more perfect [**Doc. 2, p. 86**].

The inferiority of the female body was explained more fully in classical medical texts. Renaissance medicine drew deeply from classical texts; right through the period, descriptions of sexual difference were essentially unchanged from those of Galen and Aristotle. The fundamental element of classical medicine, which remained key to early modern thinking, was the humours. Humoural theory gave every body its own complexion. Masculinity and femininity were determined by the balance in each body between hot and cold, wet and dry: heat and dryness made men, cold and wet made women. The humours provided a framework for temperament, too: the dry heat of men made them more prone to choler, or anger; the cold and wet humours of women made them susceptible to melancholy [**Doc. 3, p. 87**]. At the moment of conception, it was the domination of one set of humours that determined the sex of the child. A distinction between active and passive was established in the very elements of conception: men's seed was the more active agent, women's the passive recipient.

This model of sexual difference was based on an economy of fluids. The difference between male and female lay in the balance of humours. Some women and men were hotter, or colder, than others, and correspondingly further away from the extremes of their gender identity. The Aristotelian description of sexual organs, which provided the model for anatomy in this period, followed the same principles: male and female bodies existed on a continuum of difference, with one the physical opposite of the other. Bodies were complementary: the external genitalia of the male was the equivalent of the internal genitalia of the female. Thomas Laqueur's influential work describes this as the 'one-sex' model, and identifies it as peculiarly pre-modern, predating the world of two quite different sexes that was constructed during the eighteenth century (Laqueur, 1990).

The rhetorical description of a body which was virtually reversible, where the female anatomy was basically the male 'turned outside in', was a common thread in early modern culture, but it ran alongside many other ways of examining sexual difference. It was internally inconsistent: Jane Sharp's 1671 *Midwives Book*, for example, within a few pages compares the penis both to the womb, and to the clitoris [**Doc. 4, p. 88**]. Even in medical texts, the body was always a matter for argument and interpretation. At the popular level, where theories were dispersed through cheap print and oral culture, a greater diversity of ideas circulated. Printed medical texts repeated as orthodoxy the idea that conception required both male and female orgasm, but popular texts and everyday experience contradicted it. At every level, though, generation was a matter for debate and discovery.

It has been argued that the pre-1750 vision of sexual difference did not provide the same kind of argument for female inferiority as post-Enlightenment and Victorian models, which saw women and men as fundamentally different in anatomy and physiology: the biology of sex did not provide a stable foundation for the social roles of gender (Laqueur, 1990). However, the one-sex model was also supported by an Aristotelian inheritance, in which feminine physiology was not just different but inferior to male. Women's surplus humours caused trouble [**Doc. 3, p. 87**]. Menstruation was the key sign of this. Biblical references to menstruating women as polluted were endorsed by medical narratives which cast menstruation as the necessary purification of women's blood by the removal of excess fluids. Irregularity was dangerous. However, the end of periods at the menopause was barely discussed in the medical literature; the end of fertility was much less formally marked than it came to be in the eighteenth century.

One of the tenets of gender relations in this period was the idea of the male body as the model of perfection and the female as at best imperfect, at worst grotesque. Renaissance dramatists and satirists were mesmerised by the potential of human bodies for grotesque behaviour. The female body was often satirised as relentlessly leaky: women easily fell into both metaphorical and literal incontinence. At the same time, humoural theory also facilitated the idea of managing one's own body. Through diet, clothes and behaviour, men and women attempted to maintain and regulate their health. In practice, the contained, discreet body was an impossible aspiration for either sex. Real men were preoccupied with the wayward fluids and instability of their bodies: wind, digestion, fits, colds and headaches provided frequent evidence of humoural upset. Advice to young men stressed the importance of regulation and moderation. A balanced body was the foundation of self-control, and self-control made it possible for men to live up to the commanding position required of them. Both men and women, in different ways, were concerned with their own deviations from the model of a temperate, controlled body: but while the ultimate aspiration for the men who read bodily advice was to command others, that for women was to be able to be commanded.

Anatomically, the early modern vision of sexual difference was less binary than the modern model. In popular and academic medical texts, hermaphrodites were a common topic of discussion. The idea of a body that sat between the two extremes of male and female made sense to the humoural system, and to the one-sex model. A much-cited tale from Michel de Montaigne told of a young girl who, over-exerting herself chasing her pigs, found the extra heat of exercise turned her genitals from internal female ones, to external male ones. Sexual transformations were fantastic, not likely, but they were theoretically possible within the familiar model of sexual difference. More pragmatically, femininity and masculinity could overlap. In a world of fluid humours, weak or promiscuous men could be effeminate, and brave women manly.

This rhetorical body was beginning to be defined by race, itself in the process of construction. Without a theory of genetics, skin colour was variously described as the result of sunburn, climate or the biblical **curse of Ham**. Skin colour and ethnicity were part of the ongoing discussion of reproduction, and contemporary ideas often placed the responsibility for maintaining or threatening difference on women. Midwives' books retold a story of maternal impression, where a white woman gave birth to a black child after gazing on the picture of a black man; others said it was a confidence trick to hide adultery (Loomba and Burton, 2007: 4). The racial inflection of sexual difference was less biological, than cultural, although this did not necessarily make it more malleable. The Irish were often the prototype for images of savagery: descriptions of Irish women as drunk and immodest fuelled the English project to 'civilise'. The observations of midwives' books and travel narratives, many of them based on classical precedents, helped establish an association between hypersexuality and blackness, which would later provide one of the justifications for slavery [**Doc. 19, p. 103**].

Curse of Ham: Noah's curse on Ham's sons after Ham 'saw his father's nakedness'; used as a justification for slavery, with Black Africans interpreted as Ham's descendants.

The relationship of these various constructions of difference, most of which were confined to elite discourse, to the experience of the small but growing number of black men and, in smaller numbers, women in England is hard to construe. The London parish registers record 'blackamore' and 'negro' men and women dying and being born in the city from at least the late sixteenth century; some managed to be baptised, thought to bestow freedom from slavery; many must have married white women or men. One parish register entry, calling on the problematic understanding of the transmission of skin colour, records the birth of 'Elizabeth, a negro child, born white, the mother a negro' (St Botolph Bishopsgate, 25 Sept. 1586). By 1596 Elizabeth I was attempting, unsuccessfully, to have black slaves removed for the danger they posted to the labour market. While the term 'black' continued, until the early eighteenth century, to refer to dark-haired people, it was also beginning to mean dark-skinned. Outside the city, black slaves and servants lived in the great houses. The seventeenth century saw notions of blackness become part of English culture: race began to be codified and the English began to see themselves as 'white'.

The experience of embodiment was historically and socially variable. Workplace accidents plagued both sexes. The close work of sewing or lace-making made eye problems especially likely for women. Mortality rates were differentiated by sex, with women at high risk in the childbearing years, although if they survived those years, their life expectancy exceeded men's. After a lifetime of physical labour, old age was felt sharply: the effects of menopause, such as decreased bone density and malnutrition were likely to give older women a distinctive look, familiar in popular images of witches. Old age gave to men an authority that did not accrue to women: their know-ledge of custom made them key informants in parish affairs, especially if they could lay claim to a chain of memories from their fathers or other old men. But the effects of injury, debilitation and consequent loss of livelihood left many as reduced in status as women; past the peak of masculine achievement, old age, which could begin around 50, may have had a levelling effect. By the precepts of humoural medicine, old men were liable to melancholy as their hot, dry humours were sunk by the chilling process of ageing, bringing them closer to the natural temperaments of women.

THE SOCIAL BODY

The body was an instrument of social as well as sexual relations. A self which was embedded in family and social structures was reflected in a lack of privacy and, in some contexts at least, high levels of physical contact. Elite status provided distance and space, particularly for men; increasingly great houses included closets for personal reflection. Plebeian women and men lived closely, with little separate space and minimal privacy. Bed-sharing with others of the same sex was common both amongst plebeians and in elite households, between parents and children, masters or mistresses and servants, tutors and students, and domestic servants or apprentices. It was also a gesture of solidarity and favour. Archbishop Laud's famous dream about the king's favourite sharing his bed struck him because, in it, the rest of the court saw him gaining a great favour of trust [**Doc. 5, p. 89**].

Early modern people took care with their gestures. Not only did these cement social relations, but they were also central to business transactions. With the expansion of the market, credit depended on careful assessment of a new colleague's trustworthiness: bodily presentation was bound to matter. Drinking and eating rituals were especially important between men, since it was here that new business was likely to be done. Drinking healths was the epitome of good fellowship, and sealed both marital and business contracts: it seems to have been largely if not entirely a male practice. Contemporary manners advice addressed itself largely to children, but was most specific about the behaviour of boys in training to be gentlemen. The art of impressing was understood to be crucial to self-advancement, especially in the city or at court. Norbert Elias's narrative of the civilising process argues that the Renaissance saw an internalisation of social norms: the rules on spitting, nose blowing and farting became more demanding and eventually became part of the mechanisms of self-control (Elias, 1969). Elias's theory has been critiqued, but its suggestion of the transformation of the self remains a stimulating one, particularly for historians of masculinity (Bryson, 1998). In the literature of manners, the epitome of failure was the bumbling country bumpkin, who features in plays, ballads and jokes: his lewd ignorance is the opposite of the practised courtly gentleman.

In the rhetoric of early modern demeanour, public behaviour was not just a performance, but a mirror of the man within. Hat honour, bowing and hand-shaking all changed their meaning and their uses across different contexts and over time. Katherine Austen's angry outburst directs itself at her son's failure to raise his hat: contemporary fashion for him, in a largely male collegiate world, meant to her, in a city of merchants and lawyers, arrogance and lack of gentility [**Doc. 6, p. 90**].

Elias's narrative, like much of the manners literature, appears to focus entirely on men. The rules of public behaviour were less clear for women: the central image of good manners was that of 'honest carriage', and while the cosmetics, light feet and lack of humility that distinguished a light carriage were frequently commented on, the characteristics of an honest woman were much harder to pinpoint. The rules of female civility may have been less explicit, and less associated with the project of social mobility.

In the mid-seventeenth century, political and religious clashes were reflected in bodily styles that broke with tradition. One group broke all the rules of comportment. The **Quakers** developed their own style of speech, walking and dress. For men, in particular, it marked them off from their peers. They declined to lift their hats or use conventional marks of respect; their self-consciously measured pace was ridiculed as rustic and unrefined. Their self-presentation was the extreme end of the **Puritan** style that also drew comment. Seventeenth-century religious radicals had gone through such a wholesale personal transformation that they felt the need not just to think differently, but to *be* different. In a fairly homogenous cultural world, where the personal encounter was central to business and politics as well as social life, transgressions of personal demeanour were acutely observed.

Living in the body was also shaped by attitudes to clothes. The majority of the population owned few garments, and changed them infrequently. Particularly in the earlier part of the period, clothes were made to last and were often inherited. The passing on of used clothes was part of the informal contract between employers and servants. Men and women were recognisable

Quakers: The Religious Society of Friends, founded late 1640s by George Fox, in the conviction that individual relationships with Christ could bypass the mediation of church and clergy.

Puritans: Protestants advocating greater purity of doctrine and worship.

by their outer garments: petticoats, waistcoats, gowns and coats. With shared sleeping arrangements and infrequent bathing, inner garments like the smock that both sexes wore were almost part of the skin. The relationship between clothes and gender identities was a distinctive one. Small children's status as less clearly gendered than adults was symbolised in the long gowns that both boys and girls wore until boys were 'breeched' at around seven years old. For elite families, this could be a ceremony of grandeur and great symbolism. In a gentry household of the seventeenth century, Frank North's grandmother supervised his transition into breeches and long coats, recording his excitement for his absent father. Equally significant for the newly made boy and his family was the reaction of the minister, who, surprised at seeing him in his new clothes, was 'put to the blush'. Adult dress marked the transition of a young boy towards his place in the governing class [**Doc. 7, p. 91**].

Girls' transition to the next stage of maturity was less publicly marked. They began to wear boned bodices before the age of five, but there does not seem to have been a public recognition of this as a significant moment. A more momentous change for them came in adult life, when they married. Women's clothes were, to a variable degree, determined by marital status, in particular with relation to headcoverings. A coif and sometimes also a hat over the hair was the sign of marriage and respectability: at weddings and funerals, single women left their hair uncovered to mark their maidenhood. It was probably possible to tell from dress who was married and who was single: aprons, hats and keys distinguished the established matrons. Adam Martindale complained that fashions had changed during the seventeenth century, with single women beginning to adopt scarves and hats that had once been only appropriate for the married; this might well fit with the increasing numbers of unmarried women in their thirties and forties in these years [**Doc. 8, p. 92**]. Headcoverings for women were also a mark of modesty, and, to some, subjection [**Doc. 34, p. 118**].

Diaries, letters and paintings testify to the power of dress in signifying sex and gender. Clothes were deeply personal. The majority of clothes were tailored and specific to the wearer. The poor, with few clothes at their disposal, might be recognised by their cloaks or jackets. Long-lasting garments were often inherited, or remade and resold on the secondhand market. The meanings of clothes were individual, but their structures, shapes and patterns, were generic. The high fashion of Elizabethan and early Stuart England was mannered, with separate garments each distorted in shape: ruffs, doublets, hose, breeches, farthingales and codpieces. Favour at James I's court, critical observers noted, fell on those wearing the best-cut coats and the stiffest ruffs [**Doc. 9, p. 93**]. Display and detail was as important for men's clothes as for women's. Aside from a period of restraint in the mid-seventeenth century, flamboyance was the distinctive mark of men's clothes, from the elongated codpieces of the sixteenth century to the wide breeches and garnishing ribbons of the 1660s.

Both women and men were regularly castigated by moralists, especially by Puritans, for excessive adornment, waste of fabric and displays of pride. Men's clothes accentuated the public significance of sexuality. Codpieces grew larger and larger under Henry VIII and fell out of fashion by the reign of Elizabeth; at the turn of the century men's fashions featured padded hose and pointed doublets that made the male body look markedly more feminine. The seventeenth century saw fashionable dress increasingly determined by confessional politics. Velvet hose and tight codpieces were associated with foreign (and hence Romish) influences; reforming Protestants distinguished themselves by quiet, dark dress with plain linen collars. Their opposition to fashion created a Puritan style in itself, one which became emblematic of the politics of sobriety and reform. Its opposite, by the mid-seventeenth century, was no longer tightly cut, revealing hose, but loose, half-unbuttoned doublets, the look that became identifiable as 'cavalier'. The distinctive feature of premodern men's fashion was its elaborate, fabric-intensive nature. Modern masculinity is often denoted by minimal elaboration: it is hard to perform. Early modern male dress, in contrast, was all about show. Embroidery, ribbons, puffs and lace demonstrated status and power in concrete terms. The long hair of the seventeenth century was replaced in the eighteenth by a widespread habit of wearing wigs. It was not until the eighteenth century that men's fashionable dress became characterised by sharp lines, clean tailoring and lack of fuss. The allegation of effeminacy so often levelled at men's garments had a different meaning in this period than it would do in later centuries. Effeminacy came from too much contact with women, and too much heterosexual sex; it might undermine male authority, but it did not imply homosexuality.

It is hard to imagine the extremes of fashionable male dress reaching far outside the circles of court and metropolis, but the images of effeminate, foreign clothes did so. Daily wear for most men was unlikely to register much change from the garments of their parents, and their children and their servants were likely to inherit those same clothes to remake. Little comment survives on the gender politics of poorer men's clothes. The kind of sartorial play with effeminacy that was possible at court and on the city streets was unlikely to have much counterpart elsewhere. Nevertheless, to be careless of appearance was no part of early modern masculinity. In an economy where most clothes were still tailored, negligence was impossible.

Women's high fashion was as elaborate as men's and as sexually charged. The busks of corsets were alleged to protect the promiscuous by preventing pregnancy; the exposed breasts seen at court and the dyed and false hair constituted evidence of lust as well as pride. The loose doublets modelled on men's ones that became fashionable in the 1620s were, it was said, designed to allow easy access. Bare arms, too, began to appear for the first time in fashionable dress in the 1630s, provoking more comment on immodesty. Most of all women's dress was attacked for its deceit: perfumed gloves, velvet face masks and beauty spots, cosmetics and headdresses were all suspected of concealing the true nature of women. More than men, women were accused of counterfeiting social status with dress, causing a confusion of categories – prostitutes with gentlewomen, pretentious poor with bourgeoisie. The balance of proper dress and modest humility was not always obvious, as Mrs Jane Ratcliffe's reluctance to wear the dress her husband gave her indicates [**Doc. 10, p. 94**].

Clothes were the lineaments of social identity. Fabrics and colours were socially specific. Elizabethan England still had sumptuary laws, which prescribed who was allowed to wear what fabric and colour. Purple silk was confined to royalty, velvet coats to certain degrees of the nobility, and silk garments to men worth more than **£100** a year. Women's apparel was legislated to match the status of their husbands. By the late sixteenth century, sumptuary laws were unlikely to bind fashion, but clothing continued to be controversial. At another level, the clothing of elite women and men could constitute a visible, tangible boundary between them and their surrounding cohort. The Renaissance man of fashion combined a portly, mature stomach, the doublet sometimes filled with bombast stuffing, with the neat legs of a fencer; his sleeves were cut with a shaped bend at the elbow, to facilitate the authoritative 'Renaissance elbow' (Plate 2). Surviving portraits provide us with an image of the self-presentation of elite women and men, if not of the ways such clothing worked on the stage of court, house and street.

£, s., d.: Pounds, shillings, pence. 12 d. = 1 shilling; 20 shillings = £1.

The fashion of the streets is harder to identify. The basic construction of male and female garments followed the established structure of detachable pieces, which had some interesting implications for gender roles. Men and women wore a basic identical undergarment, the smock. Men's hose were laced to doublets: loose laces were easily noted. Men wore linen drawers; women mostly did not, allowing them to urinate more freely, as well as exposing them to unwanted touch. Linen bands and ruffs were pivotal to menswear, and their cleanliness marked both internal and external personal hygiene. The provision and cleaning of linen was a women's job and it overlapped with the provision of nappies, bandages and menstrual rags, and it also formed part of erotic exchanges; it was not accidental that Pepys's longest affair was with his laundress.

Joris Hoefnagel's painting of a Bermondsey wedding features a number of interesting vignettes: two women with masculine hats, perhaps incorporating male dress into the festivities; a mother or wet-nurse using a rich red shawl or coat to carry a baby she is breastfeeding; women wearing aprons outside

(Plate 1). In a culture where breeches were unequivocally identified as male, and complete undress was rare, it was perhaps easier for women to dress as men. Cross-dressing featured vividly in popular literature, with heroines like Moll Cutpurse roaming the streets dressed as men to claim the male privileges of work, money or marriage to a woman; it was also, as we will see in chapter 4, part of protest. In the courts, a few women were prosecuted for the crime of wearing men's clothes. Mawdlin Gawen, taken up in late Elizabethan London, was one of them [Doc. 11, p. 95]. Some cross-dressers were identified as vagrants and prostitutes; others were travelling under cover for secrecy or safety. A few, as in the ballads and stories, passed as men and married other women, and cross-dressing also featured in festive rituals and protest. Stories of men dressing as women to deceive are, in contrast, very rare.

More subtle cross-dressings than women in breeches were at issue in the print material of early modern London. Two pamphlets of the 1620s, *Hic Mulier* and *Haec Vir*, affected to condemn the fashions of women who dressed like men, and men who adopted the fashions of women. In fact, their target was particular pieces of clothing and mannish styles, none of them as sex-specific to modern eyes as breeches or skirts. *Hic Mulier* pitched on doublets and ruffs, broad-brimmed hats, bare bosoms and short hair, the same fashions that James I had urged his clergy to attack earlier that year [Doc. 12, p. 96]. Its point was not that women in men's fashions might pass as men, but that they might acquire men's prerogatives of violence and assertiveness. With doublets unbuttoned, they also became dangerously lewd: the androgyne was one of the touchpapers for desire. In a similar fashion, performances of androgyny by the boys who played women on stage, might, literary scholars have argued, provide space for re-imagining gender, and fantasising a world where gender could be in play.

SEX

Early modern popular culture was often bawdy, replete with sexual metaphor. Jokes and proverbs about sex abounded. The political tracts of the civil war period, liberated from print censorship, sometimes featured sexual satires and gossip. Pornography – literally, writing about prostitutes, which was the nature of most early pornography – was available first in manuscript, and by the 1660s in print in Latin, French and English. The evidence of jest-books suggests a verbal compass for women that was much wider than that prescribed in advice for virtuous conduct: old women, wives, widows and maidens were both subjects and speakers of bawdy humour [Doc. 13, p. 98].

Church courts: Courts enforcing canon law via litigation or disciplinary prosecutions, overseen by bishop.

Constable: Unpaid parish official, working at the orders of justices of the peace.

At the same time, sex outside marriage was powerfully proscribed. The **church courts** enforced a canon law which prohibited sex before marriage, and made adultery a cause for separation (although not remarriage); family, neighbours and parish **constables** enforced moral rules with the inevitable surveillance of a closely knit community. The articles of complaint against one illicit couple in Worcester in the 1660s presented a list of issues which focused on illicit sex, but also encompassed the man's rejection of his wife, his widowed lover's disrespect of the mother she lived with, and the rumour that she was either pregnant or had procured an abortion [**Doc. 14, p. 98**]. Privacy was not easy to achieve in most rural or urban surroundings. Mawdlin Gawen's presentment for cross-dressing and illicit sex reveals the lengths an unmarried couple had to go to to attempt a secret sexual relationship, travelling across the country and the city in disguise or pretending to be relatives [**Doc. 11, p. 95**].

Hardest to recapture through the partial records of sexual encounters must be the balance of desire, pleasure and power. Renaissance literature cast women as lustful, with overwhelming desires; but the cultural landscape also featured an ancient narrative of men as forceful warriors on the battlefield of sex and love. Leonard Wheatcroft's courtship narrative rested on this familiar story, the best way he could relate the import of love and courtship [**Doc. 15, p. 99**]. Male diarists occasionally left some evidence of their understandings of sex, most notably Samuel Pepys. Female writers left almost none. This lack of records reflects not just inhibition, but a constrained language, and a set of narratives and metaphors for sex that cast women and men persistently in predictable scripts. Some of the most explicit descriptions of sex by women come from legal records of bastardy and fornication, such as that of Elizabeth Browne in early seventeenth-century Somerset. Not surprisingly, such accounts make men the pursuers, women the passive accomplices or victims: men invariably 'take the pleasure of' or 'occupy' them, although this story also interestingly begins with some sense of wooing words and gestures [**Doc. 16, p. 100**]. The vocabulary for describing heterosexual sex was limited. Despite a medical narrative in which women were required to experience pleasure to conceive, most cultural models for female sexual assertiveness involved disorder.

Sexual knowledge was a matter of contention, guarded from the single and surrounded with controversy. Sex was intimately linked with generation: it was well established that reproduction depended on sexual pleasure. Vernacular medical books had begun to appear in the late sixteenth century, outlining the genital parts and their functions, so that a careful reader could easily put together clues about the management of fertility (and hence contraception). In the late seventeenth century, *Aristotle's Masterpiece* also offered a chapter on how to achieve the requisite sexual pleasure to ensure conception.

One of the effects of the humoural understanding of the body was to attribute particularly strong sexual desire to women. The orthodox Aristotelian view of conception was that it required both male and female partner to achieve orgasm, hence releasing seed from both parties. Not until the early twentieth century was the peculiar operation of human ovulation understood. The implications of this view of conception were considerable, even if it countered what many people must have learnt from experience. It was understood, too, that young women needed sexual fulfilment: the result of postponing marriage too long could be chlorosis, or greensickness, a disease of melancholy that was peculiar to women. Nicholas L'Estrange's mother's joke parodies a young maid who could not wait for marriage to satisfy her desires [**Doc. 13, p. 98**].

Women's lust, then, was a natural, if sinful, part of their natures: chastity was an aspiration. In this way, perceptions of the female body and nature differed significantly from later ones, which came to cast Victorian women as naturally chaste. But the effect of this difference on gender relations was not to make women's lust legitimate, except under the narrowly contained circumstances of marriage: rather, it made women's sin almost inevitable. Continence was an important value for both sexes. This was particularly so after the Reformation, when Protestants and especially Puritans stressed the significance of sexual continence to marriage. In 1650, Cromwell's government reformed the laws on adultery, fornication and bawdry to bring it firmly within the compass of secular law. Adultery was redefined, following **Mosaic law**, as sex with a married woman; men could be prosecuted, but it was the woman who was understood to be most firmly bound by marriage, and sex between a single woman and a married man was not adultery, but fornication. Under the 1650 *Act for suppressing the detestable sins of Incest, Adultery and Fornication* this new definition of adultery was a capital offence, and though executions were rare, it brought some vigorous local moral campaigns (Thomas, 1978; Capp, 2007). The Act also legislated for three months' imprisonment for fornication, and branding for bawdry.

Mosaic law: Laws attributed to Moses, set out in the first five books of the Old Testament.

The late seventeenth century seems to have seen the beginning of a shift in attitudes. From 1660, the formal regulation of sex was harder to enforce. The church courts were no longer sufficiently robust to monitor everyday sexual behaviour, and after the civil wars sexual misconduct came under the remit of criminal law. In the late seventeenth and early eighteenth centuries in London and major cities, the campaigns of the **Societies for the Reformation of Manners** pressed for brief, draconian clampdowns on fornication and sodomy, resulting in thousands of prosecutions annually; but the viability of sexual policing was being dramatically reduced. A commensurate shift in the toleration of illicit sex might be traced from contemporary literature and diaries.

Societies for the Reformation of Manners: Began in London in 1691, mobilising associations of gentlemen, tradesmen, constables and informers to prosecute vice.

One source for a history of sex outside marriage is illegitimacy rates. With a reasonably dependable system of registration from 1538, the numbers of births outside marriage should give us some idea of sexual practices. Early modern England had a surprisingly low rate of illegitimacy. In the decades between 1538 and 1750, between 2 and 4.3 per cent of recorded births were illegitimate. Peaks appeared in the early Tudor period and around the turn of the century; in the 1750s the rate was increasing again, and eighteenth-century illegitimacy rates were noticeably higher. Levels of pre-marital pregnancy were higher, with between 16 and 25 per cent of first children born to a married couple conceived before the ceremony. Recent demographic work has determined a noticeable regional pattern in illegitimacy, which has implications for the history of courtship practices. Bastardy rates were higher in the highland areas of north, west and south-west England, where pastoral farming was often underpinned by textile industry, parishes were loosely governed, and subsistence crises remained a risk into the seventeenth century. Illegitimacy was lower in the more secure arable farming areas of the lowland south-east and east, whose parishes were more closely settled and tightly governed. There, it seems, sufficient social control was exercised to keep young people from consummating relationships until they married.

However, illegitimacy levels give only a partial picture. Sex was not just reproductive; the whole concept of sexual intercourse needs historicisation. It has been suggested that the low levels of births outside marriage provide evidence of a particular sexual regime, one in which pre-marital sex was carefully non-reproductive. The eighteenth-century increase in illegitimacy, it has been argued, may represent a turn away from traditional non-penetrative sexual practices (Hitchcock, 1996). The courtship period also allowed room for some flexibility. For most couples considering marriage, there was relatively little privacy, but also a low level of supervision. Most courtships happened when young women and men were in service or apprenticeships, either on farms or in urban households. In the sixteenth century spousals, or contracts, were still a significant part of courtship practices, and it was generally accepted that after a firm promise of marriage, sex was acceptable: it bound the contract. For many couples there would also have been sufficient time and space to have some sexual encounters before they married. Masturbation, whilst well established as sinful, was barely explicable in English, until the publication of the extended warning against it, *Onania*, in the early eighteenth century: its secrecy made it safe.

One of the significant cultural changes of this period for women related to rape. In medieval England, rape had been a property offence: it concerned the abduction of a young woman from her guardians, and it was prosecuted by her father or brother. In the sixteenth century it was a crime of great severity. Classed with theft and murder, it was a capital offence with no

benefit of clergy. But in the seventeenth century it was also recognised to be a crime which was judged by the behaviour of the victim: she was required to make hue and cry, and to prove her lack of consent [**Doc. 17, p. 100**]. Pregnancy was enough to disprove rape because it meant the victim must have experienced pleasure. Very few rape cases were prosecuted, and very few of those succeeded. The majority of allegations involving adult women were dismissed before trial. The great cultural weight of virginity made it harder to prosecute any assault on it.

The close study of language and texts has enhanced our understanding of what rape and consent meant to men and women. The available language for describing rape was as limited as the opportunity to prosecute it: typically, women described their clothes being torn, their possessions destroyed, rather than articulate what had been done to their bodies. Force often seems integral to early modern descriptions of sex: in court, where of course women are defensive, men are often described as throwing women down, or having the carnal knowledge of them. Their pleasure, according to midwives' manuals, was to be passive and receptive; men's was to be active. In this way the pleasure that conception required was neutralised, and assertive female passion still emerges as disorderly. Nevertheless, the early modern period had a language for women's desire and an understanding that women required sexual satisfaction, to the extent that male impotence was a powerful fear. It is a very different sexual landscape to that of, for example, the nineteenth century.

Prostitution is well-documented in London, less so outside the city. In London, a shift in management of prostitution had come with the Reformation. Until the 1530s, brothels existed under relative tolerance on the south bank of the Thames, with their own rules and codes of dress. Prostitutes, many of whom were Flemish, provided a service on the condition their trade was contained within bawdy houses. Henry VIII's reformation abolished the zone of tolerance, and by the late sixteenth century brothels were operating all over the city, but particularly in the suburban area of Clerkenwell. Attempts to prosecute both prostitutes and clients reached a peak in the late sixteenth century. The reform of brothels also attracted apprentices, traditionally the city's rioters, legitimising assaults on working women and stigmatising sexually active women at the hands of young men. From the sixteenth century, Shrove Tuesday festivities saw licensed rampages by London's apprentices, running riot and damaging houses; brothels were a favourite target. The 'bawdy house riots' of 1668 revisited the ancient tradition, and incorporated a new understanding of **charivari** as comic performance as much as ritual protest. Pepys came to watch; disorder had become entertainment, but women remained the targets.

Heterosexuality provided the cultural, as well as the economic, context of sexuality. But heterosexuality did not necessarily preclude homosexual

Benefit of clergy: A legal fiction by which, after 1575, a felon capable of reading a verse from the Bible could be excused hanging. It was extended to women in 1624.

Charivari: Ritual of community censure, often involving 'rough music' with pots and pans.

activity. The concept of homosexuality, most historians of sexuality agree, is a modern one: the idea of sexual identity was not fully established until the nineteenth century, though the timing of its emergence is subject to debate. Renaissance law and literature was more concerned with sodomy as an unnatural crime. Henry VIII's revision of canon law to bring more spiritual offences into the criminal realm included making buggery with animals or between men a capital offence. An established public image of the sodomite, excoriated like traitors and heretics, provided a target for moral fears. But sodomites were most readily seen as strangers and enemies. The ease with which homosocial life was conducted, with men sleeping side by side and sharing bodily intimacies, suggests that it was both possible and necessary, to make a distinction between the possibility of homosexual behaviours in real life and the horrifying image of the sodomite. Feminine-behaving men were liable to be read not as homosexual, but as promiscuously heterosexual. One point of convergence of these understandings of relations between men came at the Jacobean court, where James's succession of favourites put passion between men at the heart of political favour. The most legitimate language in which that passion could be expressed was that of family and marriage [**Doc. 18, p. 102**]. Male friendship, central to political affairs, had a highly visible and charged physical side to it. The haunting danger of sodomy sometimes made it an impossible dilemma.

The first evidence that homosexuality was expected to be recognisable and allied with a subculture, or identity, comes in the late seventeenth century, with the attacks on London's molly houses, which exposed an entire culture of social and sexual relations between men and seemed to represent a sexuality that sometimes precluded sex with women. For the first time, men were arrested and executed, their trials publicly reported: sodomy became a subject of manufactured public concern.

In contrast, sex between women was never criminalised, and the evidence for it remains so sketchy that until recently it was regularly argued that passionate friendship between women occluded sexual possibilities. Sexual acts not involving male seed were not generally of interest to legislators or to reformers. When Amy Pulter managed to marry Arabella Hunt in London in 1680, for 'a frolic' as she claimed, the subsequent investigations focused on whether they shared a bed, and on the possibility that Amy Pulter was a hermaphrodite, or 'a person of a double gender', the only legal grounds for dissolution was that Pulter was already married (Mendelson and Crawford, 1995). However, lesbianism was far from culturally invisible, and the importance of female desire in contemporary models of sexuality and reproduction made it easy to imagine. Erotic fiction used scenarios of women having sex with women; travel literature and midwives' books spread stories of Egyptian or African women who 'misused' their bodies with other women.

Leo Africanus's tales of Africa described Moroccan witches as 'fricatrices', who lured women from their husbands; alongside these tales were descriptions of male innkeepers who dressed as women, and women who were absurdly pampered by their husbands. His reportage fitted into a larger picture of making gender disorder at once erotic, and foreign [**Doc. 19, p. 103**]. The sexual body was differentiated by race: a series of stories and citations helped to establish an association between blackness and hypersexuality, manifested in stories of women – always far from 'here' – who used their clitorises like penises. By the late seventeenth century, suggestions that Queen Anne's favourite, Abigail Masham, preferred to spend her nights with women than with men were defamatory, but in a carefully elusive way. There is no evidence of a similar female culture to that of the late seventeenth-century male subculture; but there is also no reason why such networks or identities would register in any records.

REPRODUCTION

The mysteries of the body were divinely ordained. The printed literature of the sixteenth century onwards bears witness to a determined attempt to make sense of those mysteries: first in the context of the 'secrets of women', and later, as part of an endeavour to open those secrets to public, and male, scrutiny. By the mid-seventeenth century, authors like the radical Nicholas Culpeper were printing their guides to generation, generically known as 'midwives' books' for the common reader.

Generation, or reproduction, was the great mystery for early modern science. The discovery of eggs in the follicles of women's ovaries, and sperm in the semen of men, provided evidence that would eventually transform the understanding of reproduction. But in the shorter term generation remained a subject of debate. Preformationists believed the foetus was already present before conception in sperm or eggs, requiring only to be nourished; Aristotelians thought menstrual blood was the nourishing fluid that made life out of seed. Interpretations varied as to whether women and men made equal partners in the business of generation; whether women's part was passively to nurture the seed that men actively produced; or whether women's eggs in fact contained the miniature of new life, to be breathed into existence by sperm. Such contests had obvious implications for the meaning of paternity. They also had religious significance: the role of the Virgin Mary in conception was one of the contested points of the early Reformation.

For sexually active women, pregnancy was hard to avoid. Contraception was scarce and ineffective. Printed sources mentioned the possibility of avoiding sex during a woman's fertile period, but that period, along with the timing of ovulation, was not correctly identified until the early twentieth century. Withdrawal was surely used, but is rarely mentioned. Breastfeeding seems to have worked fairly effectively as contraception: women who were undernourished and fed their babies on demand were likely to find their periods were delayed in returning. There was, however, a widespread awareness of the most popular means of abortion: the herb **savin** or pennyroyal [**Doc. 20, p. 105; Doc. 14, p. 98**]. Those who did not know about it probably knew someone else – a cunningwoman, an older friend, or a herbalist – to ask for advice.

Savin: Also known as pennyroyal, a herbal abortifacient.

Potency and fertility carried great weight. Impotence was one of the few grounds for the annulment of a marriage. While infertility was often attributed to women, impotence provided a male equivalent with at least as much cultural power. Almanacs provided remedies for it that encompassed both practical and magical remedies: bewitchment was always a possibility. Male potency mattered, and was hard to fix. In Sarah Jinner's almanacs, the recipes for restoring women's periods are simpler and more readily available than the much more exotic and magical remedies for restoring men's potency [**Doc. 20, p. 105**]. Samuel Pepys, dealing with infertility rather than impotence, was offered a set of more manageable routines [**Doc. 21, p. 107**]. Fertility was, it seems, largely a women's affair: it occupied a large place in the few almanacs by women, and it was wives who gave advice to Pepys. Infertility was a part of many families' lives. Many marriages were childless; fertility does not seem to have been used as a measure of masculinity or femininity.

The significance of the reproductive process was not merely personal, but collective and political. The extraordinary capability of the female body in this regard made it look sometimes magical: seeds met to make a foetus, which grew to maturity; menstrual blood was converted to breast milk; every choice a mother-to-be made, from food to entertainment, could affect her child [**Doc. 22, p. 107**]. This context made women easy to blame, and marginalised men from pregnancy. It was reflected in the practicalities of pregnancy and childbirth management.

Childbirth in early modern England was a time of magic and danger, and it took place largely in a world of women. The precarious time of labour and delivery was surrounded by rituals carefully prescribed to ensure safety, secrecy and nurture. While the actual levels of maternal mortality were relatively low, death in childbirth was a fear for almost every woman who wrote about it. Child mortality was high. Around one child in four died before the age of one, and another one in four before the age of ten (Wrigley and Schofield, 1981: 248–50).

Magical and folk beliefs provided ways of keeping the vulnerable woman and her child safe. From the 1540s, Protestant reformers pushed for the removal of traditional childbirth remedies: girdles that had been wrapped around a statue of the Virgin Mary, necklaces and saints' relics. Women continued to use magical and folk resources: herbs, and the 'eagle stone', a stone within a stone that, symbolising the pregnant body, could both keep the foetus safely in the womb, or tied to the thigh, could encourage it to move down ready for delivery [**Doc. 23, p. 109**]. Births were attended usually by a midwife and perhaps other friends, relatives or neighbours; windows and doors were closed to keep the room warm and protected from evil influences. After the birth the newly-delivered mother and her companions, the gossips, shared a specially made warm drink, caudle, of beer or wine mixed with eggs and sugar. Childbirth was a time when women from different social ranks might mix: visiting the local women lying-in was part of a gentlewoman's duties. It was a time where women collected, briefly, in a segregated world, excluding the single (usually) and men (almost always). Did this mean a time of female empowerment? To a degree: the recently delivered woman was, where possible, protected, fed and nurtured by her family and friends. Ralph Josselin's diary describes the hospitality that surrounded his wife and her gossips [**Doc. 24, p. 109**]. Some town authorities expressed concern about the extent to which this had become a time of feasting and excess consumption. Misogynist satires echoed their complaints in tales of husbands dominated by the whims of pregnant or child-bearing wives. But to read this period as a time when domestic relations turned upside down would be going too far: new mothers were elevated and protected in relation to their female neighbours, not their husbands, and it was most likely to be other women, such as maidservants or female relatives, who looked after their needs.

After the Reformation, the rituals of reproduction were politically and religiously charged. The use of gossips became, for Puritans, symbolic of old superstitions; the new ceremonies of the Commonwealth saw some women following 'the new way' of baptising without gossips. Others, like Isabella Twysden, stuck to the old ways despite their adherence to the new religion [**Doc. 25, p. 110**]. The month of childbirth and lying in culminated in another controversial ritual. Churching, the ceremony that marked the end of lying-in and the reintegration of the 'green' woman into her community, had originally been a ritual of cleansing: the mother was sometimes sprinkled with holy water and wore a white veil, as the priest accompanied her into the church. Despite the 1552 Book of Common Prayer's replacing of the term purification with thanksgiving or churching, it retained, for some Protestants, elements of its Jewish origins, superstition and popery. The wearing of the veil crystallised this, and in some cases women, and other cases ministers, refused it. The feasting that surrounded the ceremony also roused concerns, and it was often refused to single mothers; thus Jane Minors of Barking was multiply at fault, for bearing an illegitimate child and not having it baptised, and also for coming to be churched apparently for the show of it [**Doc. 26, p. 110**]. Despite some protests by women, though, the vast majority of women continued to be churched, perhaps welcoming it as a useful and supportive mark of a time of danger and significance. A ceremony that seemed to be a punitive representation of the post-partum body and a way of disciplining women actually seemed to generally fulfil important needs and continued to do so into the twentieth century.

Reproduction was women's business: but it was also a public affair. The degree to which women controlled the realm of childbirth might be seen as empowering, both in the household, and in the community. Like all areas of women's work, though, it was downgraded by the redefinition of professional skills. The status of midwifery, at the start of this period a uniquely female profession, was slowly undermined. Male physicians published works attacking midwives as superstitious and secretive; elite women began to use male midwives. The figure of the man-midwife was a controversial one; a man who meddled in childbirth, so essentially part of the female sphere, could easily be cast as not quite male. Women continued to turn, most often, to other women, and until the medicalisation of childbirth and the use of hospitals for giving birth, childbirth remained a largely female arena. But the politics of reproduction made it fertile ground for gender conflicts.

MIND AND SOUL

In humoural theory and in the popular mentality, body and mind were intimately related. The humours that determined bodily complexion also reflected mental temperaments: choleric, melancholic, sanguine and phlegmatic. Women and men were thus thought to be naturally prone to certain physical and mental behaviours. The association of choler with masculinity naturalised male violence and associated it with virtuous courage; the corollary was that women's anger was rare and unnatural. Melancholy, associated with the cold, damp humour of femininity, was characteristically female.

Our best evidence for mental worlds comes, of course, from the literate. The habit of self-reflection was facilitated by Protestantism, by literacy and by reading. Throughout our period, literacy was sharply gendered. The readiest measure, that of signing names to official documents, is inaccurate, but provides useful comparative material. In 1600, only amongst the gentry could the ability to write be taken for granted. Amongst men, yeomen and tradesmen and craftsmen began the period mostly unable to sign, and ended it mostly able to; husbandmen remained mostly illiterate. Women's literacy has gone unmeasured by social status, but it is evident that urban life, with all the cultural capital it gave to writing and reading, and the educational opportunities for girls and boys, made a considerable difference to the working women of early modern cities. These figures, though, actually denote writing ability, and not reading. At the lower social levels, where education meant attending a small local school, the habit of teaching reading and writing separately meant that those who stayed in school longer learnt to write; others, often likely to be girls, learnt only to read. Hence measuring literacy by counting those who could sign documents tells us little about functional reading ability, which must have been much wider than writing ability. The sheer amount of cheap print in circulation suggests a high level of reading amongst women as well as men.

Educational opportunities did not pretend at comparability between girls and boys. The humanist reformation of education in the sixteenth century turned elite boys' education towards independence and the development of the faculties for governing: for girls, virtue, self-occupation and restraint remained the aspiration. Amongst the elites, both boys and girls began with tutors or governesses, and boys later left for tutoring away from home, school and sometimes university; girls were also sent away, but into other elite households to learn social more than intellectual skills. Not until the early seventeenth century did boarding schools for girls appear in London and other cities and towns, and their curricula continued to focus on domestic affairs, needlework and music. By the late seventeenth century, though, a few writers on girls' education were recognising the need for some to be able to earn, and the function of education broadened somewhat. The long career of a middling status London woman, Bathsua Makin, illustrates something of the transition. Born in the early seventeenth century and educated herself by a schoolteacher father, she was rich in classical and modern languages, and after her marriage was employed to teach Princess Elizabeth, daughter of Charles I. By the 1670s, she was offering astronomy, physic, experimental philosophy and a wide range of languages to elite girls at her school in Tottenham High Cross, something which would have been unimaginable in her youth [**Doc. 27, p. 111**].

Renaissance thinking associated masculinity with reason and self-control, which enabled men to master both themselves and others; femininity meant unreason and passion. Within women, the lower self ruled the higher. Hysteria and greensickness symbolised the erratic control women had over their physical selves and their minds; by the sixteenth century love sickness, originally a male disease, had become a women's problem. Madness showed itself differently in relation to women and men. Male melancholy could distinguish men as scholars or thinkers; female melancholy appeared as a symptom of disordered or unsatisfied sexual desires.

In all sixteenth- and seventeenth-century literature, there is little identifiable trace of feminist thinking. Until the late seventeenth century, debates about the nature and role of women ran on familiar and largely rhetorical lines. While several appeared under the names of women, not all were demonstrably by women. Rather, texts like Jane Anger's represented the idea of a female voice. It was not their project to imagine a world of equality, but to defend the peculiar virtues of women, from chastity to occasional heroism. Margaret Cavendish's scientific and utopian mid-seventeenth-century writings went further, asserting that women and men were created equal and men had usurped their power. The potential for arguments that might constitute an early form of feminism was restricted by the relationship between household and state, and the necessity, for politically engaged women, of subordinating their activism to the cause of radicalism, religious reform, or **Whig** or **Tory** politics. Mary Astell, sometimes identified as the first feminist writer of the late seventeenth century, argued as a 'lover of her sex' that women needed better opportunities, and at the same time insisted, as a Tory royalist, that wives must obey their husbands as subjects in a state. Intellectual ambition was by no means incompatible with domestic subjection.

Whigs: Originally those supporting the exclusion of the Duke of York, eventually James II, from the throne in 1679–81.

Tories: Opponents of Exclusion; monarchists; supporters of the Church of England.

Women's and men's access to print remained wildly uneven throughout this period. Equally significant was the world of manuscript and the broader terrain of intellectual aspiration, embodied in part in letters. The speculative world of early Enlightenment science involved women at the margins and occasionally more centrally, at the same time as scientific proof was being more firmly defined as a masculine pursuit. At the end of the seventeenth century, another strain in the development of the self can be traced: the potency of politeness, a model for men to aspire to and women to judge. The 'man of feeling' who modelled a certain kind of masculinity in the eighteenth century could trace some roots back to the late seventeenth-century middling sort's urban world of sociability and intellectual exchange, in which sentiment, self-consciousness and reflection shaped the self.

By the end of the seventeenth century, the natural foundation of both patriarchy and inequality could no longer always be taken for granted. But challenges to them were still bound by the necessity of political and social obedience.

SPIRITUALITY

The Protestant Reformation opened the possibility of a soul free from the constraints of earthly gender. The idea of the priesthood of all believers suggested the potential of both women and men to interpret God's word for themselves. Theologians agreed that there was no division of the sexes in the immortal world; the disabilities of femininity were earthbound. But there were different images of male and female believers. Both Catholicism and Protestantism asserted that women were naturally more pious than men; in both, their piety was associated with the necessity for obedience and silence. The female worshipper was often seen as a passive vessel. Both continental and English reformers worried about women, especially servants, discussing the Bible without proper supervision; it was in this context that Henry VIII decreed that women were not to read the Bible alone [**Doc. 28, p. 113**]. St Paul's pronouncements on the constraints on women's thinking, praying and teaching were a touchstone [**Doc. 29, p. 114**].

The impact of Protestantism on gender relations is particularly hard to judge in England, where it was so piecemeal. It meant the loss of some of the practical devotions particularly associated with women, and an undermining of the potential for female sanctity that had been demonstrated by the cult of the Virgin Mary and female saints. The dissolution of monasteries and convents did much to assert the spiritual significance of marriage for both women and men. Both religions had high levels of female commitment and activism.

For both Protestant and Catholic women, resistance could fall in the domestic realm. Catholic women under Protestant regimes helped shelter priests and provided domestic support for a beleaguered religion. Rose Hickman, in exile from the Catholic regime, found ways to resist the Catholic rituals associated with baptism [**Doc. 30, p. 114**]. John Foxe's *Book of Martyrs*, reprinted through the period, featured models of more explicit female resistance, alongside men. Foxe's female martyrs were noted for their resistance, constancy, masculine courage and often, their wit. Many of his women refuse to obey their husbands, or worldly authorities. While the model of simple, uneducated women provides a convenient image of the weaker vessels God uses to perform great things, Foxe's women are also often witty, cunning and dazzling interlocutors, silencing their baffled interrogators. Alice Driver, in his account, caused her interrogator to give up and put his head down on a pillow [**Doc. 31, p. 115**]. The humility of poor women, whose education was apparently restricted to deep reading of (or listening to) the Bible, stood in sharp contrast against the subtleties of the men trying to convict them. Some of these accounts were based on records from the trials; others may have been elaborated as they were passed on. But they put a surprising variety of models for women's resistance at the heart of the core text of Protestantism. Catholics noted the dangers of domestic disorder from the early days of Reformation teaching; but women's resistance to conforming husbands was also a feature of Catholic martyr narratives.

For men, Protestant theology opened another possibility: clerical sexuality. No longer did clerical life require a commitment to celibacy. The married clergy of the Reformation years broke new ground in leading family lives that were meant to be exemplary rather than regrettable. The household was the forum for establishing and reproducing the new religion. The clerical wives of that generation made a position for themselves whose full history is yet to be written.

Puritanism had its own gender order. Its stress on active citizenship gave spiritual significance to the growing opportunities for civic authority available to middling sort men; the conflict of disorderly or lewd women with Puritan magistrates was a stock archetype of the period. The personal devotions of Puritan women were a great spur to reflective writing and sometimes to prophecy. Part of the theology of Puritanism was the duty of obedience and humility: a devotion which fitted neatly with women's natural obligation to their husbands. For both women and men, humility might, paradoxically, lead itself to self-assertion. For Puritan women and Quakers, personal humility might bring them into conflict with the authority of husbands, fathers and magistrates. Mrs Jane Ratcliffe impressed her minister with her refusal to wear the fine dress her husband had bought for her, a symbol of his local standing: her insistent humility was both an abnegation of the self and an assertion of her own Puritan identity [Doc. 10, p. 94]. Godly women were stock characters in the discourse of seventeenth-century spirituality. While some ministers praised their conformity and godliness, others attacked their insubordinate zeal, and warned of the danger of women evading the divine headship of men. The stock images of gossips, shrews and harlots were augmented by depictions of zealous arguers, whose roots came partly from the proud, stubborn women of Foxe's martyrology.

The autonomous interpretation that has been characterised as typically Protestant was by no means uniquely male; women's devotions offered a space for intellectual reflection that was rarely cherished elsewhere. But the natural piety of women was linked with an assumption of weakness and inconstancy that was to have longstanding echoes in the rhetoric of female spirituality.

By the end of the seventeenth century, this cluster of ideas about feminine spirituality had crystallised in a sense that religious conscience and internal piety were typically female. Their more violent outward manifestations were to be discouraged; the internalisation of spirituality could enhance obedience and hence, orderly family life. For Alice Thornton, royalist and conventionally pious, the framework of 'deliverances' gave a meaning to the frustrations and tragedies of marriage and childbearing [Doc. 32, p. 117]. If spirituality could promise a world of freer gender, its practical manifestations towards the end of the period were often associated with a deepening of gender divisions.

2

Patriarchal households

In theory, the household was the fundamental unit of early modern society: the heart of economic, social and gender order. In a patriarchal political system, the concepts of house, household and family carried considerable ideological weight. Every government imagined itself as ruling a nation made up of households whose order mirrored that of the state, with a father implicitly bound to protect a wife, children and servants. Obedient subjects, or families, made for peace and order. The normative ideals of femininity, and even more so those of masculinity, were premised on the patriarchal household.

The concept of patriarchy has been central to feminist criticism; it was also pivotal for early modern political theorists. For historians interested in the structures which validate and maintain gender relations, patriarchy is an invaluable analytic tool. It describes a structural system in which men dominate women through labour relations, political power, male violence, sexuality and culture (Walby, 1989). It provides a critical take on social structures and cultural practices that are all too readily naturalised, partly because so many of them remain deeply familiar.

Early modern people lived not just in a general patriarchy, but a specific one which theorised the household and the state. Patriarchalism was the dominant political theory of the sixteenth and seventeenth centuries. Perhaps its simplest articulation came in the catechism and the **Homily** on Matrimony; its fullest explication was in the political theorist Robert Filmer's *Patriarcha*. Patriarchalism presented a parallel between the household and the commonwealth, and accordingly between the father and the king. The head of the household had power over his subjects, the family, and responsibility for them, in the same way as the monarch had over his. Resistance and disobedience undid the harmony of a kingdom, and likewise of a family. All the political and religious revolutions of the period did little to undo this model. By the late seventeenth century, contract theory had established a different political model for obedience in the state: but hierarchy in the family was described as natural.

Homily: Printed sermons provided to be read to congregations.

THE SHAPE OF THE HOUSEHOLD

In practice, houses contained complex and variable groups of people, whose relationships were much more complicated than contemporary descriptions and advice allowed. If the household was the cradle of gender roles, it inculcated ambiguities, stresses and makeshifts, as much as the ideals of domestic literature.

The history of households and families has been central to that of gender relations since women and gender became historical subjects. Recent historiography has both suggested new approaches and prompted a shift of focus. The history of women has often been elided, to a greater or lesser extent, with the history of the family, with the effect of naturalising women's roles as wives and mothers, and underestimating women's roles outside the household as well as leaving men's domestic roles relatively unexamined. At the same time, the history of the family was for a long time dominated by literary and prescriptive accounts of family life, which stressed a set of rigid rules for feminine behaviour. Early attempts to historicise the emotional tenor of family life drew their evidence from high mortality rates: surely, historians reasoned, people in the past must have withheld from deep emotional commitment to the children and partners whose lives were so uncertain. Emotional detachment also fitted well with the emergent narrative of economic individualism and the self. In this story, the cultural impact of the Reformation and the early stages of capitalism provided the context for a transition from a collective society, with large, hierarchically organised family units, to a society of small nuclear households based on affective bonds and companionate marriage. Lawrence Stone described a transition, between 1400 and 1800, from a hierarchical extended family towards nuclear companionate marriage, a cultural transition which spread from the elites downwards (Stone, 1977). His narrative, supported largely by the evidence of the landed elites, has been undermined, and a more convincing model puts companionate marriage alongside hierarchical marriage throughout the period; indeed, the two were not mutually exclusive. The most eloquent sources for the emotional relations between women and men remain those of the literate elites: letters and diaries in this period begin to talk eloquently about the texture of marital relations. The emotional lives of those who did not write remain frustratingly out of reach, although court records of contracts and separations have enabled historians to start reconstructing the ordinary through the lens of the abnormal.

Alongside this set of concerns we must set the demographic history of the late twentieth century, which used the extensive records of births, deaths and marriages instigated by the Reformation to reconstitute family structures, and demonstrated a number of trends that overturned traditional expectations of pre-industrial family life. The result is a field which now stresses continuity more than change. Perspectives are still changing: feminist economic history, in particular, is prompting a rethinking of the basic assumptions that structure our understandings of households, families and individuals.

The patriarchal household was the context in which girls and boys learned their gender roles at first hand. At each stage of life, they had different models and specific parts to play. The early modern household looked surprisingly modern: it was small and nuclear, usually including one generation only and not grandparents or other extended kin. The average household size in the sixteenth and seventeenth centuries was between four and five people. Household units ranged from childless couples and single people, to couples with several children and servants. In densely populated areas like cities, households might be less discrete, with lodgers sharing a kitchen with a family. The great houses of the elite were a different matter, extending sometimes close to a hundred people. Everywhere, the distinguishing feature of early modern family life was the ubiquity of service.

Actual houses and households were complicated, and the reality of domestic life ensured that the family–state analogy that was so central to political thinking could only ever be an ideal. The household-family was necessarily flexible and sometimes fragile. High mortality rates left widowers, widows and orphans who survived in the care of other relatives. In areas of high mortality, the average length of marriage could be as short as ten years; overall it was around twenty years. Remarriages ran at a high level. At the same time, single women and widows were ordinary, not exceptional: at any one time around half the female population was unmarried, and in the seventeenth century up to a fifth of women never married. Men were more likely to marry and to remarry, but for them too, intermittent or lifetime bachelorhood was a reality if not a desirable option.

Marriage, then, meant the beginning of an economically and socially independent household. For that reason, it usually happened relatively late. In parts of central and south-eastern Europe, couples began family life with the support of kin; in England, it required independence. While the children of the elites often married in their teens, the majority of the population married first in their late twenties. Between 1550 and 1700 the average age of first marriage for men was falling from 29 to 27; for women it varied around the age of 26 (Wrigley and Schofield, 1981: 423). At the beginning of our period, marriage was a predictable life-cycle stage. By the end, it was less so. This was partly determined by economics, with hard times impacting on the age and frequency of marriage of the next generation. But it was also evident by the end of the seventeenth century that single life was becoming both more necessary and more possible.

The early modern concept of the family was a particular one: it included servants as well as the conjugal unit. Contractual bonds and domestic arrangements were more significant than blood ties in this respect. When diarists spoke of 'family', they meant the household members who shared living arrangements, especially servants and apprentices. Siblings living together, or bachelors or spinsters with servants, were families too. Ralph Josselin, an Essex clergyman, described the departure of his servant as 'the first to be married out of my family'; he replaced her with his sister [**Doc. 24, p. 109**]. Family units, it has become clear, were necessarily flexible, as servants and relatives came and went. Children grew up with powerful ties to temporary members of their households and role models who passed through. The relations between older children and servants could be close; often they shared beds, and sometimes they courted.

Wider kinship ties were powerful in a different way. The range of kin recognised in wills has been shown to be narrow, but other evidence suggests that in other circumstances, kin carried more weight. High mortality and frequent remarriage also extended the range of kin, from siblings and uncles or aunts to step-relations. High levels of mobility and migration meant that families were often isolated from relatives in their parish, but maintained connections within regional communities or at a longer distance. The single and childless were likely to leave bequests to more distant kin; single women especially often left money to nieces or younger female relations. The time of service, apprenticeship and marriage was when kinship ties were called into service. Distant family members helped find places, housing and partners for young women and men leaving home. Kinship, it seems, was not so much an obligation as a resource, and it retained emotional significance. The effect of this for gender relations was somewhat liberating, compared with other patriarchal systems. The mores of behaviour were unlikely to be enforced by a large or omnipresent group of observant older kin; indeed, as young men and women became adults, they were most likely to be away from their blood relations as well as their kin. This might have allowed some freedom to build an individual identity. Similarly, young married couples started their lives together in the context of a local neighbourhood, rather than under the eye of parents or in-laws; gender relations in adulthood must have been essentially peer-regulated. In relation to the formation of marriage, kinship connections seem to have been used not so much to suggest partners, as to provide financial investment in a new union: this was the meaning of 'friend' in the context of marriage. At the same time, the relative looseness of kin structures may well have left women in a vulnerable position. Young women migrating to London were well known to be at risk of prostitution and illegitimate pregnancy.

THE NATURE OF MARRIAGE

The European Reformation launched a reforming effort at the nature and understanding of marriage, rejecting the medieval monastic idealisation of celibacy in favour of a practical, human approach which stressed marriage as another route to salvation. Unruly sexuality, particularly that of men, was to be safeguarded by marriage. Rather than a sacrament concluded solely by the free exchange of promises, post-Reformation marriage was a secular contract as well as a spiritual one, open to the sanction of parents, and dissoluble, in the direst circumstances, on grounds of cruelty and adultery. The English Reformation did not reform marriage law as substantively as continental Protestants did, but it did result in a changed context for marriage. By the end of the sixteenth century the betrothal ceremonies which survived through medieval attempts to bring marriages more firmly into the church were falling out of use. Bigamy was brought under the aegis of the secular law, and made a capital offence. The rules on annulment and separation remained largely unchanged, but the possibility of the innocent party in a separation for adultery remarrying was being aired, and occasionally happened against the law.

One of the legacies of the Reformation's response to marriage was a great deal of printed advice. Some of this was directed at choice of partner, some at organisation of household. Robert Cleaver and John Dod's exhaustive *A godly form of household government* is perhaps the epitome of the genre, treating in turn the respective duties of husbands and wives, parents and children, and masters, mistresses and servants [**Doc. 34, p. 118**]. Many of them, like this one, were written by Protestant and later Puritan ministers, trying out their role as advisers on marriage. The basic material also reached a much wider audience through sermons preached at weddings and in the Elizabethan Homilies, provided in every church for reading when sermons were not available [**Doc. 35, p. 119**]. Almost none of this advice was new: it was essentially a commentary on key biblical texts, particularly Proverbs and the Pauline epistles. What was innovative was the detailed exposition of that advice in printed books and its frequent recapitulation in the pulpit. Sixteenth- and seventeenth-century women and men had easy access to a set of hierarchical domestic principles that were readily invoked to castigate and discipline.

The essence of those ideals was order, and the guarantee of order was obedience. Early modern society was profoundly hierarchical. Power relations were embedded in social relations, in families and in gender relations. It was, it seems, impossible to think outside a hierarchical model. The protofeminist texts of the late sixteenth century argued not for equality, but for the respective virtues of women versus men; their arguments drew on extremes to suggest not that women and men could function as equals, but that men were worse than women, or women were better. Amongst all the radicals of the 1650s, none went so far as to suggest women should stand side by side with men as equal citizens of the commonwealth. The analogy of the household as state provided everyone with a clear and comprehensible model of the contractual relations of obedience, and the relationship between husband and wife provided the model of female subordination to male authority.

At the same time, the ideals of prescriptive literature were themselves contradictory, unrealistic and sometimes extreme. The discussion of marital and domestic violence in the Homily on Matrimony portrays men beating their wives as both unacceptable and sometimes unavoidable. Its comparison with the dishonour of a man beating his servant stands in contrast to Dod and Cleaver's careful delineation of domestic discipline: for the latter work, the question was not whether to beat the servants, but who should beat them [**Doc. 34, p. 118; Doc. 36, p. 118**]. Dod and Cleaver, William Gouge, and the authors of other marital advice were Puritan clergymen preaching in a relatively narrow framework. A host of other contemporary sources offered different perspectives. We get some sense of one contemporary reaction from the prologue to William Gouge's *Domesticall Duties*, which recalls the sermons' original audience complaining about Gouge's advice on the subjection of women and their lack of control over property; Gouge's response is long and defensive [**Doc. 37, p. 123**]. Clearly, these could be matters of contention amongst churchgoers. While the Homily on Matrimony enshrines familiar principles of marital relations which were reiterated through the Tudor and Stuart period at every level of culture, it is also written with an air of debate. Historians have been apt to take Puritan household advice as either a realistic description of household order, or a reasonable prescription to aspire to; it may well be neither, and it was certainly the product of a particular set of voices at a certain moment. The balance of power between husband and wife, and the relationship between love and domination, was worked out in the pulpit, on the printing presses and in marriages.

Early modern marriage was a different institution to its modern form. It was shaped by a particular set of legal rules, some of which were under pressure from religious and political changes and by demographic realities. The ceremony of matrimony was still, as it had been for centuries, not entirely under the compass of the church. It was a process rather than a single event, often involving months if not years of courtship, an informal betrothal and sometimes a formal contract before the ceremony in church. The potential complications of this process meant that late sixteenth-century church courts were still dealing with disputed marriage contracts. A properly made contract could, in theory, undo a later church marriage, and one of the options for women and men whose courtships had gone awry was to pursue the other partner through the church courts. Such cases were infrequent, but are rich with detail about the expectations of the courtship period. The key elements for a binding contract were witnesses; the exchange of gifts, such as gloves, bowed coins or rings; and the exchange of words taken directly from the marriage service. To venture on any of these things made the tentative gestures of early courtship more formal. There were, though, plenty of ways to sidestep the final binding step of formal contracts. Promises in the future tense, or conditional ones, kept options part-way open. Sex continued to be the one binding event that made a conditional contract firm.

The rituals of courtship allocated highly gendered roles to men and women. If marriage was the time that future identity was settled, courtship was a time when women exercised a freedom to decide. They did not ask, but they responded and negotiated. Their options were still open. The rules of betrothal, which still had weight in canon law, enabled women to give men a conditional answer which they could later retract: 'if my friends agree' seems to have been a common response to a proposal. It was a time when the mixed circles of young people fell into single-sex groups, and as matters became more serious, the chaperonage of older family and friends was called for. The acceptance of rings and other gifts could be a key piece of evidence that a woman had accepted a proposal: for women especially, gift exchange could be highly compromising. The conventions of contracting left both parties room for manoeuvre, but the flexibility of informal contracts could go disastrously wrong.

Most women and men conducted their courtships in relative independence. Many were living away from home, in service or as apprentices, and by the time they married many had lost one or both parents. The influences on courtship were more likely to be contemporaries and employers. Despite the distance between many young people and their birth families, the influence of parents remained important. The power of mothers, in particular, was often cited in marriage contract litigation. Those parents who were still alive were likely to be instrumental in helping to set up a first household, alongside the friends who might contribute to a woman's marriage portion, or help a man along in his trade or profession. Even in London, where so many young people were in service away from home, marriages depended on the support of older friends and employers. Friends in marriage safeguarded the marital process from being driven by impulse, lust or unprotected individual desire. The role of parents and friends was also a useful protection at a time of great importance. The process of betrothal and marriage exemplified the depth of kinship and friendship ties for both women and men. Even remarrying widows and widowers were expected to make their decisions with reference to their friends.

The day-to-day relations between husbands and wives are some of the hardest historical experiences to recover. Even those who left personal writings were unlikely to write of the ordinary life of a marriage; quotidian days, months and years left almost no record. Letters, by their nature, were written in unusual periods of absence, and whilst family letters can be wonderfully intimate, few collections include letters from both husbands and wives.

Thus, one of the essential parts of gender relations can be glimpsed only from the margins. It is all too easy to fill in the gaps with modern assumptions. The language of courtship is one safeguard against this: most expected, it seems, to marry on the basis of choice, but to find love developing afterwards. Contrary to modern convictions, too, is the co-existence of authority, companionship and love. Amongst those elite women who left letters, the obedience required of them was sometimes a matter for jest: Maria Thynne's letters tease out the contradictions of loving marriage, and read interestingly against her mother-in-law's more conventional ones [**Doc. 38, p. 124**]. The Thynne marriage, though, was a clandestine one, much opposed by her husband's parents, and their union left a lasting bitterness between the elder Thynnes and their daughter-in-law. Neither amongst elites, nor amongst plebeians, do historians now discern a measurable shift from one type of marriage to another. The rhetoric of companionate marriage certainly became more powerful from the late seventeenth century, and is nicely reflected in the family portraits of the seventeenth and eighteenth centuries; transitions in the emotional landscape are much harder to see. Most powerful in determining the nature of marriage may be the fact that for the majority of the population, marriage was expected to be made by choice, at a relatively mature age, and with little parental pressure.

Early modern marriages were not expected to end in any way other than death. Legal separations or annulments were rare: even the large diocese of London and Middlesex dealt with fewer than ten cases a year. There were, nonetheless, a number of ways marriages could be ended, informally or formally. Informal separations were the simplest. A brief survey of women's diaries and letters might suggest a high proportion of elite women living apart from their husbands: both Anne Clifford and her sister, for example, did so (Clifford in two consecutive unhappy marriages), as did Elizabeth Freke [**Doc. 39, p. 126**]. But these were women whose writing was at least partly propelled by their marital disputes, in these cases over property and debt. At a lower social level, the church courts, while they provided a mechanism for legal separation, aspired rather to keep couples together. Living apart was an infraction of canon law, and regularly presented to courts. The rules for legal separation were ambiguous, and often depended on precedents rather than canon law. Most depended on the proof that husband or wife was incapable of marriage or that the marriage was itself null. Marriages could be annulled on grounds of physical incapacity: impotence, but not infertility. The female partner of a man alleged to be impotent was required to prove herself a virgin. After 1563, the degrees of kin within which marriages were prohibited were much simplified and rarely invoked, as was forced marriage. Child spousals were occasionally mentioned, but likely to occur only in more conservative communities. Bigamy was more common, often semi-accidental: couples had separated, lost touch or gone abroad, and presumed or hoped that their former partner was dead.

Marriage rules, then, were somewhat negotiable. Ecclesiastical law made separation unlawful, and couples known to be living apart were regularly prosecuted. The general ferment around marriage reform in mid-sixteenth century Europe seems also to have left some people with a sense that marriages could be less permanent than the church held. Some people interpreted 'separation from bed and board', the nearest the church offered to divorce, as if it entitled them to remarry. Long absences and difficulties of communication might facilitate bigamy and informal separation. The potential for losing touch was more likely to work in favour of men than women: a wife was unlikely to be able to support herself alone.

In law, a measure of violence from husband to wife was legal. Common law was understood to allow husbands to beat their wives, but not 'outrageously' or 'violently'. A woman whose husband broke those limits could bind him over to keep the peace, or sue at the church courts for separation from bed and board. Only a few did. Women who sued for separation were required to prove that the violence had been so severe they were in danger of death; accordingly, the evidence records extreme and brutal violence. Printed literature openly discussed the legitimacy of marital violence. Most agreed that, if legal, it was highly undesirable, and that a good husband should be able to persuade his wife to obey without force. In this lies the crucial difference between modern and early modern perceptions of male violence. In the seventeenth century, men's violence to their wives was often seen as a manifestation of a greater issue of subordination: men beat their wives if they could not get them to obey, and the conflicts reflected arguments about property, children and social life [**Doc. 40, p. 127**] (Plate 7). The violence that reached the courts was exceptional; cases like this tell us little about ordinary marriages and everyday disputes, but they do convey some sense of where the lines of unacceptability were drawn, in a social system that allowed men and women few ways of parting once bound together.

In the eighteenth century, a sea change in cultural representations of violence became apparent. It was no longer discussed in public discourse; the decline in acceptability of violence generally also meant the disappearance of domestic violence from the cultural radar. This says nothing, of course, about the actual levels of violence. But the degree to which violence was a matter of neighbourhood concern in the sixteenth and seventeenth centuries could be protective, as well as dangerous for women.

Neighbourly intervention in marital relations testified to the degree to which early modern marriage was a public affair. The bond between husband and wife was at the heart of the economic household. Orderly marriages were integral to that constant concern of early modern communities, keeping the peace. Partly this was due to factors of space and architecture: it was hard to ignore what happened between husband and wife, even within the walls of the household. But it also stemmed from a deeply rooted sense that marital relations were a community concern.

Far more often than any kind of separation, early modern couples were separated by death, and at an early age. Marriage was of necessity a serial institution; as many as one in three of all marriages were second unions for at least one party, and the median length of marriages was a decade.

This meant that remarriage was a live issue for most families. There does not seem to have been any actual stigma attached to remarriage: it was both an economic and a social necessity. Some men's wills even made specific reference to their wives' potential future husbands, advising them to choose well. At the same time, the cultural weight laid on women's continence meant that the remarriage of widows could arouse tensions. Ballads, plays and jokes poked fun at sexually experienced older women marrying young men.

The economic aspect of remarriage has raised some interesting historical debates, which expose some basic assumptions about marriage. The rates at which widows remarried differed, depending partly on their financial and landholding situation. Traditional demographic arguments assume that all widows wanted or needed to remarry: in fact, a more complex reasoning came into play. If poorer widows could not afford to remarry, the richest could afford not to. Both economic evidence and personal writings reveal widows making careful decisions about how to preserve inheritances in the light of custom and land tenure. Some rural widows inherited freebench, entitling them to their husband's manorial land for life: they were more likely to remarry than those living in manors which limited a widow's inheritance if she remarried.

PARENTHOOD

In theory, fatherhood was the essence of patriarchy: the domestic authority of men was the bulwark of national order. Motherhood, less charged with the rhetoric of authority, had its own political associations with protection, peace and nurture of the generations necessary to national expansion. The model of the nursing mother was strong enough to be cited not just by tracts advocating breastfeeding, but by male prophets, clergymen and monarchs describing their own role: the biblical image of the 'nursing father' united paternal authority and maternal care.

The demographic and economic realities of domestic life made the practice of parenthood socially variable. Elite families, who bore children earlier, maintained ties of dependence across generations and into the adult lives of children; newly married elite couples, often still in their teens, might start their lives together in the parental home. Poorer parents were less likely to maintain a grip of authority on children who left home in their teens and married later and more independently. The poorest were at risk of seeing their families absorbed and dispersed by the parish authority of 'civic fathers', who were authorised to bind out the children of the poor to parish work. By this manoeuvre, poor men were readily dispossessed of the authority of paternity that defined elite governors.

The emotional tenor of parental relationships is as hard to pin down as the division of parental labour. The nature of work and domestic space meant that in many households children spent much time at close quarters with their parents; while the responsibility for childcare seems to have been universally female, children worked from a young age, and children's presence was a part of street life. Amongst elite families, a greater division was apparent, between the female responsibility for early childhood and fathers' responsibility for their sons after breeching.

For women, parenthood brought them into the world of mothers and matrons, a world of sociability, conversation and secrets exchanged between gossips and around the rituals of childbirth. Paternal identity was less manifest and less collective. It was also potentially insecure. Blood ties mattered: blood was the metaphor for relatedness. But paternity was putative. It could rarely be as certain as maternity mostly was. Legal convention held that all children born in a marriage were the husband's: there was no procedure for investigating other possibilities. Medical theories about conception and the power of maternal imagination added another layer of potential uncertainty.

DOMESTIC SPACE

Examining the use of space gives historians an insight into both concrete and abstract aspects of gender relations. Contemporary ideologies of marriage and household always had a spatial dimension. The conceptual distinction between public and private spheres came into play towards the end of our period, but earlier on the distinction between outside and inside provided a touchstone for gender rules. The walls of the house were imagined to safeguard the household's honour and the wife's honesty. The role of the husband comprised work outdoors, provisioning and labouring; that of the housewife revolved around keeping and caretaking [**Doc. 36, p. 122**]. Puritan marriage manuals laid particular stress on the dangers of vanity and display: for them, the household kept the wife under her husband's governance. The symbolic weight of the walls was considerable. Prescriptions for the gender division between outdoors and indoors were rhetorically powerful, but there is no evidence that they described actual spatial practices. Every image of early modern marketplaces featured women, both selling and buying; a host of depositions describe women, both housewives and servants, going in and out of houses and up and down streets as a central part of their daily business.

Uses of actual space gave houses a history of their own, one that differentiated space by gender and by age and status. The study of household space has mostly been at the level of the great houses. There, the great shift in building styles meant a transition from houses with great halls where much of daily life was lived, towards more differentiated spaces where husbands and wives, children and servants lived and worked separately.

Women's agency in building is hard to trace, but suggestive: if architecture is apt to replicate established modes of power relations, those outside the system might be expected to design with a difference. Elite women's roles in commissioning buildings was often derived from their inheritances from a father, in the lack of male heirs; the buildings they designed tended to reflect more traditional styles (Gothic when classicism was coming into vogue), in keeping with a use of building as family memorial.

In the great houses of early modern England, changes in building style and room arrangement were becoming evident. Households were increasingly able and expected to provide a certain amount of individual space, if not privacy in the modern sense. Rooms were becoming more differentiated: the medieval hall was replaced by single function rooms, like the kitchen and the upstairs bedchambers. In the houses of the urban middling sort, room specialisation was also evident; parlours were becoming less multifunctional, although some kitchens continued to include beds throughout the seventeenth century, as well as chairs, tables and books. Vernacular housing, though, was also apt to remain fairly static in organisation; throughout our period, bedrooms were often also passages to somewhere else. Privacy in the modern sense was hard to attain. Nevertheless by the end of the period, a sense of possessive space is becoming evident. By the eighteenth century, ordinary Londoners were making regular reference to their use of keys and locked boxes; even tenants in lodging houses seemed to have some expectation of personal space. In the great houses, the growing trend for closets for reading gave elite men and women another kind of space to themselves.

In most houses, gender segregation was minimal. Despite the sermons and advice-writers' repetition of biblical advice that women should keep to the house and men to the outside world, actual patterns of work, marketing and housewifery made this unlikely to happen. In urban household workshops, domestic servants and apprentices were likely to mix with husbands, wives and children, as well as visiting customers and neighbours. Kitchens were not exclusively female space, and while workshops were largely male, female domestic servants and wives also spent plenty of time there. The closely-connected rooms ensured that women and men of all ages spent most of their time in a heterosocial world.

The marriage bed, usually the most expensive piece of furniture in the house, and hung with draperies for warmth and privacy, underlined and symbolised the bodily unity of husband and wife. Nevertheless, in houses with more space, or in unhappy marriages, men and women had rooms of their own. Lady Anne Clifford's diary records her often sleeping apart from her two husbands, sometimes with her children. In a marital dispute in seventeenth-century London, Anne Young resorted to her own room after a violent dispute with her husband; forsaking his bed was part of their relationship breakdown, and was cited by her husband as key evidence against her when she sued for a separation [**Doc. 40, p. 127**].

What imbued architectural space with gendered meanings was the blend of prescriptive ideals, building practices and social interaction. Ballads and household advice presented the domestic interior as a world of female work; the meaning of 'housewife' was fleshed out over and over in contemporary texts. The ideological power of domestic space made the doorstep a flashpoint for gender and community relations. From there, women observed their neighbours and defended their own space. However unrealistically, domestic ideals stressed that women's place was indoors, men's outdoors; the walls of the house were meant to guarantee virtue. Very few households could follow those rules, which were perhaps only remotely plausible in elite families, but their power was apparent everywhere.

DIVISIONS OF LABOUR

The household was also, most essentially, an economy. Around the relationship of husband, wife, servant and apprentice, labour relations were organised. Contemporary religious prescriptions identified husbands as workers and earners, wives as keepers and spenders; actual practice for working families was quite different, and dependent on a different model of gendered labour: more overlapping, though still restrictive. Housewifery loomed large in advice literature, with texts like Gervase Markham's *The English Housewife* (1615) setting out a model for women's work growing vegetables, making medicines, dairy work, preserving and making clothes. Much of this work was shared between mistresses and servants, although cooking, in particular, was becoming central to servants' work, and larger households were employing separate cooks or cookmaids.

Married women's work was far from entirely domestic. The best evidence for the variety of roles women undertook comes, so far, from urban sources.

In the court records of late seventeenth-century London, women's responses to questions about how they maintained themselves reveal a level of something like 60 per cent of wives keeping themselves by their own labour. The range of descriptions by women of where they worked, as much as the less dependable figures from this sample, are revealing: cleaning and washing; market selling; victualling; knitting and other textile work; nursing (Earle, 1989). Typically this was peripatetic work, or work that could be done in the home; what is invisible is the kind of labour that married women and daughters contributed to the workshops across the whole range of trades and crafts that were run by men. Where guilds regulated labour, the precise rules of female participation in guild-regulated industries were often not firmly set down, though a number of guilds periodically clamped down on mistresses, daughters and female apprentices working in competition with men, especially in times of under-employment [**Doc. 41, p. 130**]. Male artisan identity depended partly on the exclusion of women, as well as of outsiders; one complaint against French immigrants was the free training of girls in weaving who then married men in other trades, giving them an unfair range of expertise (Consitt, 1933: 313). Apprentice disputes and demonstrations show them defining their masculinity against their mistresses and against the maids of the household. Apprenticeship, however, was not exclusively a male option, and a few girls' names appear in the apprenticeship registers of a wide range of trades. Generally, widows were allowed to continue a trade after their husbands' death, but while some trades, like printing, allowed them to carry on even if they remarried a man of another occupation, others, like weaving, did not. In the seventeenth century printing was one of the few trades where women took a visible public part, their names marked on their publications. One privilege was available to married women through custom: in London and borough towns, either formal regulations or informal practice enabled married women to adopt **feme sole** trader status, which allowed them to do business with the privileges of being single.

Feme sole: Legal status of single woman.

Being unmarried did not, however, make independent work easy. For the increasing number of unmarried women, working for themselves was fraught with obstacles. In provincial towns and cities, only a few exceptions applied for and gained the freedom that allowed them to trade. Through the seventeenth century women working at their own hands were regularly forced out of communities or ordered to dispose of the tools of their trade. The situation changed somewhat in the late seventeenth century.

The reorientation of the early modern economy from a rural, household-based system towards a capitalist, urban-based economy has been pivotal in narratives of gender and change. Its precise timing remains hard to establish. Historians have seen the early signs of industrialisation and proto-capitalism, and the consequent economic marginalisation of women, at times ranging from the late fifteenth century to the late seventeenth. England was still a diverse economy; it is not inconceivable that the pace of what was in any case a gradual change could have been both slow and variable. But it should warn us to attend carefully to the precise relationship between gender relations and economic change, when the latter is so hard to pin down.

Household production remained pivotal to trade and industry. The new draperies of the early sixteenth century, readily woven at home, gave it a further boost. Within the household, gendered divisions of labour seem to have prevailed, with distinctions that varied by craft. Women's work had always also involved work outside the household; evidence from both the sixteenth and seventeenth centuries shows women working outside the house and apart from their husbands. Some of this was selling goods from the household, smallholding or workshop; some of it was entirely separate work like victualling, washing or nursing.

Much history of women's work follows one narrative: the progress of capitalism and the simultaneous exclusion of women from the most productive areas of work. Most would agree, though, that there was no medieval 'golden age' of equal economic roles for women and men: distinctions between the work suitable for women and men were a part of the gender order. What changed was the status and economic worth of particular types of work, and in line with these changes, the line between men's and women's work moved. Brewing provides a good case study. Brewing was traditionally women's work: it was a largely domestic process and the occupational term 'brewster', like other 'st' occupational words, demonstrated its association with women, but by the seventeenth century it was a largely male occupation, and women's participation had been marginalised. A combination of factors was responsible. Supervision of brewing increased, and men rather than women were licensed, often employing their wives. Ale began to be eclipsed by beer as the staple drink; the addition of hops meant more beer could be produced from one brewing, and economies of scale became evident. The need for more space and more credit to facilitate larger, less frequent brewings took beer out of the household economy, and particularly out of the reach of single women. At the same time, the older image of the alewife as a good housewife was replaced by anxieties about alewives as dishonest corrupters of both men and drink (Bennett, 1996).

Work patterns often look as if they were gendered by a consistent ideology that aligned women with work that was unpaid and/or undervalued, piecemeal and domestic. All through our period, the work that men did was recorded more fully and formally than that of women. The few women's names that appear in apprenticeship registers provide only a tantalising glimpse of the whole picture of women's work in trades and crafts. Women's work was readily elided with domestic roles: the nursing, cleaning and washing that women did in houses, whether their own or those of others, is often invisible, and apt to be read as caring, or housewifery. But there were also similarities and overlaps between women's and men's work. For most of our period, much skilled work took place in the household. While guild regulations sometimes excluded women from certain aspects of particular trades, the actual divisions of work in real households are unlikely to be recaptured. Pay is another issue. Labour regulations, issued by justices of the peace, set the rates of pay for women labourers at around one-half to two-thirds that of men: there was never any expectation that a woman would be able to support a household on her own earnings. These, however, only applied to agricultural labourers. In towns and cities, it looks increasingly as if occupations were more diverse than the names men gave their work: piecemeal work, especially for the poor, may be characteristic of men as well as women. Emerging evidence demonstrates the potential, at least from the late seventeenth century, of skilled, respectable work for women, such as millinery and clockmaking.

Midwifery constitutes a special case, as a women's occupation. The appearance of male midwives did not have a significant impact on women's midwifery until the eighteenth century, and midwives had an important legal and community role. Trained by informal apprenticeship, they were regulated by the church courts, and far from being suspected of witchcraft, they were more likely to be used as witnesses against them. The significance of reproduction for monarchy, families and communities meant midwives had a genuinely public role, whilst much of what they did was kept in secret. This made for an equivocal status.

The ease with which most men named themselves, in official circumstances, by occupation suggests a relationship between work and identity that was much more straightforward than it could be for women. However, the economic crises of the late sixteenth century complicated that relationship. With rapidly rising population and high inflation, under-employment was becoming an established problem. In many urban areas the transition through the stages of work from apprentice, through journeyman, to master was becoming harder for men to achieve. Journeymen were shut out from the opportunity to become masters, and ended up as permanent wage labourers, a position of little earning power and low repute. Agricultural labourers found it harder to establish their own smallholdings. Perpetually dependent, a significant proportion of men could not muster the economic resources to marry and support a household. Their position in communities, short of all the evidence of functional manhood, could be problematic. They were men: yet they were excluded from what has been called the 'patriarchal dividend', the advantages to men as a group from the patriarchal system (Connell, 2009: 142). Alehouse culture, gambling, violence and 'ill rule' provided an alternative means of self-assertion to the respectability of the successful householder. The fragility of male working identity was instrumental in producing the hierarchies of masculinity that characterised early modern gender relations.

ECONOMIC ROLES

The economy of marriage has been extraordinarily neglected. Economic historians are apt to rely on established assumptions about how the economy works. Men are expected to earn, women to spend; women need to marry and cannot be expected to earn a living wage; men can be independent, women cannot. Men, not women, had occupations, operated businesses and owned property. In early modern England most of those assumptions can be disproven. Levels of remarriage after widowhood make it clear that marriage was, in fact, even more economically and socially necessary for men, whose remarriages came, on the whole, sooner than women's. Women's financial contributions to households were, as we have seen, often essential. The property arrangements of marriages were subject to a whole scaffold of legal conditions, organised around **coverture**: as significant as the restrictions were women's evasions of them.

Coverture: The common law doctrine whereby a married woman's legal identity was subsumed under that of her husband.

Coverture was a peculiarly English system. After marriage, a wife's legal identity was part of her husband's, and consequently, most of her property rights were covered by his [**Doc. 42, p. 131**]. All but freehold land was transferred to the husband's ownership after marriage. Traditionally, widows were entitled to one-third of their husbands' movable property; but this 'reasonable part' was abolished in the north of England and London around 1700, and in the rest of the south before 1500 [**Doc. 43, p. 131**].

One result of this draconian regime was a flourishing variety of financial instruments to allow women to hold some goods in their own names. Bonds, settlements, contracts and trusts enabled some propertied women to evade the implications of coverture. Unless a woman had made a separate contract, she was unlikely to have any property of her own after marriage. The need to do so must have prompted a significant degree of financial awareness amongst women with property to keep. Elizabeth Freke navigated her way around the financial constraints of marriage with the help of her father, who was clear-eyed about the risks of her husband having complete financial autonomy [**Doc. 39, p. 126**]. Anne Clifford spent years fighting to inherit her family's estates; one of the eventual outcomes when she did so was the monumental 'Great Picture' which narrated her struggle and set her in the framework of her ancestors (Plate 4). Like other landed women in the period, her connection to the estates to which she was born was imperilled by her sex.

In practice, husbands and wives at many social levels seem to have maintained a quite solid sense of property ownership through marriage. Law did not necessarily determine, or reflect, popular understandings of economic relations. William Gouge's attempt to remind women that the letter of the law made marital property their husbands' to dispose of met with a distinctly frosty reception [**Doc. 37, p. 123**].

If married women were particularly economically disadvantaged in England, single women were peculiarly protected from economic inhibitions. Elsewhere in Europe single women needed guardians to engage in contracts and economic arrangements; in England they could operate exactly as men did. Their ability to do business was so useful that in some places the provision for 'feme sole traders' allowed married women to do business as if they were single. Without the need to resort to guardians, it has been argued, single women's economic activity transformed the English financial marketplace: it substantially increased the degree of economic activity, in particular, investments.

The late seventeenth century saw an expansion of personal investment activity, particularly in London. The financial revolution involved speculation on the exchanges on the part of small investors as well as major shareholders. Significant amongst those investors were single women: their investments have been traced in the Bank of England, in the stock market and in government bonds. Studies of individual entrepreneurs have illuminated the strategies of women such as Joyce Jefferies, an early seventeenth-century Herefordshire gentlewoman who managed an annual income of nearly £500 and Hester Pinney, who spent most of her life in London, dealing in lace and investing her income (Tittler, 1994; Sharpe, 1999).

More than most other fields, economic history has been slow both to historicise the effects of gender and to explore the roles of women. Recent research into responses to coverture, testamentary behaviour, credit and investment by women suggests that a significant challenge needs to be posed to standard economic narratives. In fact, Amy Erickson argues that taken together, single women's freedom to move money, and the complex financial instruments developed for and by married women, had a significant impact on the early development of capitalism in England. The peculiar combination of restrictions and freedoms on English women's property transactions actually facilitated the flow of capital that enabled the financial revolution (Erickson, 2005). In this field, gender history continues to undercut some central methodological assumptions: that women are necessarily dependents and followers of men; that domestic work is negligible; and that marriage benefits and protects women more than men.

SERVICE AND APPRENTICESHIP

In a world balanced on the side of youth, servants and apprentices took a prominent place in households and communities. Around half the households in early modern England employed servants, the majority only one. The majority of young people were in service: young men mostly in apprenticeships to crafts and trades or as farm servants, young women in domestic service either in cities or in the country. Their tasks and living situations varied, but the common features distinguished male and female servants sharply. Apprentices and male farm servants were training to become masters or husbandmen themselves: the aim was to amass enough skills to move from dependence to autonomy, the epitome of full manhood. The constraining economic circumstances of the late sixteenth century meant that many would fail to do so, and would have, instead, to achieve 'manhood' in different ways. For women, that aspiration to autonomy was never there. The definition of womanhood was not to be independent, but to be able to marry: with the skills, reputation and, preferably, portion that made a useful wife. The transition from adolescence meant a move towards independence for men; for women, it meant a greater constraining of opportunities and financial independence.

Edward Barlow left home with his parents' full support, though he remembered his mother waving him goodbye so well he drew it in his autobiography; his story of departure endows his mother with the urge to hang on to him and his father with the ability to let him go, and construes himself in the mould of a self-reliant young man whose ambitions lie far from the drudgery of agricultural labour or the uncertain rewards of apprenticeship [**Doc. 44, p. 133**] (Plate 5). Jane Martindale's ambitions, articulated only by her brother, are less clear; her family hung on more firmly to her, hoping not to lose her to the snare of London, but she too left determined [**Doc. 8, p. 92**]. Both of them trusted to the wider world, rather than their parents, to provide opportunities for them, but while Barlow's narrative employed a familiar trope of male independence, Martindale's story is haunted by the pervasive fear of the sexual dangers in wait for young women in London. Yet the possibilities of London loomed especially large for women, aware of the constraints of other opportunities; urban service almost always offered better wages than agricultural work. Once employed, servants continued to be mobile, in particular women, who were less rigidly tied to contracts and often hired annually. Before she ended up at London's **Bridewell**, Mawdlin Gawen followed a not unusual pattern of short-term contracts across two counties and with various employers, some relatives [**Doc. 11, p. 95**].

Bridewell: Converted from a palace to a prison and poorhouse in 1566.

For those in service, adolescence was characterised both by a degree of independence from parents and a bound subordination in another household. The consequent emotional complexities could include close ties between children and servants, or conflicts between mistress and maidservants. The tensions of apprenticeship were well attested to in contemporary literature. Apprentices were being trained, eventually, to become masters themselves; but in the meantime they were dependent on their employers' goodwill for everything, and subject to the orders of their mistresses, which some resented. Clothes, food and health provided perpetual sources of complaint for apprentices. Edward Barlow's reminiscences of apprenticeship in Lancashire in the mid seventeenth century describe a marginal, resented position at the end of the household table; his fellow apprentice also suggested, to his displeasure, that the reward of service was to marry a daughter of the house [**Doc. 44, p. 133**]. For young women, the risks of service included sexual harassment and, sometimes, sexual relations, rape and pregnancy. Of the illegitimacy cases that were dealt with by the courts, the majority concerned servants pregnant by masters or their friends and family: the conditions of employment put young women at risk. Service and apprenticeship also put the young in key positions in domestic disputes. Their evidence is always crucial to marriage separations and often to other legal cases, and the lines of loyalty within divided households did not fall predictably.

The nature of early modern service was peculiar to the period: intimate, familiar and unstructured, it was still part of a hierarchy. Mistresses and domestic servants, in particular, worked alongside each other; it was not until more complex hierarchical households developed that mistresses were expected to sit atop a pyramid of specialised servants. Both apprentices and servants were likely to reach sexual maturity in a household with unrelated adults: sexual contacts and suspicions were part of the cultural context of service. Given the importance of adolescence in the development of individual gender identities, it is worth considering the impact of these very particular domestic conditions.

THE SINGLE

Most sixteenth- and seventeenth-century opinion took marriage to be the linchpin of a stable, successful life. For both women and men, adulthood was expected to involve marrying, establishing a household and probably raising children. For middling-status men, marriage often marked a transition into self-sufficiency; marriage was virtually necessary to run a business or a farm. For women, marriage was additionally marked by admission into different social circles and appropriate clothes. A married woman wore a hood or hat; in church, she was allowed to sit in a pew instead of standing with the single people. She was invited to attend births and participated in the shared sexual knowledge of matrons. At the same time, her legal status changed radically: she became irrevocably a dependent.

Single life for both men and women offered some autonomy, but it still required them to be under the authority of the patriarchal household. The Statute of Artificers (1563) decreed that those between 12 and 40 years old, out of service and without a certain level of property could be compelled into service; it was invoked most often against single women working 'at their own hand', who were perceived to be particularly awkward in the late sixteenth and early seventeenth centuries, when inflation and demographic expansion were making the balance of employment fragile in many places [**Doc. 45, p. 135**]. Single women were an easy scapegoat.

By the middle of the seventeenth century, both single men and single women were a larger proportion of the population than they seem to have ever been before. Of those born between 1562–6, 4 per cent are estimated to have remained unmarried until their forties; of those born between 1602–6, the proportion was as high as 24 per cent, though this figure is probably distorted by clandestine and unofficial marriages in the mid- to late-seventeenth century. Proportions remained high through the later seventeenth century and fell again with the generations born in the 1680s (Wrigley and Schofield, 1981: 260). Of course, not marrying does not necessarily mean staying celibate: the actual relationships of the unmarried are almost entirely invisible. Living together without marriage, however, remained socially as well as spiritually unacceptable. At the least, these figures suggest that by the second half of the seventeenth century, staying single was no longer exceptional. Some of this change was forced by economic factors: marriage still meant economic independence, and it was harder for men to get to the point of being able to start their own households. By the later years of the seventeenth century, it was also becoming more feasible for women to live a single life. In London's Royal Exchange, women held stalls and ran businesses in their own name. In small towns, expanding textile industries offered opportunities that enabled women to support themselves. Proto-industrialisation is sometimes seen as encouraging early marriage, by enabling women to earn enough to marry earlier; but it also had the opposite effect of making self-sufficiency more possible.

The numbers of single people in society belie the picture often painted by contemporaries, of a world composed of nuclear households. Every household listing includes significant numbers of single women heading households, usually widows, often with spinster daughters or dependent children.

Single women were also prominent in the local economy. Probate records reveal single women lending extensively, both charitably and for business purposes. Their economic position was likely to leave them with a degree of ready money; women who could survive on their own by definition had a reliable level of personal wealth. In some areas women were increasingly allowed to access legacies at a fixed age, rather than at marriage; they were also likely to be left cash. Lending money to friends also, presumably, helped stabilise single women's social position in the local community, creating another kind of credit. In samples of wills, 42–45 per cent of urban single women mentioned money lent out, not only to individuals but to town corporations (Froide, 2005: 130–6).

The word spinster evolved in a way that reflected the priorities of social control. Originally descriptive of women who worked at spinning, by the early seventeenth century it was also being used to describe a woman who had not yet married; eventually, in the early eighteenth century, it came to denote a woman permanently single. A number of the female professional writers of the late seventeenth century celebrated the single life and their freedom from marriage. Simultaneously, the phrase 'old maid' appeared and became pejorative. Just as being a single woman was becoming more possible, the cultural images of single women were becoming more unpleasant. Satires and advice literature depicted old maids as desperate, sinister and superfluous. The reality of independent single life that some women were achieving was unlikely to be reflected in the cultural landscape of late seventeenth-century England.

Much less work has been done on bachelors, but an increasing focus on the norms and ruptures of masculinity has exposed the importance of marriage as a measure of manhood. It was firmly tied to self-sufficiency: it was difficult for either men or women to make a living, or run a smallholding, alone. Widowers remarried even faster than widows: single householding was practically hard. Unlike single women, though, bachelors did not face an array of negative stereotypes, and they were less likely to be socially or legally disciplined into marriage or service. The model of manhood was sufficiently heterogeneous to allow the pursuit of other kinds of male identity.

3

Communities

Some of the most powerful narratives of early modern history have focused on the concept of community. It is a contested, imprecise term, readily taken to represent an opposite for atomised modernity; it was also a significant term to contemporaries, readily co-opted by monarchs and radicals alike. Alongside the notion of a community of propinquity, this chapter draws on the sense of moral community that animated the villagers, townspeople and citydwellers of early modern England. Often, the period from 1450–1750 has been identified with a transition from a community of ethical neighbourly bonds to one of individualistic, commercialised stratification; with an integration of local communities into national ones; and with a redrawing of the bonds between person and community. More recently, the continuities with older habits of reciprocity have been stressed: individualism did not have to run counter to community. Much of this historiography has had little to say about gender, but community structures and social relations were deeply inflected by sexual hierarchies, in particular with relation to poverty, sexual morality, religious roles and participation. In both moral intervention, and the quietness that was understood to make for orderly neighbourhoods, women's role mattered and gender relations were a target of criticism.

THE PARISH

Tudor government highlighted the parish as the crucible of social relations. In both rural and urban areas, the parish church provided a space, a time and an identity, ordering not just social relations, but gender. Parish churches expected a predictable local weekly congregation, and well into the seventeenth century some places still had seating plans. The weekly arrangement of the congregation was both a familiar and regular ritual of community life and a point of contest. Seating was habitually arranged by status and by gender.

The elites took places in the chancel, near what was, before the Reformation, the holiest part of the church. By the medieval period, many congregations stood in single-sex groups, with men either nearer the altar and the eastern end, and women at the back, or men on the south side, nearer the door and the outside world, and women on the north side. The east/west distinction, keeping women away from the altar, confirmed a long tradition of fear of the impurity of women, particularly when menstruating, but by extension, generally. The north/south separation seems to have related, rather, to the conventional placing of the Virgin on Christ's right hand, and hence, on the north side of the church; Lady chapels and carvings of the Virgin were usually on the same side, and seem to have been, before the Reformation, the particular responsibility of female parishioners. In the post-Reformation move towards fixed seating, the north/south distinction was continued; elite women sometimes claimed seats in the chancel, but with Laudian attempts to restore a holy order in church came an insistence that women should be seated in the body of the building. While fixed seating also began a move towards family pews, reflecting the general prioritisation of the godly family over single-sex groups, separate seating seems to have remained normal through most of the seventeenth century. Not everyone had a seat: servants and single people were often expected to stand, and children's places could be a problem. The rights of people to pew space and the system of pew rents led, sometimes, to pew disputes fought out with insults, pokes and shoves. Women's prominence in these disputes suggests their role as figureheads in local hierarchies and as monitors of behaviour in church.

The relationship of men and women to the building of the church reflected different patterns of devotion and spiritual involvement. Historically, women and men had been equally likely to leave bequests to their parish church, but with a different emphasis: men were more likely to donate to the fabric of the building, women to single out particular guilds, altars or lights dedicated to saints. The Protestant doctrine of spiritual equality was often not echoed in spiritual practice, but the Reformation did undermine some of the traditional gender distinctions in parish religion, partly by abolishing previously sex-specific practices. Liturgical distinctions of gender were destabilised. In baptism, different prayers were no longer said over male and female infants. Separate seating was no longer prescribed after 1552. The walls of the church featured texts instead of the old images: in some places these featured specific reminders of the respective duties of husbands and wives, including, in one Northamptonshire inscription, the text from Colossians 3: 'Husbands, love your wives, and be not bitter to them' (Peters, 2003: 189).

Parish government demanded lay involvement. The parish was the first route through which disciplinary moral offences were prosecuted and punished. Excluded from the formal routes of presenting complaints, women participated as key witnesses, particularly as maidservants. Men might serve as overseers or constables, or as members of the vestries which governed the most local affairs; women played a less formal role, but still participated. Before 1570, a small number of women have been found in the lists of **churchwardens**; the majority held office in the 1540s and 1550s, suggesting some connection between the disruptions of the Reformation and the potential for women to hold office (Peters, 2003:182). By the late sixteenth century no female churchwardens are recorded. The secularisation of parish government after the Reformation had something of the same effect: women's role in making feasts and fasts happen was no longer significant in the new church calendar.

Churchwardens: Elected unpaid lay officials of each parish, responsible for law and order in the church, poor relief and church maintenance.

AUTHORITY

The relative stability of early modern England, in the context of dramatic demographic and economic change, has often been associated with an effective system of local government. The parish was part of a net of participatory institutions, including manors, wards and vestries. The developments which characterised the early modern state included a complex legal system and a parish-based administration of poor law, as well as taxation and religious regulation.

Recent work on early modern government has placed less stress on institutions, and more on the social relations of state formation. Authority was asserted and experienced through processes of negotiation, participation, belonging and exclusion. Participation depended explicitly on social status, and implicitly on gender. Over a period of intensive bureaucratic development, the relationship of both women and men to local authority shifted somewhat.

The expansion of local government redefined, to varying degrees, the obligations of masculinity. The incorporation of middling-status men, who were expected to internalise, transmit and police the values of the orderly state, was pivotal to the governing process. In terms of social rank, the distinction between governors and governed was narrowing, with husbandmen and craftsmen joining their superiors in taking office. With office-holding extending further down into the social hierarchy, the distinction of gender became more marked. If men of middling status and lower could expect, and be expected, to hold office, such participation was becoming a marker of masculinity. It was particularly likely to be so in administration-heavy urban parishes, and in communities where Puritan convictions of civic responsibility for reform were strong.

Formal participation in government largely excluded women. The words *respectable* and *substantial* denoted men who helped govern; they were unlikely to be used of women. And correspondingly, it was clear that women took little part in the official project of government. This was hardly new, but it was more clearly articulated. By the late sixteenth century any flexibility in officeholding had been eliminated by the establishment of more systematic patterns of administration, including the rotation of office by households. Householding, so strong a plank in the edifice of middling-sort participation, did not carry the same civic obligations for women as it did for men; female householders, of whom there were plenty, were expected to nominate a deputy to do their duties. The office of constable often rotated amongst houses, but late seventeenth-century treatises took care to clarify precisely who was not eligible, specifying that even if women were householders, they were unfit to serve (Crawford, 2001: 204). Being female came to be an active disqualification for many of the core acts of citizenship in the early modern state.

Moreover, women's place in relation to government was also defined by their being likely to be the subjects of male authority. Patriarchal theory described a system in which wives were subject to their husbands, not necessarily one in which all women were subject to all men; but local government involved repeated instances of men exercising authority over women. Many of the positions in which middling-sort men participated in government were related to the poor law, such as churchwardens and overseers. Most of the recipients of poor relief were women. Particularly in hard times, one of the central duties of the lower ranks of officeholders was dealing with the poor: they were charged with overseeing paupers and ensuring the parish did not suffer too many claims on its funds. The dynamics of local government were thus likely to be shaped sharply along lines of gender: it would have been always apparent that substantial men governed poor women.

At the same time, the wives of those substantial men were part of the governing process. Early modern conceptions of the marital unit presented husband and wife as an intertwined couple, whose credit and honour were bound together; the interdependent nature of identity must have reinforced this. It is likely that many women saw themselves as part of the governing process simply by virtue of being part of a substantial household, to whose substance they contributed. Formal officeholding might be just the tip of the iceberg.

Despite all this, women were not entirely absent from the formal and less formal processes of government. Throughout the sixteenth and most of the seventeenth centuries, women played specific, significant roles in parish and community life, their authority largely confined to areas typically associated with female responsibilities. Women's domestic roles, as mothers in particular, qualified them especially as midwives and matrons; sworn midwives held an official role regulated by the church courts, and were regularly called upon to testify to the parentage of illegitimate children. Women took a substantial part in the neighbourhood monitoring of illicit sex, illegitimacy and infanticide. Their roles as concerned mistresses, mothers, observant servants and neighbours gave them a substantial stake in the moral community [**Doc. 14, p. 98**]. Infanticide prosecutions were prompted and aided by the observant eyes of female neighbours, who sometimes went on to search the bodies of suspected single women. Outside the domestic realm, women were employed to teach in free schools and supervise pauper apprenticeships. Hospitals for the poor employed them as keepers and matrons. It was women, too, who searched the dead for signs of plague: the lists of dead by parish that were such a feature of plague-time London were, at root, the work of women [**Doc. 46, p. 136**]. Much of this authority stemmed from the established association of women with the world of reproduction and the work of nursing and washing, and some of it was exercised in a largely female world: childbirth was, throughout the period, very much a female domain, as was the disciplining of female servants. It was 'matrons', older women who were usually married, who dominated in this world. The world of women involved competition and exclusion, targeting most obviously poor women, pregnant singlewomen and maidservants. Good order required everyone to observe and intervene: women were at least as likely to do this as men, and their 'natural' sphere gave them a specific realm in which to do so. Historians might now usefully modify Keith Wrightson's influential argument for the variability of concepts of order, across the communities of governors and governed, to take account of gender (Wrightson, 1980). Women cannot, as once was assumed, be counted simply amongst those who were governed: they participated officially and unofficially in the maintenance of order, and their association with sexual morals may have given them a particular sense of priorities in local government.

POVERTY

One of the defining features of early modern society was the emergence of a stigmatised class of 'the poor': those who received relief rather than contributing to it, who were indigent rather than self-sufficient, and who constituted both the rationale for parish government, and a burden on it. Gender relations were central to the social dynamics of poverty.

The Norwich census of the poor reveals a truth that must have been plainly evident to villagers and townsfolk: the majority of recipients of poor relief were women [**Doc. 47, p. 137**]. Every list of pensions and ad hoc grants of money features a familiar profile in which poor widows were the most likely to need and receive support. In a society increasingly ready to discriminate between the deserving and the undeserving poor, widows remained, on the whole, eligible for relief. Many made themselves more so by being what parishes called 'helpful': washing and nursing the disabled or cleaning. Poor women were ubiquitous in early modern society, yet very little of the literature on poverty acknowledges its utterly gendered nature. Being single virtually guaranteed indigency for women below the middling sort: very little work would pay a woman a living wage. Live-in service was almost the only way to survive, and it was aimed at women under thirty, although increasing numbers of older women seem to have stayed in service or returned to it.

At the far end of the hierarchy of the poor was another group of women: single mothers. Judicial and parochial responses to illegitimacy in the sixteenth and seventeenth centuries penalised the poor, removing pregnant single women from parishes where they had no legal right to settle, and exacting penance or punishment on them once they had delivered their children. What became of the children is not often clear; it was often assumed that a single woman could not maintain herself and a child, and in the seventeenth century justices of the peace started imprisoning mothers, assuming and ensuring they would not be able to care for the child. Some went to a parish wetnurse, where life expectancy was often short. The ready assumption of the infanticide statute of 1624, that single women were likely to keep pregnancies secret and then kill their newborns, betrayed a conviction that single motherhood was economically and socially impossible.

The gradual construction of the Elizabethan Poor Laws, culminating in the various acts of 1599–1601, made parishes responsible for their poor. It was at parish level that relief was collected, determined and distributed. The majority of poor relief recipients were women, and particularly old women and widows; the majority of those taxed were men. Through the relief system, a particular set of charitable obligations was constructed. Parishes expected contributions from their female recipients: washing, nursing, lending domestic goods or providing housing. Old poor women were a familiar, useful feature of early modern England. Their indigence was less unsettling than that of men.

CRIME AND THE LAW

Parallel to, and deeply bound up with, the other systems of order in early modern communities was that of the law. The complex nature of early modern law made it both a system for enforcing norms of behaviour and a resource for self-defence for both women and men.

The legal system of early modern England was dependent on popular participation. The relationship of gender and the law demands an examination, not just of the degree to which legal rules determined and were shaped by gender relations, but of the ability of women and men to manipulate the law in the service of dispute and conciliation. English law derived from a variety of sources, and was practiced in a series of jurisdictions; the flexibility of the system both supported the gender order, and offered women ways around male authority.

Early modern law invoked gender not so much explicitly as implicitly. Few laws singled out women particularly and the enforcement of male superiority came through assumptions as much as literal insistence. But inherent to the legal system was an understanding of married women as subject to severe legal disabilities [**Doc. 42, p. 131**]. For women, marital status mattered at law in a way it never did to men. English coverture, the treatment of married women as subject to their husbands, was almost uniquely severe in Europe, limiting the extent to which married women could inherit, make financial transactions or pursue cases at law. But it was also dependent on jurisdictions. Not all kinds of law depended to the same degree on coverture.

The English legal system centred on common law, the body of precedents evolved in the courts. It was common law that prescribed primogeniture and coverture. But in the sixteenth and seventeenth centuries the common law ran parallel to a range of competing jurisdictions, each of which treated women somewhat differently. Canon law, used in the church courts, allowed women to prosecute their own cases. Equity, used at chancery and mayor's courts, tempered the severity of the common law, and unlike common law, recognised the property rights of married women. Manorial and borough custom was locally variable, meaning women's right to inherit could depend on where they lived. Parliamentary statutes responded to current concerns, identifying, for example, single women as responsible for a wave of infanticide, or defining the requisite punishment for bastardy. The eventual triumph of common law over ecclesiastical law and custom has been seen as undermining women's status; certainly, by clarifying the rules of inheritance and property, common law left much less room for manoeuvre. But law, in this period, was essentially responsive to community concerns. Custom depended on memory and interpretation: even where women had a well-established right to inherit, it could be readily forgotten within a few generations.

The 'common peace', that notion intrinsic to English law, was gendered. Keeping order might mean preventing women from scolding, or men from beating their wives. Disruptions to gender roles were part of the picture of disorder. Early modern laws reached deep into everyday life, and past the modern boundary of privacy. Heresy and conscience; sedition; sexual offences;

marital harmony; working on the Sabbath; all came within the remit of the law. Most of these offences of social and moral order impacted on gender relations: they both brought women and men to the courts and involved them in prosecuting them. Through marriage and sex, the law – usually canon law – regulated the relations between women and men, and the relationship of heterosexual partnerships to the community and the state. Consequently, the pace and extent of prosecution of social and moral offences was key in setting the stage of gender relations. Two factors emerge as particularly significant in determining the progress and pace of prosecution of moral and social offences: economic difficulties and religious tensions.

The role of the state and its governing elites in enforcing the law was always limited by the readiness of people to prosecute. Crimes and civil offences needed people to observe, inform and prosecute. Criminal prosecution was unlikely, therefore, to follow an elite agenda; it demanded if not consensus, then collaboration. The increasing stress on middling sort men's role in governing meant that administering justice was, for some men, part of their identity: it drew on the values of respectability, loyalty and religion. But it was not an entirely masculine endeavour. While judges, juries and magistrates were, as they always had been, men, women might be called to sit on the '**jury of matrons**', whose deliberations determined whether convicted felons were found pregnant, and hence temporarily saved from the gallows. Women were also quite ready to mobilise the law's resources. Recognizances, a way of binding over petty offenders to keep the peace, were a particularly useful resource for women. And in all courts, women's witness statements weighed as heavily as those of men, with particular potency in trials for infanticide and witchcraft.

Jury of matrons: Women appointed to search female felons for the proof of pregnancy, in which case execution would be delayed.

The sixteenth century saw a huge expansion in litigation. A variety of civil and ecclesiastical courts made it possible for even the poor to bring legal action over insult, property, debt and other complaints. At Chancery, at the church courts and at the Elizabethan Court of Requests, women became prominent as litigants, their sphere of action surpassing by far the restricted roles laid on them by common law. Law became an important tool in the negotiation of local relationships, and both women and men found in it an extraordinary potential.

In most criminal offences, men were the majority of offenders. Sometimes the figures are deceptive: prosecutions for theft have been shown to mask high levels of female activity, with women both stealing valuable goods and taking a part in detecting them. In violent crime, the popular literature of domestic homicide vastly overrepresented the tiny numbers of women actually convicted of murdering their husbands: most homicides and violent assaults were committed by men against men. While it is hard to use these convincingly as a measure of how violent early modern society was, they can provide evidence about the meaning of violence for masculinity. In early modern England violence was often legitimate: it was part of state authority. The beating of servants and, less acceptably, wives was part of a spectrum of enforced power that was also manifested in public whippings and brandings. At the level of social interaction, violence expressed competition and status. A fight was a reasonable response to an insult, and cuffs, boxes on the ears and slaps on the face could be used to restore honour. Violence was not the opposite of honest manhood, but a central part of the whole hierarchy of masculinities.

The law differentiated between the sexes in both outright and subtle ways. The murder of a husband by his wife was so heinous a reversal of order that it was deemed petty treason, and punished with burning, like heresy. A flourishing genre of cheap print and drama publicised the tales of women who killed their husbands after committing adultery, describing them as monsters, strumpets and devils. Other crimes were largely female: infanticide, usually involving the murder of newborn illegitimate children by their mothers; witchcraft; and less dramatically, scolding, an offence of disorderly speech. All these were crimes of small numbers compared to the majority of criminal law business, and in the more serious, the weight of the law was often alleviated by the reluctance of judges to convict. In other circumstances, the potential leniency of the law favoured men: homicide convictions were liable to be mitigated as manslaughter on the grounds of assumptions about honour and justifiable violence which applied only to men (Walker, 2003).

David Underdown argued that the period 1580–1640 stood out as a period of gender crisis, based particularly on the increased prosecutions of scolds and witches, skimmington rituals, and the attempts to control single working women. The actual figures prosecuted in those years were low, and the timings different, but the point remains influential. Buying a ducking stool for scolds, or renovating an existing one, was a demonstration of parishes' commitment to public order: the control of women was symbolic of orderly social relations in general (Underdown, 1985; Ingram, 1994). Much of the identification of women's crime happened not in the letter of the law, but in its administration by justices: witchcraft and illegitimacy were cases in point. While the law penalised both parents of illegitimate children, mothers generally ended up bearing the brunt of it, only partly because they were easier to track down. Imprisonment of men was avoided because of their economic responsibility, and whipping, considered by Parliament in 1593, aroused considerable opposition. Parliamentary discussions about the proposals reveal how shocking such a punishment, readily applied to the poor and especially to women, seemed in the context of men of gentle birth [Doc. 48, p. 139].

The history of witchcraft prosecution illuminates the complexity of conflicts over gender relations. The trials that took place in England, largely between 1560 and 1660, were very largely prosecutions of women. A whole cultural apparatus ensured that the stereotyped witch was female, old and poor. Witches were tempted by familiars or by the Devil himself, in relationships that had aspects of the maternal or the sexual. They damaged food, drink, children and small animals, all the arena of women's work. Yet the idea of witch-hunting as a scapegoating of poor women by elite men provides only a small part of the story. Witches were women, but so were many of the witnesses and the instigators of prosecutions. Midwives, far from being the targets of prosecution, were sometimes employed to examine women to check for teats from which familiars might have sucked. None of this means that witchcraft was not 'about' gender, but it makes for a more complex picture than a misogynistic attack on women by men. The dramas of witchcraft seemed, very often, to happen in a female-dominated world: around and in the house, over the cooking fire, in the rocking cradle, at the river where washing was done. They involved conflicts between women over scarce resources, often food: much of the damage of witchcraft was an attack on the fragile process of producing edible food and drink, with particular attention to brewing, baking and cheese-making – all processes where corruption at a crucial point could make everything go wrong. The power of familiars recalls that of disruptive children, and suggests the significance of maternity to witchcraft stories; in some narratives women speak specifically of the loss of children, and in many, witches threaten infants. Witchcraft confessions also suggest the power that being suspected to be a witch might give women. It is worth remembering how many single women and widows, and how many old poor women, lived in English communities: the witch no longer looks isolated from the local community, but integrated into it, often through networks of obligation with its women.

POPULAR RITUALS

The communal nature of early modern life meant that gender roles and relations were monitored not just by internalised controls, but by the force of community judgement. This can be seen both as a practical manifestation of the public nature of domestic life and an aspect of the way selfhood was experienced through relatedness and embeddedness. Moral offences brought shame, not just to an individual, but to a household, a street or a village. In response, communities mobilised rituals that exerted considerable force on gender relations. Supportive rituals endorsed transitional moments, such as those around childbirth: the gathering of women to help in labour and visit afterwards made 'gossips' figures of influence, and lying-in a time of gravity.

Rituals of censure drew on powerful symbolic performances, illuminating a world where concrete objects and practices held deep meanings. The horns of cuckolds, supposedly derived from the fate visited in Greek mythology on Actaeon when he caught Artemis bathing, were both imaginary and actual. Men alleged to be cuckolds were libelled with fantasies about the size of their horns; some found real animal horns left at their door or the shape of them drawn in the dust. The gesture of fingers making horns on the head must have been often used. Cuckoldry was the mark of men who had been unable to satisfy their wives or fooled by their deceit; other rituals targeted inversions of gender order. In the skimmington ritual, best documented in the west country, a man rode backwards on a horse being beaten by a 'wife', often a woman in men's clothes, sometimes using the skimming ladle women used for cheesemaking. Skimmington, or 'riding the stang' as it was also known in the north, provided an elaborate, well established ritual for humiliating men who were allegedly subordinated to their wives, and wives who 'wore the breeches'. Rough music by a crowd beating pans and basins often accompanied it. Ballads and other narratives of gender disorder drew on these familiar images; a frieze of 'riding the stang' on the wall of the Great Hall at Montacute House, Somerset, commemorated it for all visitors (Plates 3 and 10).

All these were part of a Europe-wide festive tradition of charivari, in which popular rituals overlapped with and imitated formal justice. Courts, too, sentenced sexual offenders to ride in carts, or to be led about the town with basins being rung behind them. The ducking stools that parishes exerted themselves to buy at the turn of the sixteenth century were the folkloric punishment for scolds – women who disrupted the peace by aggressive speech. David Underdown has discerned a regional pattern to such rituals, employing the distinction made by agricultural historians between 'wood-pasture' areas, of dispersed settlements, developing capitalism and less cohesive communities, and arable villages, where the old structures of manor, squire and village government persisted (Underdown, 1985). It was in the former, where the regulative structures were weaker, that rituals of punitive response to gender disorder seemed to flourish. This pattern, and the general persistence of the images of control, suggests that running parallel to the Puritan civic government that was strong in these areas in the early seventeenth century was a resonant popular tradition of regulation by other means.

Charivari does not have to be read as conservative. Its performative essence did, after all, present a vision of a woman humiliating a man. It had a humour to it which was reflected in the ballads and woodcuts that rehearsed the tale of female domination in a whole series of marital confrontations. What is perhaps most telling is the concrete nature of this kind of community gender regulation. Breeches, horns, skimming ladles, ducking stools and the often mentioned, but rarely seen, scold's bridle embodied well-known meanings; they evoked the spectre of inversions of order. Explicit confrontations about gender relations are one of the hallmarks of this period.

REPUTATION

The social bonds of early modern England were built on trust. In a culture still largely oral, the security of social relations depended on trust, and trust derived from reputation. Social historians have demonstrated the depth and variety of the culture of popular honour, a concept traditionally associated with the nobility. For the ordinary working people of early modern England, honour was a matter of gendered morals. It was fought out with words as well as blows, and it was integral to community life. The peculiar vulnerability of women to dishonour and shame made them ready both to attack misconduct, and to respond to discrediting words.

The legal system gave ample support to the culture of honour. Through lawsuits prosecuted at the church courts and other jurisdictions, ordinary women and men pursued the defence of their good names. Particularly full evidence for honour comes from the church courts, where cases of sexual slander were prosecuted. There, women fought over insults like 'whore', 'bawd' and 'quean', and men over words like 'cuckold' and 'whoremaster', with a complex of other associated insults [**Doc. 49, p. 140**]. Manifestly, women bore the main responsibility for sexual sin. To accuse a woman of unchastity undermined her whole character. Every commentary on morality placed continence at the heart of female character, and made it the proof of virtue [**Doc. 50, p. 140**]. Those same texts returned to the biblical references for dishonest women, particularly those of the book of Proverbs, and looked for the signs of harlots in contemporary life: curled hair, wayward speech, wandering feet. The whore was the archetype of sin, and unchastity the focal point of rhetoric against all sorts of other offences.

The language of whoredom also had a concrete effect. Interestingly, those who complained of being called a whore were not usually single women concerned about their marriage prospects, but married women concerned about their local standing: the insinuation of sexual trespass raised the whole spectre of neighbourhood disorder. It was related, too, to the wasting of money, spreading disease and corrupting other women or young men, as well as undermining marital households. Whether or not these women were actually suspected of illicit sex, the naming of 'whores' set people talking and made room for every other local issue to be aired. Women's responsibility for sexual honour was such that in some jurisdictions, such as London, they instigated the majority of defamation cases.

The extent and rationale of the double sexual standard has been debated: men, it has been asserted, attracted blame too, though the ready language to condemn them for unchastity was never there. Keith Thomas's original, powerful anatomy of the double standard pinned it down, ultimately, to biology: women were held responsible for sexual misconduct because women got pregnant, and because men were anxious about the paternity of their children (Thomas, 1959). The sexual blame of women also made sense on many other levels; it justified the control of women's movements and the fear of women as deceptive and secretive.

Reputation applied not only to individuals, but to households and families. The economic significance of the household meant that the personal and domestic were virtually united; husbands and wives, to a great extent, shared a joint credit. The logic of the double standard left men exposed to the impact of their wives' sexual conduct. The cultural response to this dilemma was the peculiarly early modern figure of the cuckold, the man betrayed by his wife. If the double standard which condemned women as whores is instantly recognisable, the figure of the cuckold, resonant throughout Renaissance and Restoration culture, is much less so. Given the power of marriage as a part of male identity, the notion of the married couple as one flesh, and the idea of women's natural promiscuity, cuckoldry appeared as an almost inevitable trap. Yet cuckolds were, above all, figures of ridicule: little pity or sympathy attached to them in popular culture until the eighteenth century, when a general shift of sexual and cultural attitudes made laughing at cuckolded men distasteful (though the plays that did so were still performed). Humour offered not so much a safety valve for the risks of sexual disorder, as a means to dehumanise its victims. Like the language of whoredom, that of cuckoldry had a political import: civic rituals and protests used the images of cuckoldry to poke fun at certain trades, namely cobblers and tailors, and during times of unrest, against political victims.

Reputation was not just sexual, and gossip was not exclusively female. Men's defences of their reputation uncover another set of concerns which convey something of the culture of early modern masculinity. Financial honesty and artisan skill gave men status and honour [**Doc. 51, p. 141**]. Occupational identity was not exclusive to men: women too expressed pride in their work and complained if it was undermined. They, like men, stood up for their financial honesty. But it was unusual to see women invoking the honesty of worth and substance; 'worth' came through husbands or fathers.

In an expanding economy with increasingly fierce competition for resources, social credit was aligned with financial credit. The autobiography of William Stout, a Lancaster shopkeeper in the late seventeenth century, makes much reference to the credit of his contemporaries and his employer; for him it was also tied up with their Quakerism [**Doc. 52, p. 142**]. London

Puritan Nehemiah Wallington agonised over one exchange in his shop that might have demonstrated him untrustworthy [Doc. 53, p. 143]. Credit was a chain: trustworthiness depended not only on personal morality, but on the worth of those who were prepared to extend their trust. Young men's promotion in society and business required the goodwill of their peers, their seniors and their superiors. In this way, credit was also an oral issue. It was achieved and undermined by words. Gossip about bad business could undo a household.

The collective and financial aspects of credit were most clearly described in relation to men, and have been of most concern in men's history, but they engaged women too. Widows ran households and businesses: their credit was significant to local economies, and their names mattered to them. It seems likely, given the power of sexual insult for women, that sexual and financial credit united for women in a way it did not for men; by the eighteenth century the language of whoredom was being used for dubious financial transactions as well.

FRIENDSHIP

The persistent elision of women's history, gender history and the history of the family performs a sleight of hand that undercuts a whole register of gender relations: that of friendship. In a fairly heterosocial world, relations between women and men were not bound to be sexual. Because they were of little interest to the courts, or to pamphleteers, such intimacies have a sketchy history. But they should not be ignored.

Much work on friendship has focused on its instrumental aspects. These were most visibly powerful for men. Friendship between men was a solidly established bond, the root of patronage and clientage in political and spiritual matters as well as elite society. It encompassed a physical intimacy that, in Alan Bray's phrase, made 'the gift of the body' part of social relationships: kisses, shared beds and tables, and loving letters embodied the social prestige of male homosociality (Bray 2003). Physical intimacy displayed personal and political connections. In the early seventeenth century, Thomas Howard wrote carefully to a new would-be courtier of the prevailing favourite at court, Robert Carr: his handsome bearing held King James captive, and the King's conversations were interrupted by petting him [Doc. 9, p. 93].

The archetypal stage for such display was the great elite household. The largely unspoken opposite of those transactions was the almost unspeakable danger of sodomy. Exploring the emotional terrain of friendship, rather than its dangerous erotic potential, has made it possible for historians to explore the preoccupations of betrayal and misuse that underlay contemporary relationships. It remains important to explore the fertile, unstable terrain between homosociality and homoeroticism.

The political charge of female friendship and of erotic bonds between women was much less visible, though it became prominent in one political scandal of the late seventeenth century, that of the relationships between Queen Anne, Sarah Churchill and Abigail Masham. In elite circles at least, though, where women spent their affection mattered: social relations between women were the conduit to all manner of patronage.

The instrumental powers of friendship are usually only examined amongst the elites. With less money or power at stake, they may still have functioned significantly amongst the middling sort and the poor. The gender divisions of social worlds were not absolute. Women's invitations to gossipings after childbirth were a key element of the social currency of neighbourhood life; men's purchases of gloves for midwives and gossips brought them into the bonding ritual of reproduction too. Men's sociability sealed business deals and marriage contracts. Women's comradeship also had public contexts: market-places, church and weddings, and the feasting rituals at baptisms and churchings. Women, too, built a neighbourhood of useful connections.

Amongst the young, sociability had its own gender dynamics. A few references in court records suggest the importance of intimate confidences between young women in service and daughters of the house. Young men's comradeship was notorious for its excess: drinking, gaming and dancing were common complaints against apprentices. Drinking rituals bound men together, particularly the young; they were attacked by contemporaries, and sometimes prosecuted on grounds of social disorder [Doc. 54, p. 144]. It may have been before marriage that sociability was most polarised by gender.

The post-Reformation impetus to spiritual self-examination encouraged friendships rooted in spiritual discussions: for women, increasingly identified as naturally inclined toward spirituality, spiritual friendships were particularly significant amongst the literate. Love between friends could be a way to explore deep intellectual and passionate connections without terrestrial consummation: a lifeline of platonic friendship. Margaret Blagge (later Godolphin), a maid of honour at the Restoration court, found in her six years' friendship and epistolary relationship with the diarist John Evelyn a haven in which to explore her religious commitment, and test her spiritual ideas (Harris, 2003). For the literate elites, platonic friendship, often pursued through writing, made it possible for women to explore their internal lives and to influence men without the constraints that physical presence seemed to bring. Relationships between women and priests, often slandered, were crucial to maintaining Catholicism in post-Reformation England. Protestant women of elite status also built bonds with ministers, of which letters and funeral sermons provide some memorials [Doc. 10, p. 94].

Plebeian friendship remains largely unexamined. Yet at a time of high mobility and high mortality, it was surely instrumental and emotionally significant. The practice of chain migration that brought women and men to urban communities meant they often settled close to old connections from their birthplace, establishing new kinship networks. Looking for work, finding housing and making a marriage all depended on friends. Friend remained, though, a largely formal word, used in relation to family and kin; the bonds of reciprocity that bound men and women together were often best described in the word 'neighbour'. A community of propinquity was completely bound up with one of moral obligation, in which gender relations were under constant scrutiny and in which women held a special stake.

4

Polity

The conventional political history of early modern England has had little to say about gender. Yet sexual politics were at the heart of political rhetoric. The Tudor and Stuart commonwealth was, to almost all commentators, a mirror of an ordered household, with the relationship between monarch and country reflected in that between husband and wife. The seventeenth century saw two transitions that have been taken as key to political modernity: the appearance of social contract theory and liberalism, and the distinction of private and public spheres. Both were constructed around specific forms of early modern gender relations: the idea of woman, the redefinition of manhood, the meanings of inheritance, marriage and legitimacy. The dawn of liberal democracy celebrated by Whig history was never thought to be a revolution for women: rather, it seemed to naturalise a hierarchy that was previously political and spiritual.

The historiography of gender and politics has traditionally focused on tracing the participation of women in spheres from which they were meant to be excluded. From the earliest feminist historians of the nineteenth century, whose work reconstructed a long history of women's suffrage to support their contemporary cause, through the Marxist and subsequent historians of riot, women's participation in a variety of levels of political engagement has been made visible. Framing politics around gender illuminates another set of concerns, which might include the impact of changing political participation on masculinity, and the role of gender relations in political rhetoric. Debates invoking gender permeated every level of politics: they may not have actually been about gender relations, but they played their part in determining the landscape of relations between men and women.

LANGUAGES OF POLITICS

The dominant political language was one of paternalism. Until the English Revolution, power was understood to lie in the hands of a governing patriarch, who owed his subjects care and protection in return for obedience. That relationship was a key resource for political participation: it meant men and women could argue that their rulers were obliged to protect them, using the family model as a rule.

Reflecting the political meanings of gender, the rhetoric of sex freighted political discourse. Tyranny and Catholicism were cast as feminine; slurs of effeminacy and petticoat government were meant to shame unpopular rulers. Insults like whore, cuckold and bawd permeated Reformation debates and Civil War banners and print [**Doc. 55, p. 144**]. The role of women and the power of sex were constantly at issue in debates on the conduct of the monarchy and the state. Popular demonstrations drew on gendered ideas of disorder and performed gendered roles. Always, the figure of *woman* stood alongside the acts of real women, sometimes indistinguishable. The sex-infused rhetoric of politics provided the language for ordinary women and men to engage in political discourse. The fabric of politics was woven from the engagement of rhetoric with practice.

One of the features of the seventeenth century state was the project of definition, particularly the definition of participation and rights. Often, this meant redefining concepts and groups to explicitly exclude women. As the concept of the individual became more defined, so did that of property. Holding land in freehold was becoming established as the measure of civic personhood, and the test for participation. The degree to which gender differentiated political participation is still under scrutiny. In part this is an issue of language: the false universal, where the term 'men' is used to mean people whilst excluding women, was an established feature of political discourse. Thomas Smith's description of the means of government took care to explicitly articulate the exclusion of women, along with bondmen, from governing [**Doc. 56, p. 145**]. Citizenship was equated with manhood, maturity and capacity, all of which were identified as male. As the potential for imagining the greater participation of men in the polity appeared, the capacity to imagine female citizenship seemed to contract.

The narrative of a developing public sphere, defined as civic, male and rational, leaving women in a private, domestic world, is a central theme in women's history and gender history. It no longer looks simple, if it ever did. The bourgeois public sphere of Habermas's original formulation depended on the 1688 Revolution and the creation of a space where, archetypally in coffee houses, private people came together as 'a public', to articulate and discuss political involvement (Cowan, 2001). The exclusion of women from this construct seemed almost axiomatic. But the supposedly female sphere of family was hardly nonpolitical: it was central to political discourse, and family networks key to officeholding. The classical distinction of household and polity was not convincing in relation to seventeenth-century England. The boundary between public and private was certainly significant, but it continued to be in dispute. Nor were gender roles perfectly mapped onto those distinctions. Debates continue as to the extent of women's presence in coffee-houses, as well as political demonstrations; they were clearly significantly present in petitioning and pamphleteering. The very exclusion of women from politics facilitated the voice of women's petitions, the narratives of wartime martyrdom, and the identification of women with mercy. At another level, the frequent evocation of 'ladies', 'virgins' and 'maids' in popular political literature made the female figure a key fantasy participant in political debate. Women's place in the polity was defined by conflicting and ambivalent cultural currents. Men's was less explicitly discussed in relation to gender, but political and religious changes also brought shifts in the relationship of masculinity to politics.

By the early seventeenth century, England had constituted itself rhetorically, culturally and politically as a nation. The national identity that developed in the sixteenth century and held sway through the seventeenth drew on some deep-rooted ideas of gender. The Protestantism that provided a central bulwark of national identity was a domestic religion; but much of its ideological power came from a political xenophobia. Anti-Catholicism united much of the population in support of what was still, for much of the sixteenth century, the new religion, and it had a powerful gender politics to it. The vitality of anti-Catholic feeling in the first three decades of Elizabeth's reign provided the solution to the problem of two potential queens, by tainting Mary Queen of Scots with popery. The early seventeenth century saw a further identification of the Catholic threat with both feminine government and tyranny; the Catholic queens of James I and Charles I provided lightning rods for public sentiment. National identity formed itself partly in relation to the foreign other: here, for the English, Ireland was the source of tales of savagery.

MONARCHY

Monarchs had two bodies, the mortal and the political; they also, Cynthia Herrup has argued, embodied two genders, the male and the female (Herrup, 2006). Elizabeth I referred to herself as a prince, while Mary I's funeral displayed the gauntlet and spurs of a military leader. The duality of kingship had a gendered aspect, balancing martial rigidity with tender mercy. That duality made most sense for queens; kings did not go further than to describe themselves as 'nursing fathers', which is a long way from the maternal imagery that was expected of queens. Where femininity came into the picture for kings was in the danger of tyranny: the accusation of tyranny was frequently elided with that of inconstancy, vengefulness, and effeminacy, which meant not only being like a woman, but being overly influenced by women. Lucy Hutchinson's description of the ineffectualness of Charles I draws on a typical set of anti-Catholic images [**Doc. 57, p. 146**].

The issue of queens regnant was a recurrent feature of Tudor and Stuart politics. The sixteenth century saw two examples of queens regnant; the seventeenth century likewise. Much historiography has focused on the gender politics of Elizabeth I's position, and on her development of a style of self-presentation, from speeches to portraits, that drew on such diverse elements as virginity, princehood and maternity. Before her, Mary I had assumed the position of a ruling queen, and had negotiated most of the same dilemmas. On Mary's accession, she declared herself the heir to the crown imperial, and her subjects' 'sovereign lady'. The apparent lack of contradiction in Mary's coronation proclamation was belied by the act passed less than a year later, insisting on the legitimacy of her reign [**Doc. 58, p. 147**].

For all the female monarchs of this period, the ability of a woman to rule a country was less in question than the negotiation of her marital status. If a queen, once married, became a feme covert like any other woman, many of her rights in her own name vanished; she could not hold property in her own right. There were potential implications for inheritance, too. Lawyers expressed just this anxiety early in Mary's reign, trying to prompt further parliaments by suggesting that after her marriage to Philip, she would not be able to hold the crown herself, and hence Philip would hold onto it over an heir (Richards, 1997: 904). The question had already been resolved by treaty, but it clearly remained live enough in professional minds to cause trouble.

The peculiar strategies of queens negotiating the place of power were not only the product of a female body on a throne; some derived from more generic dynastic and political strategies. The language of love that dominated at Elizabeth's court can be seen as the same strategy used by earlier male monarchs, translating feudal loyalties into affective bonds of allegiance (Richards, 1999). The domestic nature of monarchical government was also an issue. A queen regnant brought with her a household of women, who could not be given the political posts that a king's male household would have: nevertheless the women of the household and the bedchamber held significant, unexamined political roles.

By the end of the seventeenth century, the nature of monarchy and its position in public discourse had shifted. It was possible to assert publicly that the natural governing powers of men made Mary II incapable of ruling alone, and that her husband was a fitter monarch than her [**Doc. 59, p. 147**]. The rule of women had been undercut in potent new ways. The longer term effects of the events of the 1640s and 1650s kept gender politics central to national politics: the threat of female subversion was more dangerous than ever, and the power of ideologies of family, marriage and inheritance held sway across a wide range of forms of political theory and practice.

On the throne, queens have always had a gender; that of kings has rarely been noticed. The dynastic struggles of Henry VIII, the passionate favouritism of James I and the alleged subordination of Charles II to the sexual power of women are all worth examining through the lens of masculinity. The divisions of the civil war also divided ideas of masculinity and power: the gulf between the very different masculinities of Charles I, Cromwell and Charles II suggests some of the deep fissures in the notion of manhood.

PARTICIPATION

The formal mechanisms of government included little popular participation. The question of the qualification of women to participate in government was largely irrelevant when democracy was not an issue. The radicals of the English Revolution brought participation into question. However, when the Putney debates discussed the participation of commoners in the commonwealth, the commoners in question were universally taken to be male. Very few men and women in early modern England expected to participate actively in the polity in terms that are consonant with modern political identity: a minority participated in elections; a tiny number of men stood for parliament. They did, however, understand themselves to be political subjects of the monarch, of the government, and members of the church. The obligations of those roles were sometimes in dispute. The political dramas of the sixteenth and seventeenth centuries put the role of subject under sharp scrutiny. Women were unlikely to see themselves as political actors; but so were most men. Moreover, by the late seventeenth the impact of the penal laws was to make Catholic men almost as legally disempowered as married women.

Historians and political theorists have seen in the late seventeenth century a process of exclusion of women from formal politics that was not reversed until the twentieth century. From the mechanisms of parliamentary selection to political theory, politics was being more firmly identified as masculine. That formal exclusion meant not that women were depoliticised, but that their relationship to politics was likely to be expressed in complex ways: this might be demonstrated both through writing, and in words and actions.

The capacity to vote for parliamentary representation is a touchstone of modern political participation, but it occupied a quite different status in sixteenth and seventeenth-century England. Members of parliament were chosen by a process more akin to selection than election, in which, for most of this period, consensus was a mark of a successful political process. Consequently, the voices of electors and selectors are particularly hard to trace. There is, however, evidence that participation in the process of election was not defined as exclusively male until the late seventeenth century.

The female suffrage campaigners of the late nineteenth century drew on evidence mobilised by historians for a long history of women participating and voting. To the first generation of feminist historians in the early twentieth century, the seventeenth century was the time when women's historic freedoms were constricted. The medieval statutes that defined the workings of parliamentary selection did not exclude women from participating in elections to parliament, as freeholders holding land worth forty shillings, on the same basis as men. At least three legal cases in the reign of James I upheld the right of femes soles to vote for parliamentary representatives; if married, their husbands were to have their votes. Edward Coke's much-cited opinion of the legal incapacity of women to vote, therefore, seems to have been in conflict with other contemporary understandings [**Doc. 60, p. 148**]. In elections without an outright contest, the voice of propertied women was both uncontroversial and invisible. Only in the contests which became more likely from the 1640s was the right of women to use their vote likely to be debated. This was what happened in Ipswich in 1640, where Sir Simonds D'Ewes presided over the elections of representatives for Suffolk to the Long Parliament [**Doc. 61, p. 149**]. D'Ewes's description of the status of those would-be voters is revealing. The clerk did not know to turn them away immediately; D'Ewes, as sheriff, protests that he did so not because they were not legally entitled to vote, but because it was dishonourable to accept their votes. More significant than the numbers of women who 'voted' before 1660 was the lack of any structures forbidding them to do so.

After 1660, those structures began to be put into place through the redrawing of charters and the establishment of more predictable voting practices. There is no evidence of women voting in the elections of the late seventeenth century, and in 1690 Coke's exclusion of women was quoted, seemingly uncontroversially, in George Petyt's *Lex parliamentaria*. Voting had become, without question, a male prerogative. But the significance of that prerogative was confined to the limited numbers of men who held sufficient property to vote. Arguably, property remained more significant than gender in enfranchisement.

Other political activities provide a better measure of gendered participation. The divided loyalties of the mid-seventeenth century brought a series of public tests for householders, such as the **Protestation Oath** in 1641–2, and the Covenant in 1643. Women are recorded as subscribing to these, in numbers that vary greatly by parish and oath. In some places all adult householders seem to have taken the oath; in some up to half of the subscribers were female; in others the only women who did were widows. Clearly, loyalty was a different matter from influence; indeed, one aspect of the political battles of the 1640s was the characterisation of female influence as a dangerous part of royalism.

Protestation Oaths: Oaths of allegiance to the Commonwealth.

RESISTANCE

The political consensus of early modern England involved a degree of acceptable protest, with a line of unacceptability drawn at the peak of riotous demonstrations. Petitions and protests were part of the relation between subject and state. An established set of understandings about gendered responsibilities and roles determined women's and men's behaviour in crowds and protests. Habitually described, in court, as 'riot' or 'riotous', much of that behaviour was conventional and part of the consensus that maintained authority. It was also, though, part of a coherent, long-lasting exchange that brought local issues into national politics. Occasionally, when dire circumstances coincided, protests resulted in severe responses and executions.

As in other political arenas, the participation of women was both an accepted part of the politics of protest and a marker of disorder. The conventions of protest were governed, to a great degree, by custom, and custom prescribed certain roles and powers for men and women. The language of patriarchalism at the heart of so much political discourse was also used in protest, enabling both women and men to engage with national politics: as the subjects of a patriarchal monarch, they were owed protection, as well as being obligated to obedience. Women's role in provisioning the household and as mothers provided a rationale for participation in food riots and peace petitions. The festive inversion of charivari offered another route to expressing complaint through the female figure, with men participating dressed as women: inversions of the natural order allowed room for protest. The community ritual of skimmington could also shade over into politics, with protests, leaders and victims respectively all sometimes identified as 'skimmingtons'; the rhetoric of popular politics drew on the familiar language of neighbourhood relations. A long tradition of role reversal in protest put gender relations at the heart of protest rituals.

The staging and prosecution of protest brought the issue of women's legal liability to the fore. Custom had long held that women were not legally responsible for damage in such cases; it was reiterated both in legal texts and in some riot cases [**Doc. 62, p. 149**]. Events such as the hanging of 'Captain' Ann Carter after her leadership of the second Maldon riots in 1629 proved this to be utterly misconceived. But it remained a feature of popular political discourse through the first half of the seventeenth century. Drawing on this custom, some women led protests using the title of Captain; other demonstrations were led by men dressed as women, or involved cross-dressing as charivari.

In the records of protest, the voices of women and men emerge with different inflections. With food and supply a primary concern, all protesters complained about profiteering: merchants and middle men were always the target. Men, though, were seemingly more able to articulate both individual concerns, such as a conviction that only a king could solve the nation's problems, and a plebeian solidarity. Women were more apt to represent mothers and families; their voice was most audible when they stood in the familiar role of providers and nurturers.

No kind of protest was exclusively male, but the nature of complaints made some difference. Food was a familiar ground of protest for women: in sixteenth- and seventeenth-century England they protested over scarcity, high prices or the quality of grain. Recent interpretations describe food protests as a form of negotiation, rather than desperation, which changes too our understanding of female involvement. Women participated not just because it was an emergency of subsistence; they expected to bargain through demonstration. Enclosure protests are more conspicuously male, but still feature regular complaints of women pulling down fences, destroying ditches and throwing stones. The protests on Grewelthorpe Moor, near Ripon in Yorkshire, in 1612 involved a number of middle-aged women, led by 'Captain Dorothy' Dawson, who broke down the new ditches erected to enclose the common land. Their responses clarify the defence offered by women accused of protest. They insisted they went 'two by two' – not, in other words, riotously; that no one in particular had led them; and that their husbands had not known what they were doing. Dorothy's deposition, by far the longest, describes at length her defence of a poor woman who needed the grazing on the land to live [Doc. 63, p. 150].

The precise balance of gender roles in protests is complicated by the politics of court reportage. Given the issue of female culpability, legal questions were often asked about whether women took part alone or with their husbands. Historians' interpretations have sometimes underplayed the leadership of women, and read their participation as figureheads for the grievances of men. The leadership of protests was far more likely to be by men than women, but partly because of the role that cross-dressing and gender politics played in practices of protest, it was one of the places where men and women seemed to claim equivalent or parallel voices. When they were questioned, women protesters articulated a claim to protest for themselves, their families and the community. The more subtle analyses of early modern politics, and the rethinking of the state, that have emerged with recent historiography make it hard to dismiss any crowd action, however local in focus, as lacking in ideological depth or political nous. The weapons of the weak often had a resonance outside their immediate context. The right of women to protest over economic want, and to defend their families, gave them a lasting political voice, whose echoes continued to be felt first in the activism of the civil war years, and later in the female-dominated food riots of the eighteenth and nineteenth centuries.

Muttering beneath the explicit petitions and protests were the exchanges of political conversation. In a highly oral culture, seditious words were a serious matter and, particularly before 1640, they were severely punished. But no government could aspire to control the constant flow of political debate. That governors even attempted to do so testifies to the significance of speech in popular politics. Seditious words provide extensive evidence of the political voices of women. Those prosecuted were mostly attacks on monarchs, but they suggest a wider sphere of political discussion in which a range of people participated.

On the evidence of prosecutions, seditious words often highlighted sexual misconduct: in violent conversation monarchs were called whores, bastards, pimps and cuckolds. Elizabeth I was frequently alleged to have had children by Leicester, which in some versions she had had murdered and hidden in a chimney. For monarchs, unlike ordinary women and men, infertility was another dangerous slur. A suggestion in the 1680s that Queen Mary thought she could not conceive without drinking of the blood of Monmouth raised both the spectre of royal infertility and an image of the monarchs as bound to a poisonous popular culture of magical remedies [**Doc. 64, p. 151**]. While gossip was habitually characterised as female, sedition was a crime of both sexes, and inattention to women's speech may have meant that seditious words from women were actually less likely to be prosecuted. Much of what appears in the archival record concerns brief words, presented as if one person spoke once. In reality, the danger of sedition was that, in a largely oral culture, it was also news. It spread fast, and it was remembered.

Clearly, women and men talked politics together, and political sedition was a sphere of discourse in which both sexes participated. They may have stressed different aspects; women seem to have been particularly, though by no means exclusively, active in sexual rumours and stories about secret births or infertility. That, after all, was understood to be their special sphere of expertise. But women also voiced complaints in which they assumed roles very far from the 'female' sphere. In Newcastle in 1663, Sarah Walker told people in 1663 that she would get a petition and raise an army to fight the king and his **hearth tax** [Doc. 65, p. 152]. Political talk of all slants could include women as well as men. The defamatory image of women as gossips also played a part in constructing female speech as significant and weighty.

> **Hearth tax:** Imposed in 1662, at a rate of 2s. per hearth per year.

Recusancy had its own sexual politics. Contemporaries often suggested, and historians have agreed, that English Catholicism survived through the work of women. In the domestic realm Catholic women sheltered priests and preserved the material objects of the mass; in the outer world, it was often postulated, they attended church for conformity to shelter the recusancy of their husbands. Penal laws were constructed on a tricky tightrope between maintaining the structure of coverture, whereby men were responsible for

> **Recusancy:** Refusal to attend church services.

their wives' dissent, and bringing non-conforming wives to book through financial penalties. Recent widows were a particular target. Anti-Catholic rhetoric drew on the conventional image of the disorderly wife, compelling the henpecked husband to shelter her dissent.

THE ENGLISH REVOLUTION

The exceptional activities of women in the 1640s and 1650s have long provided a high point of female activism for historical memory; more recent histories have expanded the political sphere to include the worlds of news, local politics and popular opinion, making room for a deeper politics of gender.

Most obviously, an ongoing war both reinforced and altered the existing association of masculinity with violence, war and military culture. War is apt to polarise gender roles. Recent historiography has stressed the depth of military involvement: one estimate suggests between a quarter and a third of the adult male population were mobilised (Morrill, 1999: 190). After decades of peace, Englishmen were much less heavily experienced in fighting than their European, Scottish and Irish counterparts. Perhaps as a consequence, appeals to the manliness of war were not frequent. (Carlton, 1992: 47)

The armies that fought the civil wars represented a new kind of organisation; it was the first time for generations that Englishmen had armed themselves and fought on their home soil. The parliamentary armies, in particular, constituted a departure from all previous military structures. Men were supposed to be advanced on merit; they prayed and fasted together; their victories came from God. Together they worked out a new kind of militaristic and egalitarian masculinity, in aspiration at least.

Women's engagement in the civil wars also expanded their familiar realm of action. Soldiers billeted on households throughout the country meant a wide range of families dealt with military men and their weapons, including guns, in their houses. In cities and towns, women defended fortifications, and in Norwich women sold their jewellery to fund a 'Maiden Troop'. Elite women found themselves defending houses and castles against besieging forces. When, in 1643, Brilliana Harley was facing the siege of her house at Brampton Bryan, her letters show her bringing the role of obedient wife into unison with the defence of Parliament and what she understood to be the true religion [Doc. 66, p. 152]. The story of women's radicalism became part of revolutionary legend and later mockery: a pack of playing cards in 1679 satirising the Rump Parliament included, for the Knave of Hearts, a preacher holding up 'the bodkins and thimbles given by the wives of Wapping for the good old cause' (Crawford, 2001: 212).

Like the Reformation, the civil wars were a battle of conscience. For the majority, loyalty was regional: royalism was strongest in the north and west, parliamentarianism in the south and east. But as the possibility of consensus receded, opinions and convictions proliferated. The political storms of the early seventeenth century were accompanied by an outbreak of news. Through the 1640s, newsbooks were published regularly and circulated nationally; there was plenty of room for sectarian debate, and a growing audience for it. While the loyal support of wives leant ammunition to the weapons of both sides, husbands and wives did not always speak with one voice, and religious radicals both male and female had a spiritual justification for leaving the ties of family to follow the Lord. Revolution, like reformation, could provoke divisive dilemmas for married life.

The radical religious sects of the 1640s were renowned for their high levels of female participation. At least 300 women prophets can be identified through their printed works, two-thirds of them Quakers. Women prophets both defied and reinforced the conventions of gender. Identifying themselves as prophets like the men of the Old Testament, they spoke in a trance, sometimes using male voices, and claiming to articulate the voice of God. In that sense, they spoke out more audibly and with fewer constraints than most seventeenth century women were able to. At the same time, the governing principle of female prophecy was that it emerged from, and was justified by, the idea of the 'weaker vessel'. The text 1 Corinthians 1:27 gave God's word most authentically to the weakest [**Doc. 67, p. 154**]. The empty vessel of the female mind received, and reproduced, the divine message with clarity. Yet Quaker women still had to be reminded to be both brave and deferential. Most importantly, female prophets were not aspiring feminists; prophecy was not a way to claim a public role, but was experienced, rather, as a forcible overwhelming by God's word. Women were always defined by their weakness, and to attribute any self-conscious self-assertion to women of the sects misses much of the essential nature of seventeenth-century spirituality. Nevertheless, the result was a public space in which women's voices were heard, considered and discussed.

Men prophesied too. To do so was not so great a leap; interpreting God's word was already part of the early modern male role. In the moving world of sectarian discourse, men, like women, adopted new roles, sometimes crossing gender to do so. Male prophets spoke of themselves as nursing mothers, as warriors and as babies, using metaphors of sex and the body that most women shrank from. Sometimes their masculinity gave them a freedom that allowed them to challenge social order more deeply than their female counterparts. An exchange of letters between the **Ranter** leader, Abiezer Coppe and one of his female followers is revealing: while she dreams of growing strong like an eagle, it is he who insists there is no difference between male and female in Christ [**Doc. 68, p. 154**]. But the voice of male prophets came from an

Ranters: Heretical sect of the Revolutionary period, seen as a threat to social order.

established identity, while that of women tended instead to be characterised by a tone of alienation.

Prophesying, particularly by women, was never mainstream; it remained, for many, upsetting, offensive or plain wrong. But it was part of two important strands of the early modern polity. One was the historic spiritual role of women, which endowed them with a particular intuition to the divine. The prophets of the 1650s were in part the heirs of Elizabeth Barton, the poor woman who prophesied to Henry VIII and his ministers in the 1530s, and they reaped both positive and ill effects from the long history of female visionaries. The other was the enlarged political sphere of the mid-seventeenth century. Evidence of the circulation of news and popular responses to international and national events, suggests a long history for the new public of the 1640s. This was less apparent in relation to women, if only because of our lack of knowledge about women's literacy; historians are apt to assume the main consumers of newsbooks were men. It may have been in the 1640s, when fresh and dramatic news was appearing on a daily basis, that ordinary women's reading habits transformed. It was in those years that printed materials by women rose so fast in numbers that they constituted a whole new genre, mostly of religious prophecy; it was the first time that works authored by women were in print in any quantity. The voice of women in the politics of the 1640s left its fullest record in the petitions to parliament, presented by groups describing themselves as wives, maids or honest gentlewomen. Petitioning to parliament put them in one position in particular: advocating for peace, and an end to the wartime disruptions of trade and communities. They drew on the long history of women protestors, who had traditionally assumed responsibility for the supply of food: subsistence was the common preoccupation of most of the petitions. Women petitioners also drew on the rhetoric of anti-Catholicism, hostility towards the episcopacy, and the investment of mothers in peace and national security.

Petitioning gave women a physical presence in the political world of Westminster: petitioners habitually gathered a large crowd on the steps of parliament, outside the doors and in Westminster house. Some demonstrations became violent, such as that in 1643, and some resulted in arrests. Members of Parliament rarely responded positively to women's demonstrations; Pym notoriously told one group to go back to their houses [**Doc. 69, p. 155**]. Critical newsbook accounts described the female crowds, in one instance reported to number five thousand, as composed of whores, bawds, oysterwomen and beggars [**Doc. 70, p. 159**]. By 1646, demonstrations of women were most often associated with the Leveller cause, often on behalf of imprisoned men and women.

The idea of a political collective of women, hanging about on the stairs of parliament is so pervasive in revolutionary rhetoric that it is hard to pin down how many and how often women were involved, and how significant their sex was in practice. Mixed and male public gatherings were seemingly less worthy of comment. But the female crowd was also significant because it signified disorder and spatial promiscuity, however familiar the political voice of women was.

The actual participation of women in public politics in the 1640s was paralleled by a parody of gender relations which drew on and revivified the old stereotypes of disorderly women, concerned only with sex. A whole series of 'Parliaments of Women' pamphlets took the petitioning activities of London women and turned them into an extended jest about women using parliament to legislate for cuckoldry **[Doc. 71, p. 160]**. The habitual rendering of the people as a subordinate wife, and the monarch as a masterful husband, made domestic relations an excellent source for political comment. The Puritan concern with sexual morality provided as much fodder for satire as the actual misdeeds alleged of sectarian groups. Newsbooks reported on the supposed sexual misconduct of prominent men on both sides, or claimed that London women were running wild out of men's control. In London pornographic fantasy blurred with gossip to libel public figures; news was both sexual and political. A petition of 1660, 'The Royall Virgine. Or the Declaration of Several Maydens' claimed to be printed for Virgin Hope-well, and sold at the Maiden-Starre: it used the idea of maidenly virtue to disclaim the dishonourable behaviour of the Rump Parliament (Plate 9). Whether or not any real women were behind it, it called upon the nominal authority of virgins – a matter of jest, but not without political meaning. On both sides, the figure of the disorderly woman loomed large. The newsbook *Mercurius Democritus* satirised Puritan obsessions with unruly, sexually voracious femininity; its expansive imagining of the grotesque excesses of city wives enhanced an already familiar script **[Doc. 55, p. 144]**. The horror of disorderly households, epitomised in imperious women, was a powerful weapon in every quarter.

Within a few years, the public role of women in the commonwealth had become more parody than real. The influence of women on royal government was identified as dangerous, provoking intrigue and mistrust. The long-running discourse of anti-Catholicism elided femininity with misgovernment, tyranny and popery. In contrast, Parliamentarian politics drew on fraternal and civic connections, and on the shared world of men who had been in parliament and in the army together (Hughes, 2011). The new style of government meant men working together in a meritocracy; it did not mean men working with women. The most radical female voices had been in the sects; over time, those voices were marginalised and characterised as eccentric and unreliable precisely because of their articulation of a conscience that was once true, and swiftly became dangerous. The Restoration in 1660 has been seen as a reinstatement of male political authority, with greater constraints on women's political voice. Keith Thomas concluded, in a path-breaking early article on women in the civil war, that the sectarian radicalism of women seemed to have had no lasting effects; subsequent historians have agreed (Thomas, 1958). As a basis for equality, spiritual claims proved to be unreliable.

The English Revolution, then, saw challenges to gender order, and new roles for both women and men. But it did not transform gender relations. Even in the radical sects, the interactions of men and women often fell back into familiar patterns: women acting as 'mothers in Israel', organising and facilitating, while men made the boldest ventures. In some marriages, the wars brought new divisions of labour; women like Brilliana Harley and Lucy Hutchinson offer an elite view of shared political involvement that must have been echoed further down the social scale. For the Harleys, as for other couples, another pattern also emerged: husbands' absence and wives' responsibility. More than relations between the sexes, relations within them were changed. The actions of women in the 1640s and 1650s drew on a collectivity of women that was novel; men, too, found new kinds of all-male groups. Sexual relations, marriage and the family, despite the claims of some contemporaries, remained largely the same. The old ceremonies of marriage and baptism were missed, and even when new forms were developed, the essence of marriage was unchanged. The fantasies of sexual disorder and gender overturned were more powerful than the reality.

SOCIAL CONTRACT AND SEXUAL CONTRACT

The political theories of seventeenth-century England put the family at the centre of politics. The patriarchalism of Robert Filmer and others, compared the tie between husband and wife to that between monarch and subject, and from this basic connection a whole net of comparisons between family and state sprang forth. Habitually, the question of loyalty, authority and obedience which was tested so hard in both sixteenth and seventeenth centuries was one that resonated with family ties. Marriage contracts, parental responsibilities, inheritance and adultery all had political meanings, and made for stirring connections between household and polity. The ordered family was the heart of the nation.

But this was also an era in which the 'ordered family' was a contentious matter. For Tudor monarchs, securing a male dynasty proved fraught with problems. The desperation with which Henry VIII attempted to consolidate his inheritance was followed by a series of dynastic crises in which the monarchy was faced with queens regnant, queens marrying foreigners, and queens with no heirs. In the early seventeenth century, the roles of two subsequent

Catholic queens made the royal household a focus for anti-Catholic sentiment, and in the rhetoric of the civil war years, absolutism and female power were cast hand-in-hand. In the late seventeenth century, the questions of legitimacy and resistance were pivotal in national politics, and they continued to have ties to the politics of the family. Whether, and how, a woman was subject to a man; how her subjection could, or should, be compelled; and whether their contractual relationship could ever be dissolved remained matters of great political import.

Through the sixteenth and the seventeenth centuries, the family was a political battleground. The orderly households envisaged by Puritan reformers were the prototypes of patriachalism, with every father acting like a monarch in his own commonwealth; their basic claims came from St Paul and Xenophon. We might reasonably expect the events of the 1640s, and especially the regicide of 1649, to have undermined the ties between family and state. The English Revolution brought an obvious parallel that worked both ways: between political rebellion against an alleged tyrant and the right of an abused wife to resist or divorce her husband; and between regicide and petty treason. The execution of a king by his subjects seems to vitiate the whole basis of patriarchalism. It might also reinforce it. The late seventeenth century saw the parallel between household and state become more contested. Political parties in parliament emerged in part in response to a crisis of inheritance: the emerging Whig party's attempts, in 1685, to exclude Charles II's Catholic brother from the throne, potentially in favour of the Duke of Monmouth, one of Charles II's illegitimate children, challenged the meaning of inheritance and legitimacy. The 'warming pan scandal' of 1688 saw a print furore and a public fantasy about the illegitimacy of the Catholic heir to the throne. Rumours circulated that Mary of Modena had never been pregnant at all, and that the child had been smuggled into her bed in a warming pan; the equivocation of the best witnesses, midwives and women at court helped the story stick (Plate 8). The unrelated crime of Mary Hobry, a French midwife who was burnt for the murder of her husband in the same year, was drawn into the rhetoric of women's dangerous part in Catholic conspiracy; the alleged role of Elizabeth Cellier, 'the popish midwife', in the popish plots of 1679 had a similar effect. The public authority of women in the drama of reproduction was at the heart of the political crisis of the 1680s.

The political developments of the later seventeenth century undercut the long-cherished political theory of patriarchalism. At the beginning of our period, the political order was commonly explained by anology: the authority of the king was not just comparable to, but the same as, that of a father in a household. From this root much of the domestic advice of the Puritan reformers sprang. By the end of the seventeenth century, the patriarchalist vision of Filmer was eclipsed by those of Hobbes, Locke and others, in which political authority was dependent on the consent of the governed in a social contract. Filmer's understanding of what a father and hence a king was came up against Whig writers' challenges to sovereign power as paternal. The rise of social contract theory was associated, in varying degrees depending on historians' views, with the Revolution of 1688, when the Catholic James II was ousted in favour of William of Orange and his wife, James's daughter Mary.

The political meaning of that revolution and its relationship to a modern polity remains in contest. Its implications for gender have been interrogated in relation to the impact of social contract on theories of the family, and the peculiar configurations of the politics of family life in the late seventeenth century. Carole Pateman argues that the social contract of Locke continued dependent on a 'sexual contract', in which women are subjected to men. The civil freedom that contract establishes is, in this formulation, a masculine freedom, and it brings with it a continuation of the same patriarchal order that underlay patriarchalism. The absence of any discussion of that sexual contract in contract theory means it can be presumed to be natural – more so than it was in patriarchalism. The liberalism of the Whigs thus emerges as at least as socially conservative as patriarchalism, and has the further consequence of privatising family life (Pateman, 1988). At the same time, Whigs and Tories, contractarians and patriarchalists held a diversity of sometimes unpredictable views (Weil, 1999). The high-profile dramas of succession put marriage and inheritance at the centre of public debate: no clear line could be drawn around the privacy of the family.

Plate 1 A Fete at Bermondsey by Joris Hoefnagel (1542–1600). See pp. 14–15. Oil on panel, c.1570, 73.8 × 99 cm.

Source: © Hatfield House, Hertfordshire, UK/The Bridgeman Art Library

Plate 2 Sir Philip Sidney (1554–86) by an unknown artist.
See p. 14.
Oil on panel, c.1576 is uncertain, 113.9 × 84 cm.
National Portrait Gallery.

Source: © Lebrecht Music and Arts Photo Library/Alamy

Plate 3 Skimmington frieze in the Great Hall at Montacute House, Somerset, featuring a husband beaten by his wife made to ride on a broom. See p. 59.
Plaster, c.1600.

Source: © NTPL/W H Rendell

Plate 4 The Great Picture by Jan van Belcamp (1610–53) (attr.)
Commissioned by Lady Anne Clifford in 1646, when she attained her inheritance, the centre panel depicts her parents, the Countess and Earl of Cumberland, and brothers before her birth; the side panels show herself in youth and age. The portraits on the wall show her family and her tutor and governess. See p. 45.

Oil on canvas, 1646. Centre panel: 254 × 254 cm; side panels: 254 × 119.38 cm.

Source: © Abbot Hall Art Gallery, Kendal, Cumbria, UK/The Bridgeman Art Library

Plate 5 Edward Barlow leaving home, with his mother behind him. See p. 47.
Drawing in Barlow's journal, 1695–1703.
Ink on paper, 36 × 24 cm.

Source: © National Maritime Museum, Greenwich, UK

Plate 6 The Prodigal Sifted. A commonplace image of parents sieving their son of his vices, surrounded by images of gambling, duelling, drinking, smoking, a brothel, sickness and jail.

Etching, 1677 (this impression 1740s), 19.7 cm × 30.6 cm.

Source: © The Trustees of the British Museum. All rights reserved

Plate 7 A New Yeare's Gift for Shrews. A popular story, depicting a wife who 'will not be good' beaten by her husband and eventually sent to the devil.
See p. 37.
Print, 1625–40, 18.9 × 20.6 cm.

Plate 8 Playing card from a set illustrating the events leading to the Revolution of 1688.
See p. 81.
Etching on pasteboard, 1688–9, 8.8 × 5.3 cm.

The Royall Virgine.

OR THE

DECLARATION

OF SEVFRAL

MAYDENS

In and about the once Honourable City of
LONDON,

 FORASMUCH as, (since that moſt horrible, unnatural, nnrighteous, unjuſt, and moſt hainous murder, committed upon the perſon of Our moſt Renowned, Honourable, Inocent, Harmleſs, Good diſpo-
ſitioned KING CHARLES the firſt ; And ſince the baniſhing, diſowning, diſinheriting and
diſpoſſeſſing of Our three moſt Illuſtrious, Virtuous, and inefable Princes) We ſay, for as much as
(ſince theſe abominable, unſufferable Acts) ENGLAND, SCOTLAND and IRELAND,
have had Experience of ſeveral Subtle, Covetous, Ambitious, ſelf-ſeeking Guardians, and Governours
ver Them. Who (inſtead of ſaving their LIBERTIES, preſerving their TRADE, and upholding the
ood of theſe NATIONS) have cheated the People, ſtinted their Trade, ſpilt mnch Inocent Blood, and have done
nothing viewable, but evil in theſe Nations.) We do Declare,

FIRST,

That it is infinitely below Us, To cover or gloſſe over Our Intentions, with ſpecious pretences ; And therefore,
We do manifeſt to the whole World, That this Our Declaration is, neither for a Free PARLIAMENT, a full
PARLIAMENT, or a Piece of a PARLIAMENT, (We leave that to the diſcretion of him) who onely
has Power to Call a PARLIAMENT) We do therefore Declare, That the onely meanes, (in Our Judgments)
to bring theſe NATIONS to out of Bondage: For the preſerving of Peace, and the upholding of every good
thing, will be, the ſpeedy Reſtauration of the Baniſhed, We mean, that the Government be of theſe Nations be caſt
upon the Shoulders of him that ought to bear it ; that the People of ENGLAND, SCOTLAND and
IRELAND, may be obedient to Him, to whom Obedience is due, and that the Crown may be ſet upon His head
whoſe Right it is. C. R.

SECONDLY,

We do Declare, That as for this preſent Power (which men call the Rump) We do utterly diſown it, accounting it
aboundantly below our Sphere, to ſtoop to that Tail, whence the Head is forced to abſent it Self.

THIRDLY, and LASTLY,

We do Declare, That if this Our Declaration be granted, We will undertake to procure an Act of Indemnity, for
all ſuch perſons as have tranſgreſſed in theſe latter dayes, (ſave five); bnt if it be not granted, by fair means, Take what
follows. And if you reject the Virgins Counſel, as thk late Lord Lambert did his Wives, you may repent at your lea-
ſure as he dos and after all, do as Alderman Hoyle did, Hang your ſelves for madneſs.

Behold O Men, we aime at Preſervation,	Signed by many thouſands of Maidens in the Cities of
Unleſſe you ſtand unto Our Declaration	London and Weſtminſter, aud the Borough of Southwark,
Your Aonour is condemn'd, and you Behold	and other adjacent parts : which to nominate here, would
Are qnite undone, Your Fortunes are foretold.	be to tedious.

Printed for Virgin Hope-well, and are to be ſold at
the Maiden-Starre. 1660.

Plate 9 *The Royal Virgin*, a royalist declaration claiming to be by the virgins of London.
See p. 79.

The Cuckold's Complaint:

OR,

The Turbulent WIVES severe Cruelty.

To the Tune of, I marry and thank ye too.   Licensed according to Order.

I Marry'd a Wife of late,
which sinks my heart full low,
She laid a Ladle o'er my Pate,
a Curse of a cruel Shrow.

Before I'd been Wed a Week
her Cruelty she did show,
And would not suffer me to speak,
a Curse, &c.

I am forc'd to clean her Shoes
before she abroad doth goe,
Or else my person she'll abuse,
a Curse of a cruel Shrow.

I am forc'd to wash her Smock,
and the Child's Shitten Clouts also,
Though I sit up till Twelve a Clock,
a Curse of &c.

Her Gallant comes every day,
and they to the Tavern goe,
But I poor heart must nothing say,
a Curse of, &c.

Those Dainties is all her Farr,
while I with a hard Crust goe;
With this and ten times more I bear,
a Curse of a cruel Shrow.

One night as I went to Bed,
I happen'd to touch her Toe,
She with the Piss-pot brake my head,
a Curse of a cruel Shrow.

My Money she spends in Pride,
while I in Rags do go,
She Cudgels me if once I chide,
curse of a cruel Shrow.

Sometimes I would her embrace,
then straitway she'll fling and throw,
And call me Cuckold to my face,
a Curse, &c.

My Gullet she often tares,
and luggs my Ears also,
nd kicks me beating down the Stairs,
a Curse, &c.

Wish I had ne'er bin Wed,
irh Sorrows I undergo,
comfort now is from me fled,
Curse of a cruel Shrow.

When I led a single Life,
I rebell'd from Town to Town,
But since I am married to this cross Wife,
the world is turn'd upside down.

I formerly with a Friend,
could merrily spit a Crown,
But now one Groat I dare not spend,
the World, &c.

Rich Robes I was us'd to wear,
but Fortune hath sent a frown,
My head and heart is filled with care,
the World is turn'd up side down.

I formerly lived at ease,
and kept both my Hawk and Hound,
But now I have a Wife I cannot ple
the World, &c.

There's nothing like Liberty,
but here I am ty'd and bound
fast to the sowre Apple-Tree,
the World is turn'd upside down.

Printed for P. Brooksby. J. Deacon. J. Blare. J. Back.

Conclusion

Assessment

At the end of the early modern period the shape of gender relations does not look significantly different than at the beginning. Indeed, they are recognisable in modern terms: the length of marital relationships, the age and frequency of marriage, the earning power of women compared to that of men, and the disparity in sexual standards applied to women and to men are startlingly familiar. The differences are harder to see. Concepts of the body, the self, the community and the polity were integral to gender relations and made for a particularity of time and place. One aspect of that is the degree to which gender was confronted publicly: both sex and marriage were matters of community intervention. Another is the power of rituals and symbolic objects: the breeches, the ducking stool, the cuckold's horn. Distinctive, too, is the potential overlap between maleness and effeminacy, femaleness and masculinity: the qualities of gender were not the same as the distinctions of sex.

We have seen how gender relations were shaped by four forces: structures, beliefs, practices and transformations. Beliefs about gender were slow to change. The humoural body provided a basis for a scale of sexual difference that encompassed extremes of masculinity and femininity, allowing for a flexible understanding of what composed a man or a woman. Biblical texts provided a more rigid foundation for the subordination of women. The structures of church and state were complex, leaving some room for individual manoeuvre; at some points, like equity and church courts, women found a surprising opportunity, at others, like testamentary law, male authority was buttressed. The practices of daily life are the hardest to recover and the most relevant for our grasp of gender relations in the past. The most evident aspects of popular experience are not likely to be the most ordinary ones: customs were recorded because they were unusual, court cases dealt with contested issues, and personal writings were unlikely to recall the most familiar daily exchanges. It is sometimes the passing revelations of evidence that are the most informative about difference: where people worked, where they slept, who they confided in and what they dreamt.

In this era of metamorphoses, did anything transform gender roles? Not permanently. The Reformation had rather less immediate impact on relations between women and men in England than elsewhere: marriage law remained unreformed and practices of worship shifted piecemeal; one of the most tangible effects may have been the attack on reproductive rituals and the eclipse of Mary as maternal model. In the longer term the self-reflective nature of Protestant spirituality encouraged autobiography, and for women writers the form of spiritual reckoning gave a new weight to the minutiae of daily life. A greater revolution came with the 1640s. The spiritual authority of women, and their traditional political responsibilities, enabled them to claim a public voice amidst the turmoil of war, though often in a context of self-abnegation. The realignments of Restoration closed down most of these avenues. By 1700 a new set of justifications was in place to endorse the limitations of existing gender roles. Rather than looking back for a golden age of more equal gender roles, or forward for steadily gathering momentum towards parity, the most likely model seems to be that which imagines a cycle of changes through the premodern period, readjusting towards an equilibrium of inequality (Bennett, 2006).

The seventeenth century saw the beginnings of an articulation of women's collective voice. Jane Anger, whoever she was, spoke of 'we women'; the women petitioners asserted their rights to speak to be equal to men's; at the end of the century Mary Astell wrote against the inequality of marriage. The balance of power, justified on different terms and manifested in various ways, remained equivalent and recognisable, but it was challengeable through jest, rhetoric, protest and print.

Part 2

DOCUMENTS

Document 1   GENESIS 2:18–25

The second chapter of Genesis described the making of woman as a helpmeet for man. Its words were a point of departure for both attacks on women and proto-feminist writers.

18.   And the Lord God said, It is not good that the man should be alone; I will make him an help meet for him.

19.   And out of the ground the Lord God formed every beast of the field, and every fowl of the air; and brought them unto Adam to see what he would call them: and whatsoever Adam called every living creature, that was the name thereof.

20.   And Adam gave names to all cattle, and to the fowl of the air, and to every beast of the field; but for Adam there was not found an help meet for him.

21.   And the Lord God caused a deep sleep to fall upon Adam, and he slept: and he took one of his ribs, and closed up the flesh instead thereof;

22.   And the rib, which the Lord God had taken from man, made he a woman, and brought her unto the man.

23.   And Adam said, This is now bone of my bones, and flesh of my flesh: she shall be called Woman, because she was taken out of Man.

24.   Therefore shall a man leave his father and his mother, and shall cleave unto his wife: and they shall be one flesh.

25.   And they were both naked, the man and his wife, and were not ashamed.

Source: Genesis 2:18–25, King James Version.

Document 2   JANE ANGER

Jane Anger's pamphlet in defence of women was one of the earliest contributions to the English 'querelle des femmes'. Addressed 'to the gentlewomen of England', it countered a previous pamphlet's insults of women and set forth some familiar, and some novel, defences of the virtues of women. There is no evidence that Anger was a real author, although the name is not implausible.

The creation of man and woman at the first, he being formed in principio of dross and filthy clay, did so remain until God saw that in him his workmanship was good, and therefore by the transformation of the dust which was loathsome unto flesh, it became purified. Then lacking a help for him, God making woman of men's flesh, that she might be purer than he, does evidently show, how far we women are more excellent than men. Our bodies are fruitful, whereby the world increases, and our care wonderful, by which man is preserved. From woman sprang man's salvation. A woman was the first that believed, and a woman likewise the first that revered of him.

Source: Jane Anger Her Protection for Women, 1589, in The Women's Sharp Revenge: Five Women's Pamphlets from the Renaissance, *ed. Simon Shepherd, London: Fourth Estate, 1985, p. 39.*

LEVINUS LEMNIUS   **Document 3**

Levinus Lemnius's 400-page work, The Secret Miracles of Nature, *was first published in Antwerp in 1559, and translated into English in 1658. Offering both a philosophical and an anatomical discussion of the body and nature, it provided much of the material for midwives' books, including* Aristotle's Masterpiece. *This extract is from a chapter in Book IV entitled 'Of the nature of women'.*

For a woman's mind is not so strong as a man's, nor is she so full of under-standing and reason and judgement, and upon every small occasion she casts off the bridle of reason, and like a mad dog, forgeting all decency, and her self, without choice, she sets upon all, be they known or unknown. If any man desires a natural reason for it, I answer him thus, that a woman's flesh is loose, soft and tender, so that the choler being kindled, presently spreads all the body over, and causeth a sudden boiling of the blood about the heart. For as fire soonest take hold of light straw, and makes a great flame, but it is soon at an end, and quieter; so a woman is quickly angry and flaming hot, and rageth strangely; but this rage and crying out, is soon abated, and grows calm in a body that is not so strong and valiant, and that is more moist; and all her heat and fury is quenched by her shedding of tears, as if you should throw water upon fire to put it out. Which we see also in some effeminate men, whose magnanimity and fierceness ends almost as children's do in weeping, when the adversary doth strongly oppose himself against them. If any man would more nearly have the cause of this thing explaned, and desires a more exact reason; I can find no nearer cause that can be imagined, than the venom and collection of humours, that she every month heaps together, and purgeth forth by the course of the moon; For when she chanceth to be angry, as she will presently be, all that sink of humours being stirred fumeth, and runs through the body, so that the heart and brain are affected with the smoky vapours of it, and the spirits both vital and animal, that serve those parts are inflamed, and thence it is that women stirred up, especially the younger women (for the elder that are past childing, are more quiet and calm, because their **terms** are ended) will bark, and brawl like mad dogs,

Terms: Menstrual periods.

and clap their hands and behave themselves very unseemly in their actions and speeches, and reason being but weak in them, and their judgement feeble, and their mind not well ordered, they are sharply enraged, and cannot rule their passions. And the baser any woman is in that sex, the more she scolds and rails, and is unplacable in her anger, hence the vulgar women and whores (for noble women and gentlewomen will usually observe a decorum, though oft times they will be silent, and bend their brows, and scarce vouchsafe to give their husbands an answer, the Dutch call it *Proncken*) because their bodies are commonly polluted with faulty humours, are full of impudence, joined with equal malice, as if the Devil drove them, and they cannot be persuaded by counsel, reason, shame, flattery, admonition (that will ordinarily make wild beasts quiet) and you cannot hold them from their cruelty, or make them forbear their mad and loud exclamations.

Source: Levinus Lemnius, *The Secret Miracles of Nature: in Four Books*, 1658, pp. 274–5.

Document 4   JANE SHARP

Jane Sharp's midwives' book of 1671 presented a familiar view of the female body, unusual only in that it was written by a woman; its sources are sixteenth-century and classical.

Book I, Chap. XII *Of the likeness of the privities of both sexes*
But to handle these things more particularly, *Galen* saith that women have all the parts of Generation that Men have, but Mens are outwardly, womens inwardly.

The womb is like to a man's cod, turned the inside outward, and thrust inward between the bladder and the right gut, for then the stones which were in the cod, will stick on the outsides of it, so that what was a cod before will be a matrix, so the neck of the womb which is the passage for the yard to enter, resembleth a yard turned inwards, for they are both one length, only they differ like a pipe, and the case for it; so then it is plain, that when the woman conceives, the same members are made in both sexes, but the child proves to be a boy or a girl as the seed is in temper; and the parts are either thrust forth by heat, or kept in for want of heat; so a woman is not so perfect as a man, because her heat is weaker, but the man can do nothing without the woman to beget children, though some idle coxcombs will needs undertake to shew how children may be had without use of the woman.

Book II, Chap. 1 *What things are required for the procreation of Children*
The two principles then that are necessary in this case are the seed of both sexes, and the mother's blood; the seed of the male is more active than that of the female in forming the creature, though both be fruitful, but the female adds blood as well as seed out of which the fleshy parts are made, and both the fleshy and spermatick parts are maintained and preserved. What *Hippocrates* speaks of two sorts of Seed in both kinds, strong and weak seed, hot and cold, is to be understood only of strong and weak people, and as the seed is mingled, so are boys and girls begotten.

The mother's blood is another principle of children to be made; but the blood hath no active quality in this great work, but the seed works upon it, and of this blood are the chief parts of the bowels and the flesh of the muscles formed, and with this both the spermatical and fleshy parts are fed; this blood and the menstrual blood, or monthly terms are the same, which is a blood ordained by Nature for the procreation and feeding of the infant in the womb, and is at set times purged forth what is superfluous; and it is an excrement of the last nutriment of the fleshy parts, for what is too much for nature's use she casts it forth; for women have soft loose flesh and small heat, and cannot concoct all the blood she provides, nor discuss it but by this way of purgation.

Source: Jane Sharp, *The Midwives Book*, 1671, ed. Elaine Hobby, Oxford: Oxford University Press, 1999. By permission of Oxford University Press, Inc.

ARCHBISHOP LAUD'S DREAM **Document 5**

After his arrest and imprisonment in the Tower of London, William Laud's diary was translated and published by his opponent William Prynne in 1644. Comparisons with the original show few differences in this section, which records a period when he thought and dreamed much about the Duke of Buckingham, the King's favourite, and his family.

August 21 [1625]. I stayed at Brecon in Wales: that night in a dream the Duke of Buckingham seemed to me to ascend into my bed; where he carried himself with much love towards me, after such rest wherein wearied men are wont exceedingly to rejoice: And likewise many seemed to me to enter the Chamber who did see this. Not many days before, I seemed to see the Duchess of Buckingham that excellent lady, in a dream: at first she was much perplexed about her husband, but afterwards merry, and rejoicing, that she was freed from the fear of abortion[1]; that in due time she might be a mother again.

Source: William Prynne, *A Breviat of the Life of William Laud, Arch-Bishop of Canterbury*, 1644, p. 6.

Document 6   KATHERINE AUSTEN

Katherine Austen was born into a London draper's family in 1629, and was married and widowed by the age of thirty. During her widowhood she composed a manuscript book of poems, reflections and advice to her children: this piece, written in the 1660s, is addressed to her son Thomas who, as his father had been, was enrolled at an Oxford college.

To my Son Thomas Austen

A fellow of a College is made up of pride and unmannerliness (in diverse of them). And they that are fellow commoners, learn those ill habits. I repent me of nothing more I made you one. I had better have took the good counsel of Dr Wilbe not for the charges, as the diverse dangers is in it. What makes noble men to be so extremely civil but being used from all men to receive a great respect by observance and keeping their hats off in their presence. Which does not exclude them theirs by their dignity above others. But civility and good breeding obliges the same answerable return. As the Lord Manchester to Cousin T.K. put off his hat all the time he had business to my Lord. And truly in my estimation this very rude fashion creates abundance of pride in Colleges. Either all lordly. Nay Kingly. Or else vassals, and lavish in the royalty of Colleges.

And certainly for the ill breeding and unaccomplishments in colleges, enforces Gentlemen of quality to send their sons to travel to learn civility and sweetness of deportment, for by the early habit of pride, and surliness and stoutness of carriage they hardly ever forget it while they live. . . .

Whatever the fashion is I would have your demeanour other ways. And though you may go scot free, hat free, be not so rude in your carriage but if a beggar put off his hat, give the like.

Source: BL Add. Mss. 4454, f. 40.

---

[1] Abortion here means miscarriage.

FRANK NORTH

Document 7

Anne North took her grandchildren to live with her in Suffolk when her son Francis North, Lord Chief Justice, was widowed in 1678. She was about sixty-five and had herself been widowed the previous year. These letters to the children's father record the progress of her grandson Frank into breeches. The end of the second letter refers to a disagreement between herself and her eldest son over her right to present to the local church.

For the Rt Honorable the Lord Chief Justice at his house in Chancery Lane.

These.

[Tostock] 10 October, '79

Dear Son,

Nobody believed that you could make so short a stay here, so that the letters are directed hither still, and this enclosed was brought me yesterday. You cannot believe the great concern that was in the whole family here last Wednesday, it being the day that the tailor was to help to dress little Frank in his breeches in order to the making an everyday suit by it. Never had any bride that was to be dressed upon her wedding night more hands about her, some the legs and some the arms, the tailor buttoning and others putting on the sword, and so many lookers on that had I not had a finger amongst them I could not have seen him. When he was quite dressed he acted his part as well as any of them, for he desired he might go down to inquire for the little gentleman that was there the day before in a black coat, and speak to the men to tell the gentleman when he came from school that here was a gallant with very fine clothes and a sword to have waited upon him and would come again upon Sunday next. But this was not all, for there was great contriving while he was dressing who should have the first salute, but he said if old Lane had been here she should, but he gave it me to quiet them all. They are very fit, everything, and he looks taller and prettier than in his coats. Little Charles rejoiced as much as he did, for he jumped all the while about him and took notice of everything. I went to Bury and bought everything for another suit, which will be finished upon Saturday, so the coats are to be quite left off upon Sunday. I consider it is not yet term time and since you could not have the pleasure of the first sight I have resolved you should have a full relation from

Your most affectionate Mother,
A. North.

When he was dressed he asked Buckle whether muffs were out of fashion because they had not sent him one.

For [as above]

[Tostock] 12 October, '79

Dear Son,

I thank you for sending me so particular an account of the little ones' ages, which I think as forward children for these times as can be. I gave you an account in my last that this day was designed wholly to throw off the coats and write man, and great good fortune it was to have it a fair day. It was carried with a great deal of privacy purposely to surprise Mr. Camborne, and it took so well as to put him to the blush as soon as he saw him in the church, which pleased Frank not a little. I perceive it proves as I thought, that your brother North would think I infringed upon his right when I presented to Drinkston. But I wonder he should declare so much when he knows it is my unquestionable due: it looks as if he grudged at what I have, though it be but the honour and gratifying of another, without any profit to myself, and indeed I cannot take it well of him for he lays an aspersion both upon my dear Lord and myself, but I shall look upon it only as selfishness and let him say his pleasure. . . .

Source: Roger North, *The Autobiography of the Hon. Roger North*, ed. Augustus Jessopp, D. Nutt, 1887, pp. 215–7.

Document 8 JANE MARTINDALE

Adam Martindale was born in Lancashire in 1623, to yeoman parents who had fallen on hard times. He went to grammar school and became a teacher, and then a Presbyterian preacher in the 1640s. Near the end of his life, in 1685, he recorded his life story; this is an extract from the early section, describing his sister leaving home after the plague of 1625, and reflecting on the changing habits of single women in the era.

There had lately been a great plague in London, causing many that had friends in the country to come down, who having employments to return unto, were full as hasty to go up as consisted with safety; and my sister Jane having conversed with some of them, was as forward as they. Our parents and other prudent friends were against her going for many substantial reasons:

1. She wanted nothing at home, nor was likely to lack anything; and if she had a mind to be married, my father was then in a good ordinary capacity to prefer her.
2. She had no friends in London to go to.

3. It was feared the City was not clear of the plague, as it proved to her cost.
4. She had been bred in a most pure air, and being of a fresh complexion and not very hardly, 'twas much to be questioned whether the city air would agree with her in the most healthful times.

But all these would not back her. She measured not a competency by the same mete-wand that they did. Freeholders' daughters were then confined to their felts, petticoats and waistcoats, cross handkerchiefs about their necks, and white cross-cloths upon their heads, with coifs under them wrought with black silk or worsted. 'Tis true the finest sort of them wore gold or silver lace upon their waistcoats, good silk laces (and store of them) about their petticoats, and bone laces or works about their linens. But the proudest of them (below the gentry) durst not have offered to wear an hood, or a scarf (which now every beggar's brat that can get them thinks not above her) no, nor so much as a gown til her wedding day. And if any of them had transgressed these bounds, she would have been accounted an ambitious fool. These limitations I suppose she did not very well approve, but having her father's spirit, and her mother's beauty, no persuasion would serve, but up she would to serve a lady as she hoped to do, being ingenious at her needle. Monies to carry her up and to subsist on awhile, till she got a place, was all she could handsomely desire, seeing she went against her parents' will, and that she was furnished with.

Source: Adam Martindale, *The Life of Adam Martindale: By Himself*, ed. Richard Parkinson, Manchester: Chetham Society, 1845; BiblioBazaar, 2008, pp. 6–7.

JAMES I AND ROBERT CARR   **Document 9**

A letter written in 1611 from Lord Thomas Howard to Sir John Harington, who was hoping to move back into court circles under James I, describes Carr's success with the King.

I will now premise certain things to be observed by you, toward well gaining our Prince's good affection: – He doth wondrously covet learned discourse, of which you can furnish out ample means; he doth admire good fashion in clothes, I pray you give good heed hereunto; strange devices oft come into man's conceit; some one regardeth the endowments of the inward sort, wit, valour, or virtue; another hath, perchance, special affection towards outward things, clothes, deportment, and good countenance. I would wish you to be well trimmed; get a new jerkin well bordered, and not too short; the King saith, he liketh a flowing garment; be sure it be not all of one sort, but diversely coloured, the collar falling somewhat down, and your ruff well stiffened and bushy. We have lately had many gallants who failed in their suits, for want of due observance of these matters. The King is nicely heedful of such points, and dwelleth on good looks and handsome accoutrements. Eighteen servants were lately discharged, and many more will be discarded, who are not to his liking in these matters. I wish you to follow my directions, as I wish you to gain all you desire. Carr is now most likely to win the Prince's affection, and doth it wondrously in a little time. The Prince leaneth on his arm, pinches his cheek, smoothes his ruffled garment, and, when he looketh at Carr, directeth discourse to divers others. This young man doth much study all art and device; he hath changed his tailors and tiremen many times, and all to please the Prince, who laugheth at the long grown fashion of our young courtiers, and wisheth for change every day.

Source: Sir John Harington, *Nugæ antiquæ*, ed. Henry Harington, Bath: T. Cadell and L. Bull, 1792, pp. 271–2.

Document 10   MRS JANE RATCLIFFE

Mrs Jane Ratcliffe, Puritan wife of an alderman in seventeenth-century Cheshire, was memorialised in a funeral sermon by her minister John Lay.

And whereas some out of a rebellious reluctancy to rule, cannot abide any abridgement of liberty, and so like things the worse (though otherwise unoffensive and faultless) because they are commanded; she liked the performance of such things rather by humble obedience than by liberty of choice, and that self denial was the principal exercise of humility, which could not consist with self will, when we like better to do what we list, than what (for things that are lawful) they would have us to do whom God hath set over us. Yet once I observed her a little to stick at an imposition, and rather to require a dispensation than readily to yield to an observation of it.

But it was in such a case as might commend her humility the more, and the case was this, a new gown was brought her to put on, and presented as a gift from her husband, wherein his kindness had put him to more cost than she wished, to make her more fine than she desired to be, for she would have been clothed with humility, as the Apostle prescribeth, 1.Pet.5.5 *viz.* as I may apply rather than expound the phrase, she would have worn a meaner habit both for matter and fashion than that was, and she humbly besought, with trickling tears on her cheeks, that it might not come upon her back, I was present and stood silent with some marvell at the matter, because I had never seen such a sight before.

For it is more usual a great deal for women to be too much affected to fine clothes, and offended if they may not have them, than to make a grief of an outward glory as she did: she said little with her tongue (but with her eyes spoke much) because she was loath to contradict him whom she was bound to obey, yet she suffered a contradiction within her self (and that a strong one) where the strife was not (betwixt pride and covetuousness or two adverse vices, as many times it is) but betwixt two humilities, whether the humility of prompt obedience without gainsaying, or the humility of refusing gay clothes should prevail, and at the last the resolution was, that she did submit to her husband's mind against her own, not only because that habit was no better than others of her rank did wear, yea some that in divers respects (besides the desert of her own worth) were inferiors unto her, but because it was a testimony of her husband's love and of her own loyal and obsequious subjection to his will . . .

Source: John Ley, *A patterne of pietie. Or The religious life and death of that grave and gracious matron, Mrs. Jane Ratcliffe widow and citizen of Chester*, 1640, pp. 128–131.

MAWDLIN GAWEN

Document 11

Mawdlin Gawen appeared at London's Bridewell in 1575 on the charge of wearing men's clothes.

Mawdlin Gawen sent in by my Lord Mayor and the aldermen his brethren for going and putting herself into man's apparel she being of the age of 22 years or thereabouts born in the parish of Thame in Oxfordshire. Saith that she was in service with one Goodwife Oliver in the said town of Thame an innkeeper where she dwelled two years. And from thence she said she went to Teddington in Bedfordshire to an uncle of hers to which place she came on Monday in Whitsun week last. And by her said uncle was placed with one Mr Chaunce the Lord Chenye's Steward. And there remained until Michaelmas last. And then came to one Smith a tanner dwelling in Teddington aforesaid and was hired with him for one year.

And that she then by the enticement of one Thomas Ashwell also servant with the said Smith did consent to roam from her said master with the same Thomas, and so they two came from thence to Stansted in Hertfordshire where they tarried three days. And from thence they came to London to one Thomas Balle's house in Finche Lane, the saide Thomas Ashwell by the way always said she was his kinswoman. And being in Finche Lane she was brought to one Mr Fluett where she was placed in service, the said Ashwell coming to her to the said Mr Fluett's house. The said Mr Fluett asking, what countrywoman she was she said she was borne in Collyweston which the said Ashwell also affirmed. And in asking them how far it was from Stamford because the truth might be known, the said Ashwell could not tell. Nevertheless the said Fluett received her into service where she remained about three weeks. But the said Gawen saith she spake not with the said Ashwell from the time she was there placed in service until Thursday last, at which time he persuaded her to meet him at Paul's Wharf the Tuesday next following in the morning by four of the clock. She answered him again she would not come in her own apparel. And he told her, that what apparel soever she came in he would receive her and put on her own.

And the time appointed she changed her self into man's apparel which she had in her said mistress's house being about two of the clock after midnight and came away and so came to Paul's Wharf being the place appointed but the said Ashwell was not there present nor came not according to his appointment, she calling there for a boat to go down westward a waterman looking out of a window said it was too early and she said she would stay until it were time and that he would go. Whereupon the waterman came down and opened his door and she went in to his house with her farthingale under her arm which she cast down upon the ground within the door. And then she desired the waterman himself to do so much as to poll her and

Groat: Four pence.

she said she would give him a **groat** for his labour. And the waterman made her believe he would so do but he sent his man for the constable when he perceived what she was and so made a strife saying he lacked his scissors and so made as though he sent his man for them as he told her, and his man tarrying long went himself for the constable, and when the constable came she was apprehended and she saith she told the constable that she dwelled in Philpott Lane with one Goodwife Osborne.

Also she saith that the said Thomas Ashwell began to live wickedly with her from Shrovetide last until such time as she was placed in service here in London. And that he had the use of her body carnally divers and sundry times as at Stansted aforesaid and other places more for the which wickedness she had by order of the Lord Mayor and the bench correction.

Source: London Metropolitan Archives, Bridewell Court Book II, fos 114v–115v, 20 April 1575 (microfilm).

————————◀●▶————————

Document 12   *HIC MULIER*

The anonymous short pamphlet attacking the cross-gendered fashions of early seventeenth-century London uses a masculine article (hic) for a feminine noun (mulier).

Come, then, you masculine women, for you are my subject, you that have made admiration an ass and fooled him with a deformity never before dreamed of; that have made yourselves stranger things than ever Noah's Ark unloaded or Nile engendered, whom to name, he that named all things might study an age to give you a right attribute; whose like are not found in any antiquary's study, in any seaman's travel, nor in any painter's cunning. You that are stranger than strangeness itself; whom wise men wonder at, boys shout at, and goblins themselves start at; you that are the gilt dirt which embroiders playhouses, the painted statues which adorn caroches,[2] and the perfumed carrion that bad men feed on in brothels: 'tis of you I entreat and of your monstrous deformity. You that have made your bodies like antique boscage or crotesco work,[3] not half man/half woman, half fish/half flesh, half beast/half monster, but all odious, all devil; that have cast off the ornaments of your sexes to put on the garments of shame; that have laid by the bashfulness of your natures to gather the impudence of harlots, that have buried silence to revive slander; that are all things but that which you should be, and nothing less than friends to virtue and goodness; that have made the foundation of your highest detested work from the lowest despised creatures that record can give testimony of: the one cut from the commonwealth at the gallows; the other is well known. From the first you got the false armoury of yellow starch (for to wear yellow on white or white upon yellow is by the rules of heraldry baseness, bastardy, and indignity), the folly of imitation, the deceitfulness of flattery, and the grossest baseness of all baseness, to do whatever a greater power will command you. From the other you have taken the monstrousness of your deformity in apparel, exchanging the modest attire of the comely hood, cowl, coif, handsome dress or kerchief, to the cloudy ruffianly broad-brimmed hat and wanton feather; the modest upper parts of a concealing straight gown, to the loose, lascivious civil embracement of a French doublet being all unbuttoned to entice, all of one shape to hide deformity, and extreme short waisted to give a most easy way to every luxurious action; the glory of a fair large hair, to the shame of most ruffianly short locks; the side, thick gathered, and close guarding safeguards to the short, weak, thin, loose, and every hand-entertaining short bases; for needles, swords; for prayerbooks, bawdy legs; for modest gestures, giantlike behaviours; and for women's modesty, all mimic and apish incivility. These are your founders, from these you took your copies, and, without amendment, with these you shall come to perdition.

Source: *Hic Mulier*, 1620, sig. A3v–B1.

[2] Luxurius coach.
[3] Grotesque ornaments (Montaigne).

Document 13   A JOKE

Sir Nicholas L'Estrange, a Norfolk baronet, kept a book of his favourite jests, with attributions for each.

A plain country fellow, following his daughter to church to be married: well go thy ways says he, for there goes as pure a virgin as ever man laid leg over; but at dinner in all the mirth and jollity, our bride grew quamish in her stomach, and (striving to smother her disease) swooned away for a goose rump; and within few weeks after, this pure virgin was delivered of a most goodly knave-child [My Mother].

Source: Nicholas L'Estrange, *'Merry Passages and Jeasts': A Manuscript Jestbook of Sir Nicholas Le Strange, 1603–1655*, Salzburg: University of Salzburg, 1974, p. 105.

Document 14   EDWARD LACY AND ELIZABETH INKBERROW

Edward Lacy, a husband, and Elizabeth Inkberrow, a widow, were bound over to behave by their neighbours in Riple, Worcestershire, in 1661; the names of the complainants are beside each article of the complaint.

Worcester county	Articles of the Good Behaviour exhibited September 6 1661 against Edward Lacy of Riple labourer and Elizabeth Inkberrow of the same parish widow before Henry Bromley esq . . . Justice of the Peace
Isabell Morris jun Thomas Clarke jun	1. That the said Edward Lacy did threaten to go away from his wife and leave her nothing but a bed and the rags on her back as he himself expressed, whereby she may become a charge to the parish
Robert Tustian Thomas Best jun William Morris	2. That he the said Lacy will not cohabit with his wife, but hath lain for the most part of twenty weeks last past at the widow Inkberrow's house giving a great cause of scandal and offence to the neighbourhood, who generally suspect that they live together in incontinency
Margaret Fairelock	3. That besides the general fame the said Lacy hath been seen in the bed with the said widow Inkberrow, and hath been heard to wish his knife in his heart if he lay with his wife again
Anne Land	4. That the said Lacy when a difference happened betwixt the said widow Inkberrow and her mother, did provoke and encourage her to offer abuse and violence to her said mother.

The Articles against the aforesaid Elizabeth Inkberrow widow are

Anne Land	1. That upon a difference betwixt her mother and her self the said Elizabeth Inkberrow did assault hurt and abuse her said Mother
Robert Tustian Thomas Best	2. That the said Elizabeth Inkberrow by her lewd carriage doth give great offence to the neighbourhood and a general cause of suspicion that she lived in whoredom with the aforesaid Lacy, having entertained him at her house almost this half year last past, and lodging him there from his wife though his own house is very near adjoining to hers: whereby his affection is alienated from his wife, which hath been a great cause of sadness and affliction to her
Margaret Fairelock	3. That besides the general suspicion it is known that she hath gone to bed to the said Lacy, having been seen in his bed with him
Robert Tustian	4. That she is much suspected to be with child, and that there is great suspicion and fear that she hath a design to destroy her child there having been savin found in her bed, and she having been known to have tampered with those that pretend to give physic.

Source: Worcestershire Record Office, QS 98/37.

LEONARD WHEATCROFT

Document 15

Leonard Wheatcroft (1627–1707), a Derbyshire yeoman, kept a manuscript notebook with a narrative of his courtship of his wife, Elizabeth. This extract is from one of the earliest entries, where a journey from London brings him to the parish festival known as the wakes at Ashover.

And I being present at that wakes, I had some intelligence of a young maid that would be there by one of her relations, who told me she was very fortunate, besides beautiful lovely.

So in process of time she came, and many more with her, both relations and friends, and being all drawn up into a garden, where was a famous arbour which at that time held 28 people, amongst whom was placed this beautiful damsel. Then after I had saluted several of my friends and acquaintance, I drew a little nearer this young lady, whom I had never seen before. So after we had parled awhile and could not agree we parted and she returned to her castle again; from which hold she sent me a challenge, and withall hang her flag of defiance against me; which I no sooner perceiving all this, I mustered up all my man forces, and close siege to her, which siege lasted for the space 23 months and more, before she would yield I should enter, etc. But what happened in this long and tedious siege was as followeth.

After I had enclosed her in her castle called by the name of Winster (not far from Bakewell in the Peak) we had several parleys, but in many of them we could not agree, and she like a courageous commander always cheered up her resolved and commanded thoughts to resist poor me. But being as then a never-daunted soldier in the wars of Mars, I played several cannon-like letters against the main tower of her heart, and every day laying closer siege than other, as you shall hear hereafter.

Source: The Courtship Narrative of Leonard Wheatcroft, Derbyshire Yeoman, ed. George Parfitt and Ralph Hourbrooke, Reading: Whiteknights Press, 1986, pp. 41–2.

Document 16   ELIZABETH BROWNE

Quarter sessions: Criminal courts held quarterly for lesser offences.

*The examination of a pregnant Somerset servant at the **Quarter Sessions** in 1607.*

The Examination of Elizabeth Browne of Wisterton spinster . . . 10 August 1607

She saith that she was the Saturday before St Luketide last retained into the service of one John Norris of Wisterton and within one month next after her retaining the said Norris service, one William Norris dwelling at home with his father made love to this examinant and had to do with her in his father's hall floor in the night time when his father was abed, and about sevenight after the said William Norris being on his father's mow, caused this examinant to come up to throw sheaves to him, at which time the said William Norris had to do with her again and from that time forth, he had his pleasure of her, sometimes when she was making the beds and sometime elsewhere, as often as pleased him.

Source: Somerset Archives, Q/SR 2/12.

Document 17   *THE COUNTRY JUSTICE*

Michael Dalton's book was a guide for magistrates; these sections cover bastardy and the felony of rape.

Chapter 2 *Bastardy*

Every Justice of Peace, upon his discretion, may (as it seemeth) bind to the good behaviour, him that is charged, or suspected to have begotten a bastard child, to the end that he may be forthcoming when the child shall be borne; otherwise there will be no putative father, when the two justices (after the birth of the child) shall come to take order according to the Statute of 18 Eliz. c. 3. The like may be done after the birth of the child, and before such order taken. . . .

Also it seemeth the mother may be examined upon oath, concerning the reputed father, and of the time, and other circumstances, for that in this case the matter and the trial thereof dependeth chiefly upon the examination and testimony of the mother . . .

By the Statute 7. Jac. it appeareth that the Justices of the peace shall now commit such lewd women to the house of correction, there to be punished, etc. And therefore it seemeth that the Justices of Peace may not punish (by corporal punishment) the mother by force of this Statute of 18 Eliz. 3 and then to send them to the house of correction. . . .

But such corporal punishment, or commitment to the house of correction, is not to be until after that the woman is delivered of her child, neither are the Justices of Peace to meddle with the woman until that the child be born (and she strong again) lest the woman being weak, or the child wherewith she is, happen to miscarry; for you shall find that about 31. Eliz. a woman great with child, and suspected for incontinency, was commanded (by the Master of Bridewell in London) to be whipped there, by reason whereof she travailled, and was delivered of her child before her time, etc. And for this the said masters of Bridewell were in the Star-Chamber fined to the Queen at a great sum, and were further ordered to pay a sum of money to the said woman . . .

Every lewd woman which shall have a bastard, which may be chargeable to the parish, the justices of peace shall commit such woman unto the house of correction, there to be punished and set on work for one year: and if she shall eftsoons offend again; then to be committed to the house of correction, as aforesaid; and there to remain until she can put in good sureties for her good behaviour, not to offend again. . . .

It seemeth also (by the words of this statute 7. *Jacobi*) that such a woman shall not be sent to the house of correction, until after the child be born, and that it be living; for it must be such a child as may be chargeable to the parish.

Also it seemeth that such a bastard child, is not to be sent with the mother to the house of correction, but rather that the child should remain in the town where it was born (or settled with the mother) and there to be relieved by the work of the mother, or by relief from the reputed father . . . and yet the common opinion and practice is otherwise, *sc.* to send the child, with the mother, to the house of correction; And this may also seem reasonable, where the child sucketh on the mother. . . .

Chapter 107 *Felonies by Statute*

Women, *sc.* to ravish a woman where she doth neither consent before nor after, or to ravish any woman with force, though she do consent after, it is felony: and the offender shall have no benefit of clergy . . .

Now Ravishment is here taken in one and the same signification with Rape, which is a violent defllowering of a woman, or a carnal knowledge had of the body of a woman against her will . . .

A woman that is ravished, ought presently to levy open hue and cry, or to complain thereof presently to some credible persons as it seemeth . . .

If a woman at the time of the supposed rape, do conceive with child, by the ravisher, this is no rape, for a woman cannot conceive with child, except she do consent. . . .

And yet if a man ravish a woman, who consenteth for fear of death or duress, this is ravishment against her will, for that consent ought to be voluntary and free.

Source: Michael Dalton, *The Countrey Justice, Containing the Practice of the Justices of the Peace out of their Sessions*, 1635, pp. 37–9; 281.

Document 18   JAMES I AND GEORGE VILLIERS

James I's letters to Villiers, Duke of Buckingham, cast a love widely assumed to be sexual in the terms of family relations; Buckingham wrote to him as 'Dear dad and gossip'.

[December 1623?]

My only sweet and dear child,

Notwithstanding of your desiring me not to write yesterday, yet had I written in the evening if, at my coming out of the park, such a drowsiness had not come upon me as I was forced to set and sleep in my chair half an hour. And yet I cannot content myself without sending you this present, praying God that I may have a joyful and comfortable meeting with you and that we may make at this Christmas a new marriage ever to be kept hereafter; for, God so love me, as I desire only to live in this world for your sake, and that I had rather live banished in any part of the earth with you than live a sorrowful widow's life without you. And so God bless you, my sweet child and wife, and grant that ye may ever be a comfort to your dear dad and husband.

James R.

Source: *Letters of King James VI and I*, ed. G.P.V. Akrigg, Berkeley: University of California Press, 1984, p. 431.

LEO AFRICANUS   **Document 19**

The Moroccan traveller Leo Africanus's Geographical History of Africa (first published in Venice in 1550; translated into English in 1600) introduced European readers to tales of the exotic practices of African culture, repeating suggestions of reversed gender roles that were as old as Herodotus. These extracts dealing with gender inversions are from the sections on Morocco and Egypt.

Of the Inns of Fez.
In this city are almost two hundred inns, the greatest wherof are in the principal part of the city near unto the chief temple. Every of these inns are three stories high, and contain an hundred and twenty or more chambers apiece. Likewise each one hath a fountain together with sinks and water-pipes, which make avoidance of all the filth . . . In these inns certain poor widows of Fez, which have neither wealth nor friends to succour them, are relieved: sometimes one, and sometimes two of them together are allowed a chamber; for which courtesy they play both the chamberlains and cooks of the inn. The inn-keepers of Fez being all of one family called Elcheua, go apparelled like women, and shave their beards, and are so delighted to imitate women, that they will not only counterfeit their speech, but will sometimes also sit down and spin. Each one of these hath his concubine, whom he accompanieth as if she were his own lawful wife; albeit the said concubines are not only ill-favoured in countenance, but notorious for their bad life and behaviour.

Of the fortune-tellers and some other artisans in Fez.
. . . The third kind of diviners are women-witches, which are affirmed to have familiarity with devils: some devils they call red, some white, and some black devils: and when they will tell any man's fortune, they perfume themselves with certain odours, saying, that then they possess themselves with that devil which they called for: afterward changing their voice, they

feign the devil to speak within them: then they which come to enquire, ought with great fear and trembling ask these vile and abominable witches such questions as they mean to propound, and lastly offering some fee unto the devil, they depart. But the wiser and honester sort of people call these women *Sahaoat*, which in Latin signifieth *Fricatrices*, because they have a damnable custom to commit unlawful venery among themselves, which I cannot express in any modester terms. If fair women come unto them at any time, these abominable witches will burn in lust towards them no otherwise than lusty younkers do towards young maids, and will in the devil's behalf demand for a reward, that they may lie with them: and so by this means it often falleth out, that thinking thereby to fulfil the devil's command they lie with the witches. Yea some there are, which being allured with the delight of this abominable vice, will desire the company of these witches, and feigning themselves to be sick, will either call one of the witches home to them, or will send their husbands for the same purpose: and so the witches perceiving how the matter stands, will say that the woman is possessed with a devil, and that she can no way be cured, unless she be admitted into their society. With these words her silly husband being persuaded, doth not only permit her so to do, but makes also a sumptuous banquet unto the damned crew of witches: which being done, they use to dance very strangely at the noise of drums: and so the poor man commits his false wife to their filthy disposition. Howbeit some there are that will soon conjure the devil with a good cudgel out of their wives: others feigning themselves to be possessed with a devil, will deceive the said witches, as their wives have been deceived by them.

[Cairo]

The women go costly attired, adorning their foreheads and necks with frontlets and chains of pearl, and on their heads they wear a sharp and slender bonnet of a span high, being very precious and rich. Gowns they wear of woollen cloth with straight sleeves, being curiously embroidered with needlework, over which they cast certain veils of most excellent fine cloth of India. They cover their heads and faces with a kind of black scarf, through which beholding others, they cannot be seen themselves. Upon their feet they wear fine shoes and pantofles, somewhat after the Turkish fashion. These women are so ambitious and proud, that all of them disdain either to spin or to play the cooks: wherefore their husbands are constrained to buy victuals ready dressed at the cooks' shops: for very few, except such as have a great family, use to prepare and dress their victuals in their own houses. Also they vouchsafe great liberty unto their wives: for the good man being gone to the tavern or victualling-house, his wife tricking up her self in costly apparel, and being perfumed with sweet and precious odours, walketh about the city to solace her self, and parley with her kinsfolks and friends. They use to ride upon asses more than horses, which are broke to such a gentle pace, that they go easier than any ambling horse. These asses they cover with most costly furniture, and let them out unto women to ride upon, together with a boy to lead the ass, and certain footmen to run by. . . . The citizens in their common talk use ribald and filthy speeches: and (that I may pass over the rest in silence) it falleth out oftentimes that the wife will complain of her husband unto the judge, that he doth not his duty nor contenteth her sufficiently in the night season, whereupon (as it is permitted by the Mahometan law) the women are divorced and married unto other husbands.

Source: Leo Africanus, *A geographical historie of Africa . . . gathered partly out of his owne diligent obseruations, and partly out of the ancient records and chronicles of the Arabians and Mores . . .* , trans. John Pory, 1600, pp. 130–1; 148–9; 314–5.

SARAH JINNER   **Document 20**

Sarah Jinner, a London astrologer, published annual almanacs (perhaps the most widely used form of cheap print) for several years in the 1650s and 1660s. Her remedies, many of which dealt with reproductive health, were followed by a calendar of useful dates.

Common syrups which remove obstruction of the terms are
Syrup of mugwort, of maidenhair, of chicory with rhubarb, and the syrup of the five roots; these you may have ready at the apothecary's.

Another to move the terms
Take mints, balm, penny-royal, marjoram and southernwood, of each an handful: aniseeds, fennel and caraway seeds, of each an ounce; polipody, an ounce and an half; chicory roots, an ounce; cut the roots and herbs very small, and boil them all together in a quart of water till a third part be consumed; then strain it, and sweeten it with sugar to your own liking, and take thereof as you please.

   . . .

A confection to cause fruitfulness in man or woman
Take rapes, ivory shaven, ashkeys, sesely, behen red and white, of each one dram: cinnamon, downicum, mace, cloves, galangal, long pepper, rosemary flowers, balsam wood, blattis, byzantine marjoram gentle, penny royal, of each two scruples:[4] balm-bugles, citron pieces, of each one scruple: spica indie,

---

[4] A scruple: 20 grains, or 3 drams.

amber, pearls of each half a scruple: sugar a pound; decoct the sugar in malmsey, and the other things; and make them into a confection, use of it a little at a time.

A powder for the same to be strewed on meat
Take nutmegs, cubebbes, ginger, of each half a dram: long pepper, mastic, cinnamon, red behen, white behen, of each a scruple: mix them all together, and make them into a fine powder, and strew a little of it upon the party's meat.

. . .

A Plaster to remedy the corrupt humours
Take roses, cypress nuts, burnt ivory, sandarac, of each one dram, rosin 2 ounces: boil the rosin in red vinegar, till the vinegar be consumed, then mix the other things with it, and make two plasters of it, and apply one to the back, and the other to the womb.

Another excellent good plaster to strengthen women with child, that do not use to go out half their times
Take oil of quinces, oil of roses, oil of mints, of each one ounces and a half, comfrey, blood-stone, red-coral, sandarac, date stones burnt: of each one dram mix it with a sufficient quantity of wax to make a salve thereof: and with this anoint the kidneys and mother.[5]

An Almanac and Prognostication for the year of our Lord 1664
For such as think themselves bewitched, that they cannot do the act of Venery.
Take flying ants, mixed with the oil of cider, and anoint the defective instrument.

To take away the desire of a Woman to the Act of Venery
Take of a red bull's pizzle, and powder it, and put in wine or broth, the quantity of a crown weight of silver, and she will abhor the desire of lying with a man: this may be a good medicine for the preventing of young girls throwing themselves away upon mad-cap fellows. The same ingredient given to men, will provoke venery in them that are dull and impotent.

Source: Sarah Jinner, *An Almanack and Prognostication for the year of our Lord 1659* and Sarah Jinner, *An Almanack and Prognostication for the year of our Lord 1664* in *Almanacs, The Early Modern Englishwoman: A Facsimile Library of Essential Works*, ed. Alan S. Weber, Aldershot: Ashgate, 2002.

—◆—

[5] Mother: womb.

SAMUEL PEPYS **Document 21**

At a dinner to celebrate the birth of his friends' child, Pepys found himself being advised about his own apparent infertility.

26 July 1664.

All the morning at the office. At noon to Anth. Joyce's to our gossips' dinner; I had sent a dozen and a half of bottles of wine thither and paid my double share besides, which is 18s. Very merry we were, and when the women were merry and ris from table, I above with them, ne'er a man but I; I begin discourse of my not getting with children and prayed them to give me their opinions and advice; and they freely and merrily did give me these ten among them. 1. Do not hug my wife too hard nor too much. 2. Eat no late suppers. 3. Drink juice of sage. 4. Tent and toast. 5. Wear cool Holland-drawers. 6. Keep stomach warm and back cool. 7. Upon my query whether it was best to do at night or morn, they answered me neither one nor another, but when we have most mind to it. 8. Wife not to go too straight-laced. 9. Myself to drink Mum[6] and sugar. 10. Mrs Ward did give me to change my plate. The 3rd, 4th, 6th, 7th and 10th they all did seriously declare and lay much stress upon them, as rules fit to be observed indeed, and especially the last: to lie with our heads where our heels do, or at least to make the bed high at feet and low at head.

Source: *The Diary of Samuel Pepys*, vol. v, 1664, ed. Robert Latham and William Matthews, London: HarperCollins, 1995, p. 222.

ARISTOTLE'S MASTERPIECE **Document 22**

Aristotle's Masterpiece, *a pseudo-Aristotelian popular guide to sex and reproduction, was reprinted in various editions from the late seventeenth century into the twentieth century. Its summary of beliefs about 'the secrets of generation' combined ancient learning and popular knowledge. This discussion of the question of parental resemblance also stresses the alignment of femininity with the left hand side and masculinity with the right, a fundamental principle of pre-modern gender relations.*

Chap. III *The reason why children are often like their parents, and what the mother's imagination contributes thereto: how the mother contributes seed, and is*

[6] A kind of beer.

a companion in the whole generation; and whence grows the kind, viz. whether the man or the woman is the cause of the male or female child, etc.

It is the opinion of learned physicians, grounded upon reason, that if a woman in the act of copulation afford most seed, her likeness will have the greatest impression upon the child; but if on the contrary, then will follow the contrary effects; or if a proportionable quantity proceed from either, then will the similitude depend upon either.

Lactantius is of opinion, that when a man's seed falls on the left side of the womb a male child may be gotten: but by reason it is the proper place for a female, there will be something in it greatly resembling a woman, viz, it will be fairer, whiter, and smoother, not very subject to have hair on the body or chin, long lank hair on the head, the voice small and sharp, and the courage feeble; and arguing yet further, he says, that a female may perchance be procreated if the seed fall on the right side; but then through extraordinary heat, she will be very large boned, full of courage, endued with a big voice, and have her chin and bosom hairy, not being so clear as others of the sex; subject to quarrel with her husband when married, for the superiority, etc. Yet in case of the similitude, nothing is more powerful than the imagination of the mother; for if she conceive in her mind, or do by chance fasten her eyes upon any object, and imprint it in her memory, the child in its outward parts frequently has some representation thereof; so whilst a man and woman are in the act of copulation, if the woman earnestly behold his countenance and fix her mind thereon, without all peradventure, the child will resemble the father; nay so powerful is its operation, that though a woman be in unlawful copulation, yet if fear or any thing else causes her to fix her mind upon her husband, the child will resemble him, though he never got it. The same effect, according to the opinion of the learned, proceeds from imagination in cause of warts, mouldspots, stains, dashes, and the figures of strange things, though indeed they sometimes happen thro' frights and extravagant longings. Many women there are, that seeing a hare cross them when great with child, will, through the strength of imagination, bring forth a child with a hairy-lip. Some children again are born with flat noses, wry mouths, great blubber lips, and ill shaped bodies, and most ascribe the reason to the strange conceit of the mother, who has busied her eyes and mind upon some ill shaped or distorted creature; therefore it greatly behoves all woman with child to avoid any monstrous sight, or at least to have a steadfast mind, not easily fixed upon any one thing more than another.

Source: Aristoteles Master-piece, or, The secrets of generation displayed in all the parts thereof, 1684, pp. 24–6.

THE EAGLE STONE **Document 23**

Thomas Lupton's A thousand notable things *compiled a list of magical and spiritually powerful objects.*

52. Aetites, called the Eagles Stone, tied to the left arm or side: it bringeth this benefit to women with child, that they shall not be delivered before their time. Besides that, it brings love between the man and the wife. And if a woman have a painful travail in the birth of her child, this stone tied to her thigh, brings an easy and light birth; but you must take it away quickly after the birth.

Source: Thomas Lupton, *A thousand notable things, of sundry sortes*, 1579, p. 38.

RALPH JOSSELIN **Document 24**

Ralph Josselin kept a diary during the years he was vicar of Earls Colne, Essex from 1641–83. The section below comes from the early part, which was written retrospectively.

My wife now growing big and ill my mother came from Olney to us upon a Tuesday lecture day April 12 [1642] after sermon having waited upon God in his house, my wife called her women and God was merciful to me in my house giving her a safe deliverance, and a daughter which on Thursday April 21ˢᵗ was baptized by the name of Mary: Mr Rich: Harlakenden: Mr John Litle: Mrs Mary Mildmay and my wife's mother being witnesses. I entertained my neighbours all about it cost me £6 and 13s. 4d. at least: they shewed much love to me from all parts. God blessed my wife to be a nurse, and our child thrived, and was even then a pleasant comfort to us. God wash it from corruption and sanctify it and make it his own. But it pleased God my wives' breasts were sore which was a grievance and sad cut to her but with use of means in some distance of time they healed up. This spring times grew fearful in the rising of the year about Midsummer we began to raise private arms: I found a musket for my part and the King was beginning to raise an army. The Parliament did the like . . .

1643: In spring now my wife weaned her daughter and began to breed again. God gave us both our health in a greater measure than I had before or my wife of late days . . .

August 2: being Wed: I was taken very ill with a quotidian ague I had three fits, the physician told me I would have one harsh one more but on Friday night seeking God for my health that if it pleased him I might still go on in my calling I was strangely persuaded I should have no more fits neither had I: Lord let me never forget thy goodness but let me because he hath heard my cry answered my request. . . .

Aug 8: 1644: I have bought a part in a ship it cost me £14.10s. God send me good speed with the same. I have sent my part in a bag of hops to Sunderland. My sister Mary is come under my roof as a servant, but my respect is and shall be towards her as a sister, God might have made me a waiter upon others. Our former maid Lydia Weston having dwelt with me one year and almost three quarters married into our town, the first that married out of my family.

Source: *The Diary of Ralph Josselin 1616–1683*, ed. Alan McFarlane, Oxford: Oxford University Press, 1976, pp. 14–15. © The British Academy 1976, reproduced with permission.

Document 25   ISABELLA TWYSDEN

Lady Isabella Twysden, of Royden Hall, Peckham, in Kent, wife of the royalist MP Sir Roger Twysden, kept a diary between 1645–7.

The 6th of March 1644 between one and two in the morning I was brought abed of a boy, the 7th he was christened and named Charles, the gossips were my brothers Thomas and Francis Twysden and my Lady Astley, James stood for her. He was born at Peckham being Thursday.

. . .

The 17th September 1647 my sister Twysden was brought a bed of a girl at a quarter past five a clock in the morning being Friday. It was christened that afternoon, and named Margaret, it was born at Peckham, it was christened without gossips, the new way.

Source: 'The Diary of Isabella, Wife of Sir Roger Twysden, Baronet, of Royden Hall, East Peckham, 1645–1651', *Archaeologia Cantiana*, 51, 1939–40, pp. 117, 121.

Document 26   JANE MINORS

Jane Minors of Barking was presented to the archdeaconry court of Essex on 29 April 1597 for failing to baptise her child and for misconduct during the service of churching.

We present Jane the wife of John Minors for keeping her child unbaptised a whole month . . .

Also detected, for that she very unwomanlike, came to be churched at the end of the said month, together with her child to be baptised, and feasted at a tavern four or five hours in the forenoon: and in the afternoon came to the church, rather to be seen, than upon any devotion, as it seemed; for whilst the minister was burying a corpse, she went out of the church, unchurched, unto the tavern again. And when she was spoken unto by the clerk to return to church again and to give God thanks after her committal of delivery, she answered it was a ceremony. The which abuses of the said Jane, seeing they are so public and notorious, and the example unpunished, may prove dangerous, we pray that your worship would enjoin, that her satisfaction may be also public; to the content of many of good worth.

Source: William Hale Hale, *A Series of Precedents And Proceedings in Criminal Causes: Extending From the Year 1475 to 1640, Extracted From The Act-Books of Ecclesiastical Courts in the Diocese of London*, F. and J. Rivington, 1847, p. 216.

BATHSUA MAKIN   **Document 27**

Bathsua Makin, née Reginald (c.1600–after 1675) published her first work, a book of poetry, at 16, and married at 21. Educated by her father, a school-master, she became tutor to Charles I's daughter Princess Elizabeth, and was kept in custody with her in the 1640s. This essay of 1673 proposed a revival of gentlewomen's education, and set out the prospectus of her own school, about which little else is known.

If any desire distinctly to know what they should be instructed in?
I answer, I cannot tell where to begin to admit women, nor from what part of learning to exclude them, in regard of their capacities. The whole encyclopedia of learning may be useful some way or other to them. Respect indeed is to be had to the nature and dignity of each art and science, as they are more or less subservient to religion, and may be useful to them in their station. I would not deny them the knowledge of Grammar and Rhetoric, because they dispose to speak handsomely. Logic must be allowed, because it is the key to all sciences. Physic, especially visible, as herbs, plants, shrubs, drugs, etc must be studied, because this will exceedingly please themselves, and fit them to be helpful to others. The tongues ought to be studied, especially the Greek and Hebrew, these will enable to the better understanding of the scriptures.

The Mathematics, more especially Geography, will be useful: this puts life into History. Music, Painting, Poetry, etc are a great ornament and pleasure. Some things that are more practical, are not so material, because public employments in the field and courts, are usually denied to women: Yet some have not been inferior to many men even in these things also. Witness Semiramis among the Babylonians; The Queen of Sheba in Arabia; Miriam and Deborah among the Israelites; Catherine de Medici in France; Queen Elizabeth in England . . .

In these late times there are several instances of women, when their husbands were serving their King and country, defended their houses, and did all things, as soldiers, with prudence and valour, like men.

They appeared before committees, and pleaded their own causes with good success.

This kind of education will be very useful to women . . .

This will be a hedge against heresies. Men are furnished with arts and tongues for this purpose, that they may stop the mouths of their adversaries. And women ought to be learned, that they may stop their ears against seducers. It cannot be imagined so many persons of quality would be so easily carried aside with every wind of doctrine, had they been furnished with these defensive arms; I mean, had they been instructed in the plain rules of artificial reasoning, so as to distinguish a true and forcible argument, from a vain and captious fallacy. . . .

POSTSCRIPT

If any enquire where this education may be performed, such may be informed, That a school is lately erected for gentlewomen at Tottenham High Cross, within four miles of London, in the road to Ware; where Mrs Makin is Governess, who was sometimes tutoress to the Princess Elisabeth, daughter to King Charles the First; Where, by the blessing of God, gentlewomen may be instructed in the principles of religion, and in all manner of sober and virtuous education: more particularly, in all things ordinarily taught in other schools: as works of all sorts, dancing, music, singing, writing, keeping accounts. Half the time to be spent in these things. The other half to be employed in gaining the Latin and French Tongues: and those that please, may learn Greek and Hebrew, the Italian and Spanish: in all which this Gentlewoman hath a competent knowledge.

Gentlewomen of eight or nine years old, that can read well, may be instructed in a year or two (according to their parts) in the Latin and French Tongues; by such plain and short rules, accommodated to the grammar of the English Tongue, that they may easily keep what they have learned, and recover what they shall lose; as those that learn music by notes.

Those that will bestow longer time, may learn the other languages, aforementioned, as they please.

Repositories also for Visibles shall be prepared; by which, from beholding the things, Gentlewomen may learn the names, natures, values and use of herbs, shrubs, trees, mineral-juices, metals and stones.

Those that please, may learn Limning, Preserving, Pastry and Cookery.

Those that will allow longer time, may attain some general knowledge in Astronomy, Geography; but especially in Arithmetic and History.

Those that think one language enough for a woman, may forbear the languages, and learn only Experimental Philosophy; and more, or fewer, of the other things aforementioned, as they incline.

Source: Bathsua Makin, *An essay to revive the ancient education of gentlewomen in religion, manners, arts & tongues with an answer to the objections against this way of education*, 1673, pp. 24–5, 42–3.

AN ACT FOR THE ADVANCEMENT OF TRUE RELIGION AND FOR THE ABOLISHMENT OF THE CONTRARY, 1543

Document 28

Passed under Henry VIII, this statute restricted the reading of the Bible in the vernacular. It was repealed under Edward VI.

Recourse must be had to the Catholic and Apostolic Church for the decision of controversies; and therefore all books of the Old and New Testament in English, being of Tyndale's false translation, or comprising any matter of Christian Religion, Articles of the Faith, or holy Scripture, contrary to the Doctrine set forth thence *Anno Domini* 1540, or to be set forth by the King, shall be abolished. No printer or bookseller shall utter any of the aforesaid books. No persons shall play in interlude, sing or rhyme, contrary to the said doctrine. No person shall retain any English books or writings concerning matter against the holy and blessed sacrament of the altar, or for the maintenance of Anabaptists, or other books abolished by the King's proclamation. There shall be no annotation or preambles in Bibles or New Testaments in English. The Bible shall not be read in English in any church. No woman or artificers prentices journeymen servingmen of the degree of yeomen or under, husbandmen nor labourers, shall read the New Testament in English. Nothing shall be taught or maintained contrary to the King's instructions. And if any spiritual person preach, teach, or maintain anything contrary to the King's instructions or determinations, made or to be made, and shall be thereof convict, he shall for his first offence recant, for his second abjure and bear a faggot, and for his third shall be adjudged an heretic, and be burned and lose all his goods and chattels.

Source: 34, 35 Henry VIII c.1, *Statutes of the Realm*.

Document 29   1 TIMOTHY 2:9–15

St Paul's letter to Timothy included the prescriptions for female behaviour that were used to limit women's public roles, dress, and intellectual authority.

9.   In like manner also, that women adorn themselves in modest apparel, with shamefacedness and sobriety; not with braided hair, or gold, or pearls, or costly array;

10.   But (which becometh women professing godliness) with good works.

11.   Let the woman learn in silence with all subjection.

12.   But I suffer not a woman to teach, nor to usurp authority over the man, but to be in silence.

13.   For Adam was first formed, then Eve.

14.   And Adam was not deceived, but the woman being deceived was in the transgression.

15.   Notwithstanding she shall be saved in childbearing, if they continue in faith and charity and holiness with sobriety.

Source: 1 Timothy 2: 9–15, King James Version.

Document 30   ROSE HICKMAN

Rose Hickman, who died in 1613, left a manuscript autobiographical account of her experiences as the wife of a Protestant merchant in the mid-sixteenth century.

Afterwards my husband (to drive away the wicked days) went to Antwerp, where he had a fair house which he rented for £40 a year, and I being with child went into Oxfordshire to a gentleman's house that was a lodge and stood far off from any church or town (the name whereof was Chilswell) and there I was delivered. And from thence I sent to Oxford to the bishops (who were then and there in prison, and did afterwards suffer martyrdom there) to be advised by them whether I might suffer my child to be baptized after the popish manner: who answered me that the sacrament of baptism, as it was used by the papists, was the least corrupted, and therefore I might. But therewithall they said that I might have been gone out of England before that time, if I had done well. And so my child was there baptized by a popish priest but because I would avoid the popish stuff as much as I could, I did not put salt into the handkerchief that was to be delivered to the priest at the baptism, but put sugar in it instead of salt.

Source: Maria Dowling and Joy Shakespeare, 'Religion and Politics in mid-Tudor England through the eyes of an English Protestant Woman: the Recollections of Rose Hickman', *Bulletin of the Institute of Historical Research* 55, 1982, p. 100.

ALICE DRIVER   **Document 31**

Foxe's Book of Martyrs recorded the story of Alice Driver, executed at Ipswich in 1558 alongside Alexander Gouche. This is the first of two examinations.

The examination of Driver's wife, before Dr Spenser the Chancellor of Norwich.

First, she coming into the place where she should be examined, with a smiling countenance, Dr Spenser said: Why woman, doest thou laugh us to scorn?

Driver's wife. Whether I do, or no, I might well enough, to see what fools ye be.

Dr Spenser. Then the Chancellor asked her wherefore she was brought before him, and why she was laid in prison.

Dri. Wherefore I think I need not to tell you: for ye know it better than I.

Spenser. No by my troth woman, I know not why.

Dri. Then have ye done me much wrong (quoth she) thus to imprison me, and know no cause why: for I know no evil that I have done, I thank God, and I hope there is no man that can accuse me of any notorious fact that I have done justly:

Spenser. Woman, woman, what saiest thou to the blessed Sacrament of the altar? Doest thou not believe that it is very flesh and blood, after the words be spoken of consecration?

Driver's wife at those words held her peace, and made no answer. Then a great chuff headed priest that stood by, spake, and asked her why she made not the Chancellor an answer. With that, the said Driver's wife looked upon him austerely, and said: Why priest, I come not to talk with thee, but I come to talk with thy master: but if thou wilt I shall talk with thee, command thy master to hold his peace. And with that ye priest put his nose in his cap, and spake never a word more. Then the Chancellor bade her make answer to that he demanded of her.

Dri. Sir, said she, pardon me though I make no answer, for I cannot tell what you mean thereby; for in all my life I never heard nor read of any such Sacrament in all the Scripture.

Spenser. Why, what scriptures have you read, I pray you?

Dri. I have (I thank God) read God's book.

Spenser. Why, what manner of book is that you call God's book?

Dri. It is the old and new Testament. What call you it?

Spenser. That is God's book indeed, I cannot deny.

Dri. That same book have I read throughout, but yet never could find any such sacrament there: and for that cause I cannot make you answer to that thing I know not. Notwithstanding, for all that, I will grant you a sacrament, called the Lord's supper: and therefore seeing I have granted you a Sacrament, I pray you shew me what a sacrament is.

Spenser. It is a sign.

And one D. Gascoine being by, confirmed the same, that it was the sign of an holy thing.

Dri. You have said the truth sir, said she. It is a sign indeed, I must needs grant it: and therefore seeing it is a sign, it cannot be the thing signified also. Thus far we do agree: for I have granted your own saying. Then stood up the said Gascoine, and made an oration with many fair words, but little to purpose, both offensive and odious to the minds of the godly. In the end of which long tale, he asked her if she did not believe the omnipotency of God, and that he was almighty, and able to perform that he spake. She answered, yes, and said I do believe that God is almighty, and able to perform that he spake and promised.

Gasc. Very well. Then he said to his disciples: Take, eat, this is my body: Ergo, it was his body. For he was able to performed that he spake, and God useth not to lie.

Dri. I pray you did he ever make any such promise to his disciples, that he would make the bread his body?

Gasc. Those be the words. Can you deny it?

Dri. No, they be the very words indeed, I cannot deny it: but I pray you, was it not bread that he gave unto them?

Gasc. No, it was his body.

Dri. Then was it his body that they did eat over night?

Gasc. Yea, it was his body.

Dri. What body was it then that was crucified the next day?

Gasc. It was Christ's body.

Dri. How could that be, when his disciples had eaten him up over night? except he had two bodies, as by your argument he had: one they did eat over night, and another was crucified the next day. Such a doctor, such doctrine. Be you not ashamed to teach the people, that Christ had two bodies? In the 22. of Luke, He took bread and brake it, and gave it to his disciples, saying, Take, etc. and do this in the remembrance of me. St Paul also saith, 1. Cor 11, Do this in the remembrance of me: for as often as ye shall eat this bread, and drink this cup, ye shall shew the Lords death till he come: and therefore I marvel ye blush not before all this people, to lie so manifestly as ye do. With that Gascoine held his peace, and made her no answer: for, as it seemed, he was ashamed of his doings. Then the Chancellor lift up his head from his cushion, and commanded the gaoler to take her away.

Dri. Now, said she, ye be not able to resist the truth, ye command me to prison again. Well, the Lord in the end that judge our cause, and to him

I leave it. Iwisse, Iwisse, this gear will go for no payment then. So went she with the gaoler away.

Source: John Foxe, *Actes and Monuments*, 1583 edition, hriOnline, Sheffield 2004, Book 12, pp. 2048–9. Available from: http://www.hrionline.shef.ac.uk/foxe/

ALICE THORNTON   **Document 32**

Alice Thornton (1626–1707) was the daughter of the Lord Lieutenant of Ireland; after marriage she settled in Yorkshire with her husband. Her 800-page manuscript recollections of her life, which she shared with family, records the tribulations and deliverances of childhood, married life and widowhood.

Of my ninth child it was the pleasure of God to give me a weak and sickly time in breeding, from the February till the 10th of May following, I not having fully recruited my last September weakness; and if it had been good in the eyes of my God I should much rather (because of that) not to have been in this condition. But it is not a Christian's part to choose anything of this nature, but what shall be the will of our heavenly Father, be it never so contrary to our own desires. Therefore did I desire to submit in this dispensation, and depend upon His providence for the preservation of my life, Who had delivered me in all my extremities and afflictions.

Source: *The Autobiography of Mrs. Alice Thornton of East Newton, Co. York*, ed. Charles Jackson, Surtees Society 62, York: Surtees Society, 1875, pp. 164–5.

THE INFANTICIDE ACT   **Document 33**

Passed in 1624, this implied an epidemic of infanticide amongst single mothers.

An Act to prevent the Destroying and Murdering of Bastard Children
Whereas many lewd women that have been delivered of bastard children, to avoid their shame, and to escape punishment, do secretly bury or conceal the death of their children, and after, if the child be found dead, the said women do allege, that the said child was born dead; whereas it falleth out sometimes (although hardly it is to be proved) that the said child or children were murdered by the said women, their lewd mothers, or by their assent or procurement:

For the preventing therefore of this great mischief, be it enacted by the authority of this present Parliament, That if any woman after one month next ensuing the end of this session of Parliament be delivered of any issue of her body, male or female, which being born alive, should by the laws of this realm be a bastard, and that she endeavour privately, either by drowning or by secret burying thereof, or any other way, either by herself or the procuring of others, so to conceal the death thereof, as that it may not come to light, whether it were born alive or not, but be concealed: In every such case the said mother so offending shall suffer death as in case of murder, except such mother can make proof by one witness at the least, that the child (whose death was by her so intended to be concealed) was born dead.

Source: 21 Jac.I c. 27, *Statutes of the Realm*.

Document 34   DOD AND CLEAVER ON MARRIAGE

Puritan preachers John Dod and Robert Cleaver's 400-odd page volume of domestic advice enlarged from biblical precepts was first published in 1598 and reprinted eight times. Its length made it prohibitive to all but the social elite, but its ideas would have been widely familiar from sermons and homilies. The following extract is from the sections on the duty of husbands to wives.

The duty of the husband is to get goods: and of the wife to gather them together, and save them. The duty of the husband is to travel abroad, to seek living: and the wife's duty is to keep the house. The duty of the husband is to get money and provision: and of the wives, not vainly to spend it. The duty of the husband is to deal with many men: and of the wives to talk with few. The duty of the husband is to be intermeddling: and of the wife, to be solitary and withdrawn. The duty of the man is, to be skilful in talk: and of wife, to boast of silence. The duty of the husband is to be a giver: and of the wife, to be a saver. The duty of the man is, to apparell himself as he may: and of the woman, as it becometh her. The duty of the husband, is to be lord of all: and of the wife, to give account of all. The duty of the husband is, to dispatch all things without door: and of the wife, to oversee and give order for all things within the house. Now, where the husband and wife performeth these duties in their house, we may call it a college of quietness: the house wherein these are neglected, we may term it a hell.

It is to be noted, and noted again, that as the provision of household dependeth only on the husband: even so the honour of all dependeth only of the woman: in such sort, that there is no honour within the house, longer than a man's wife is honourable. And therefore the Apostle calleth the woman,

The glory of the man. But here it must be noted and remembered, that we do not entitle honourable to such, as be only beautiful, comely of face, of gentility, of comely personage, and a good housewife: but only, to her that is virtuous, honest of life, temperate, and advised in her speech.

Source: John Dod and Robert Cleaver, *A godlie forme of householde government*, 1612, pp. 167–9.

HOMILY OF THE STATE OF MATRIMONY

Document 35

This homily, whose authorship is uncertain, was one of a series published by the Elizabethan church in 1563 to be read in church services where no sermon was being preached. This extract is from the beginning.

The word of almighty God doth testify and declare, whence the original beginning of matrimony cometh, and why it is ordained. It is instituted of God, to ye intent that man and woman should live lawfully in a perpetual friendly fellowship, to bring forth fruit, and to avoid fornication. By which means a good conscience might be preserved on both parties, in bridling the corrupt inclinations of the flesh, within ye limits of honesty. For God hath straitly forbidden all whoredom and uncleanness, and hath from time to time taken grievous punishments of this inordinate lust, as all stories and ages hath declared. Furthermore it is also ordained, that the church of God and his kingdom might by this kind of life be conserved and enlarged, not only in that God giveth children by his blessing, but also in that they be brought up by ye parents godly, in the knowledge of God's word, that thus the knowledge of God and true religion might be delivered by succession from one to another, that finally many might enjoy that everlasting immortality.

Wherefore, forasmuch as matrimony serveth as well to avoid sin and offence, as to increase the kingdom of God: you, as all other which enter that state, must acknowledge this benefit of God, with pure and thankful minds, for that he hath so ruled our hearts, that ye follow not the example of the wicked world, who set their delight in filthiness of sin, where both of you stand in the fear of God, and abhor all filthiness. For that is surely the singular gift of God, where the common example of the world declareth how the devil hath their hearts bound and entangled in diverse snares, so that they in their wifeless state run into open abominations, without any grudge of their conscience. Which sort of men that liveth so desperately and filthily, what damnation tarrieth for them, St Paul describeth it to them, saying: Neither whoremongers, neither adulterers, shall inherit the kingdom of God. This horrible judgement of God ye be escaped through his mercy, if so be that ye live inseparately, according to God's ordinance. But yet I would not have you careless without watching. For the devil will assay to attempt all things to interrupt and hinder your hearts and godly purpose, if ye will give him any entry. For he will either labour to break this godly knot once begun betwixt you, or else at the least he will labour to encumber it with diverse griefs and displeasures.

Learn thou therefore, if thou desirest to be void of all these miseries, if thou desirest to live peaceably and comfortably in wedlock, how to make thy earnest prayer to God, that he would govern both your hearts by his holy spirit, to restrain the devil's power, whereby your concord may remain perpetually. But to this prayer must be joined a singular diligence, whereof St Peter giveth this precept, saying, You husbands, deal with your weaker vessel, and as unto them that are heirs also of the grace of life, that your prayers be not hindered. This precept doth particularly pertain to the husband: for he ought to be the leader and author of love, in cherishing and increasing concord, which then shall take place, if he will use moderation and not tyranny, and if he yield some thing to the woman. For the woman is a weak creature, not endued with like strength and constancy of mind, therefore they be the sooner disquieted, and they be the more prone to all weak affections and dispositions of mind, more than men be, and lighter they be, and more vain in their fantasies and opinions. These things must be considered of the man, that he be not too stiff, so that he ought to wink at some things, and must gently expound all things, and to forbear. Howbeit the common sort of men doeth judge, that such moderation should not become a man: For they say that it is a token of womanish cowardness, and therefore they think that it is a man's part to fume in anger, to fight with fist and staff. Howbeit, howsoever they imagine, undoubtedly St Peter doth better judge what should be seeming to a man, and what he should most reasonably perform. For he saith, reasoning should be used, and not fighting. Yea he saith more, that the woman ought to have a certain honour attributed to her, that is to say, she must be spared and borne with, the rather for that she is the weaker vessel, of a frail heart, inconstant, and with a word soon stirred to wrath. And therefore considering these her frailties, she is to be the rather spared. By this means, thou shalt not only nourish concord: but shalt have her heart in thy power and will.

. . .

Now as concerning the wife's duty. What shall become her? Shall she abuse the gentleness and humanity of her husband and, at her pleasure, turn all things upside down? No surely. For that is far repugnant against God's commandment, For thus doeth St Peter preach to them, Ye wives, be ye in subjection to obey your own husbands. To obey, is another thing than to control or command, which yet they may doe, to their children, and to their family: But as for their husbands, them must they obey, and cease from commanding, and perform subjection. For this surely doth nourish concord very much, when the wife is ready at hand at her husband's commandment, when she will apply her self to his will, when she endeavoureth her self to seek his contentation, and to do him pleasure, when she will eschew all things that might offend him: For thus will most truly be verified the saying of the poet, A good wife by obeying her husband, shall bear the rule, so that he shall have a delight and a gladness, the sooner at all times to return home to her. But on the contrary part, when the wives be stubborn, froward, and malapert, their husbands are compelled thereby to abhor and flee from their own houses, even as they should have battle with their enemies. Howbeit, it can scantly be, but that some offences shall sometime chance betwixt them: For no man doth live without fault, specially for that the woman is the more frail party. Therefore let them beware that they stand not in their faults and wilfulness: but rather let them acknowledge their follies, and say, My husband, so it is, that by my anger I was compelled to do this or that forgive it me, and hereafter I will take better heed. Thus ought the woman more readily to do, the more they be ready to offend. And they shall not do this only to avoid strife and debate: but rather in the respect of the commandment of God, as St Paul expresseth it in this form of words, Let women be subject to their husbands as to the Lord: for the husband is the head of the woman, as Christ is the head of the Church. Here you understand, that God hath commanded that ye should acknowledge the authority of the husband, and refer to him the honour of obedience. And Saint Peter saith in that place before rehearsed, that holy matrons did in former time deck themselves, not with gold and silver, but in putting their whole hope in God, and in obeying their husbands, as Sara obeyed Abraham, calling him lord, whose daughters ye be (saith he) if ye follow her example. This sentence is very meet for women to print in their remembrance. Truth it is, that they must specially feel the grief and pains of their Matrimony, in that they relinquish the liberty of their own rule, in the pain of their travailing, in the bringing up of their children. In which offices they be in great perils, and be grieved with great afflictions, which they might be without if they lived out of Matrimony. But St. Peter saith, that this is the chief ornament of holy matrons, in that they set their hope and trust in God, that is to say, in that they refused not from marriage for the business thereof, for the gifts and perils thereof: but committed all such adventures to God, in most sure trust of help, after that they have called upon his aid. O woman, do thou the like, and so shalt thou be most excellently beautified before God and all his Angels and Saints, and thou needest not to seek further for doing any better works. For, obey thy husband, take regard of his requests, and give heed unto him in perceive what he requireth of thee, and so shalt thou honour God and live peaceably in thy house. . . .

This let the wife have ever in mind, the rather admonished thereto by the apparel of her head, whereby is signified, that she is under covert or obedience of her husband as that apparel is of nature so appointed, to declare her subjection: so biddeth Saint Paul that all other of her raiment should express both shamefastness and sobriety. For if it be not lawful for the woman to have her head bare, but to bear thereon the sign of her power, wheresoever she goeth: more is it required that she declare the thing that is meant thereby. And therefore these ancient women of the old world called their husbands lords, and shewed them reverence in obeying them. . . .

Yet I speak not these things that I would wish the husbands to be sharp towards their wives: But I exhort the women that they would patiently bear the sharpness of their husbands. For when either part do their best to perform their duties the one to the other, then followeth thereon great profit to their neighbours for their examples sake. For when the woman is ready to suffer a sharp husband, and the man will not extremely entreat his stubborn and troublesome wife, then be all things in quiet, as in a most sure haven. Even thus was it done in old time, that every one did their own duty and office, and was not busy to require the duty of their neighbours . . .

But yet I mean not that a man should beat his wife, God forbid that, for that is the greatest shame that can be, not so much to her that is beaten, as to him that doth the deed, but if by such fortune thou chancest upon such an husband, take it not to heavily, but suppose thou, that thereby is laid up no small reward hereafter, and in this life time no small commendation to thee, if thou canst be quiet. But yet to you that be men, thus I speak, Let there be none so grievous fault to compel you to beat your wives. But what say I your wives, no, it is not to be born with, that an honest man should lay hands on his maid servant to beat her. Wherefore if it be a great shame for a man to beat his bond servant, much more rebuke it is, to lay violent hands upon his free woman. And this thing may be well understood by the laws which the Painims hath made, which doth discharge her any longer to dwell with such an husband, as unworthy to have any further company with her that doth smite her.

Source: The second tome of homilees of such matters as were promised, and intituled in the former part of homilees. Set out by the aucthoritie of the Queenes Maiestie: and to be read in euery parishe church agreeably, 1571, pp. 476–95.

Document 36   DOD AND CLEAVER ON SERVANTS

From the section on 'What duties masters and mistresses owe to their servants'.

It is very meet and convenient, that the mistress or dame, do not make herself too familiar with her servants, or household-folks, lest they should be too bold, to talk, to jest, or unreverently and unmannerly to behave themselves towards her: and so modestly and wisely to bear her self among her servants, that they may fear, reverence, and so stand in awe of her, as the mistresse and mother of the house.

And as it is not comely or beseeming, that the wife should take upon her to rule and correct the men-servants; so likewise, it is not comely or meet, that the husband should meddle with the punishing or chastising of the maid-servants: so that it is most meet and acceptable to the offender, that the master should correct the men, and the mistress her maids: for a man's nature scorneth and disdaineth to be beaten of a woman, and a maid's nature is corrupted with the stripes of a man. Therefore we read, that *Abraham* would not meddle with his maid, but committed her to his wife, and said: *Do with her as it pleaseth thee.*

Source: John Dod and Robert Cleaver, *A godlie forme of householde government*, 1612, pp. 378–9.

WILLIAM GOUGE   **Document 37**

William Gouge's Of Domesticall Duties: Eight Treatises, *first published in 1622, offered a lengthy outline of the respective duties of family members. This extract from the prologue to the reader describes the reaction of members of his congregation in St Helen's, Bishopsgate, to some of the advice when it was first given as sermons.*

I remember that when these *Domesticall Duties* were first uttered out of the pulpit, much exception was taken against the application of a wives subjection to the restraining of her from disposing the common goods of the family without, or against her husbands consent. But surely they that made those exceptions did not well think of the cautions and limitations which were then delivered, and are now again expressly noted: which are, that the foresaid restraint be not extended to the **proper goods of a wife**, no nor overstrictly to such goods as are set apart for the use of the family, nor to extraordinary cases, nor always to an express consent, not to the consent of such husbands as are impotent, or far and long absent. . . . Other exceptions were made against some other particular duties of wives. For many that can patiently enough hear their duties declared in general terms cannot endure to hear those generals exemplified in their particular branches. This cometh too near to the quick, and pierceth too deep. But (to interpret all, according to the rule of love, in the better part) I take the main reason of the many exceptions which were taken, to be this, that wives' duties (according to

Proper goods of a wife: Paraphernalia.

the Apostle's method) being in the first place handled, there was taught (as must have been taught, except the truth should have been betrayed) what a wife, in the uttermost extent of that subjection under which God hath put her, is bound unto, in case her husband will stand upon the uttermost of his authority: which was so taken, as if I had taught that an husband might, and ought to exact the uttermost, and that a wife was bound-in that uttermost extent to do all that was delivered as duty, whether her husband exact it or no. But when I came to deliver husband's duties, I shewed, that he ought not to exact whatsoever his wife was bound unto in case it were exacted by him but that he ought to make her a joint governor of the family with himself, and refer the ordering of many things to her discretion, and with all honourable and kind respect to carry himself towards her. In a word, I so set down a husband's duties, as if he be wise and conscionable in observing them, his wife can have no just cause to complain of her subjection. That which maketh a wife's yoke heavy and hard, is a husband's abuse of his authority: and more pressing his wife's duty, than performing his own: which is directly contrary to the Apostle's rule. This just Apology I have been forced to make that I might not ever be judged (as some have censured me) *an hater of women.*

Source: William Gouge, *Of Domesticall Duties: Eight Treatises*, 1634, fos. 3v–4.

Document 38   MARIA THYNNE

Maria Touchet and Thomas Thynne were married clandestinely in 1594, aged sixteen; the marriage was finally legalised in 1601. This letter is dated sometime after August 1604.

Mine own sweet Thomken, I have no longer ago than the very last night written such a large volume in praise of thy kindness to me, thy dogs, thy hawks, the hare and the foxes, and also in commendation of thy great care of thy businesses in the country, that I think I need not amplify any more on that text, for I have crowned thee for an admirable good husband with poetical laurel, and admired the inexpressible singularity of thy love in the cogitations of *piamater*,[7] I can say no more but that in way of gratuity, the dogs shall without interruption expel their excremental corruption in the best room (which is thy bed) whensoever full feeding makes their bellies ache, and for my own part since you have in all your letters given me authority to

---

[7] Tender mother: possibly suggesting pregnancy.

care enough, I will promise to be inferior to none of my Deverill neighbours in playing the good housewife, though they strive till they stink. Now if for my better encouragement and in requital thou will at my earnest entreaty but for this time spare Digory, I shall be so much bound, that nothing but a strong purgation can loose me. For if you will believe me in sober sadness, my cousin Stantor hath upon speech with me, made it appear that he hath digested many uncivil and unbecoming words from three of your servants. He doth not desire you to remit Digory's fault, but to dispense with his appearance for his sake this time, because it concerns him in his profit, and when you come into the country my cousin will come and thoroughly satisfy all matters in controversy between you. I will not entreat too earnestly because I known thou art choleric with me ever in these cases, but though thou doth many times call me fool for yielding to the enticing of fair words, yet if you mark it, I have never yet craved anything of such great importance as hath ever been prejudicial to your reputation or profit. If so (as it is too true it is so) name me any man that hath a wife of that rare temper. No, in good faith this age will not help you to an equal, I mean for a wife. Alas I sit at home and let thy dogs eat part with me, and wear clothes that have worn out their prenticeship a year and half sithence; when my sisters will be in London at their pleasure, I am talking of foxes and ruder beasts at home. Well, do but make haste home and make much of thy Mall when thou dost come home. I will not be melancholy, but with good courage spend my life and waste my spirits in any course to lease thee, except fighting, and in this business satisfy my request as you think I deserve, and do not be angry with me for importuning you, but ask all the husbands in London, or ask the question in the Lower House, what requests they grant their wives, and then good husband think upon your fool at home as there is cause.

Thine,
Maria Thynne.

I will say nothing of any business, for I have this last night written you a whole sheet of paper and given you knowledge, according to your appointments, of all your affairs. If your leisure will not serve, good sweet, cause Exall to write in his own name but this and this is my mistress' pleasure and it shall serve the turn, for I know your trouble in matters of more weight there is great, and I like not his writing in your name for it is as though thou were angry. God in heaven send thee well and speedily home.

Source: Two Elizabethan women: Correspondence of Joan and Maria Thynne 1575–1611, ed. Alison D. Wall, Wiltshire Record Society 38, Devizes: Wiltshire Record Society, 1983, pp. 32–3.

Document 39   ELIZABETH FREKE'S REMEMBRANCES

Elizabeth Freke (1642–1714), a Norfolk gentlewoman, left two successive versions of 'Some few remembrances of my misfortunes that have attended me in my unhappy life since I were married'. She started writing in 1702; the earlier entries are probably made with reference to previous notes. Married in 1672 by choice and for love to a cousin, Percy Freke, she recorded a married life beset with struggles to keep her land and money intact from her husband's debts and borrowing. This extract records her father's attempt to help her, and three years later, her exile in Bilney, the Norfolk house that she held in trust for her son.

July 7 [1682] So soon as I came to my dear father, he made me promise him that I would not leave him whilst I lived, which I readily and gladly did. And then he bid me take no care for I should want for nothing his life, who made his words good with the greatest kindness to me and my son. A great alteration it was to what I found in Ireland from a husband.

August 15 And on my looking a little melancholy on some past reflections, he fancied it was my want of money; and my dear father, without saying a word to me, went up into his closet and brought me down presently in two bags two hundred pounds, which £200 he charged me to keep private from my husband's knowledge and buy needles and pins[8] with it. This was very kind in my father; and which the very next post I informed Mr Freke of, who presently found a use for it. But I, that had not two and twenty shillings from my husband in the last two and twenty months I were in Ireland with my son, kept it for my own use. Which with more my father had given me and the interest, all which made up eight hundred pounds, [Mr Freke] took from me the year after my son married and so left me at Bilney a beggar again.

. . .

December 24 [1685] Mr Freke came over by Dublin from Ireland, I having hardly heard of him or from him in three quarters of a year. As he came unlooked for by me, so he was very angry with me for being on this side of the country, though in all his times of his being from me he never took care for a penny for my subsistence or his sons. For which God forgive him. My husband's errand for England was to join with him in the sale of West Bilney to Sir Standish Hartstonge for the like in Ireland. But I being left the only trustee for my self and my son, God gave me the courage to keep what I had rather than part with it and be kept by the charity of my friends or trust to his or any one's kindness. So in a great anger Mr Freke left me alone again and went for Ireland, where he stayed from me almost two years.

---

[8] A reference to pin money.

Source: The Remembrances of Elizabeth Freke, 1671–1714 ed. Raymond A. Anselment, Camden Society, Fifth Series, Volume 18, Cambridge: Cambridge University Press, 2001, pp. 49, 55.

ANNE AND JAMES YOUNG

Document 40

Anne Young, née Lingham, sued her husband James for separation at the London consistory court in 1608, on the grounds of his cruelty to her. The following documents represent one of her witnesses' statements, and his response to her claims. (Italic sections are translated from Latin.)

Margaret Bonefant, *wife of James Bonefant, woolman, of St Olave Southwark, whose wife she has been for about 12 years; she has been married to him 12 years and is about 32; she has known Anne Young for 9 or 10 years and James Young for 3 months.*

. . . *To the 2nd and 3rd articles she deposes and says* that in the month of February last past upon a Sunday in the afternoon . . . this deponent went to the articulate[9] Anne Young alias Lingham to her own house in St Bride's parish in London to visit her and to see how she did and coming to her she found the said Anne Young alias Lingham so beaten and bruised and swollen about her head face and body that she was not able to speak nor go nor stir any of her limbs to help her self and her jaws were displaced or otherwise so hurt with beating that she was not able to stir them and the gristle of her nose was so bruised that until by the help of a surgeon it was raised and the flesh suppled she could not well fetch or take any breath at the nose, but seemed as though she were more like to die of that beating than to recover and live. And soon after that this jurate came and saw the said Anne in this miserable case the said James Young her husband came in, to whom this Jurate said she was sorry to see his wife in this miserable case. Whereunto he answered that he did think her estate had been better when he married her than he did then find it as he said and then she this deponent asking him if he had so used her, he said that that which was done to her he had done, and so she this deponent then said unto him that was not the way to know or under-stand of her estate but if he would know that it must be his kind usage of her and not that severity for that was a way to make an end of them both. 'Aye', quoth he the same Young, 'I am told I shall be hanged if she die within a year and a day but if I be there is but one out of the way'. And this speech of his acknowledging his so beating of his said wife he the same Young did avouch

---

[9] Said (a legal term).

once or twice after within as then a week after walking with this deponent in the street homeward towards her this deponent's house in St Olave's parish from his the same Young's house. And she saith there was present and saw her the same Anne Young alias Lyngham in that pitiful sort as aforesaid, Mrs Anne Cotes one Mr Gralce and divers others . . .

To the 5th she says that both at the time afore by her deposed of upon the Sunday and twice after after the same week when she this deponent came to see her the same Ann Young alias Lyngham she hath been in sad want as that she this deponent did see Mrs Cotes and others that came to her give her money and send for drink wood and coals and for meat and likewise for ointments for her and for diverse things that was fit for her comfort she having no money her self but being in great want and need . . .

To the 6th article she says that for the reasons by her deposed of she saith that she verily believeth and that not without cause the said Anne dareth not nor maye not live safely with her said husband in one house for fear of death or at least such cruel usage as she is not able to. . . .

To the 13th . . . she saith she never heard any body ever say better of him than that he was and is such a severe cruel man to his wife.

To the 14th she says that at such time as the articulate James Young and his said wife lay in her this deponent's house . . . he hath acknowledged and confessed both to her this deponent and in her hearing that he was worth four hundred pounds . . .

Ann Cotes, *wife of Edward Cotes of St Dunstan in the West, poulterer, where she has lived for 18 years and more, born in Buckinghamshire, aged 37 . . . she has known Anne Young for 26 years and James Young since Michaelmas last.*

To the first article of the said libel she says and deposes that she this deponent doth know that the articulate James Young and Alice Young alias Lyngham are commonly accounted lawful man and wife together and so have been ever since about Michaelmas last or a little before . . .

To the 2 and 3 articles . . . she says and deposes that in the month of February and about the beginning of February last as she now remembreth the time otherwise she remembreth not, one Sara a maidservant of the articulate James Young and his wife came to her this deponent being a neighbour, by her and told her that her master and mistress were fallen out and that they being alone in the house, 'I fear' quoth she 'that he will kill her or do her some great mischief, he hath thrust me out at doors', whereupon she this deponent going thither did then find her the same Ann Young alias Lyngham articulate in a most pitiful case so beaten about the face and head that her cheeks and part of her face by her nose were swollen above her nose and is black as a black sloe the gristle of her nose (as it seemed) broken, and she said that she had sent for a surgeon that had lifted it up for before he had done so she told her this deponent that she could not speak and it seemed to be true the face and nose was so exceedingly battered and bruised insomuch as she was so weak and in such a pitiful case as she this deponent and all the women that were there did verily think she would have died as she this deponent thinketh she will ever hardly recover it for thereby and ever since she hath used to have such strange fits of shaking and quaking as that she is for the time when the fit cometh blind and senseless very strange to see. And this deponent so seeing her at that time she talked with James Young her husband then there present who confessed unto her this deponent that he had so broken her and that she was in that sort by his breaking of her but seemed not to be sorry or care for it . . .

To the 5th article she says that both the time afore by her deposed of and sundry times since she this deponent seeing her the articulate Anne Young to be in need of sustenance she saith that she this deponent hath given her money to send her such necessaries as she wanted both meat drink firing and such like . . .

To the 6th article she says that she does not know . . . saving she saith that . . . when she found Anne Young cruelly beaten as aforesaid she the same Anne Young said in presence of her said husband that he would have run at her with a rapier or sword that was there and she this deponent telling him of it and reproving him for that his cruel using of his wife he did not deny it or gainsay it but seemed to ratify it to be true . . .

Personal Answers of James Young
6 June 1608

To the 2nd and 3rd articles he responds that Ann Young this respondent's wife articulate having given him this respondent many vile and bad speeches, he this respondent hath sundry times in the time articulate chidden her and given her many angry words again. And he saith that the week before Shrovetide last she . . . having taken up a thing of wood like unto a bowl to strike him this respondent, he this respondent saith that he did strike her the same Ann with his fist in so much as her face was black and blue. Whereupon she the same Ann forsook his this respondent's bed, and that night the next following lay by her self and the next morning he this respondent going up into her chamber and seeing her purse lying there took out two rings or three that was in it and when she arose and found that he this respondent had taken away her rings she became so sullen that she counterfeited her self sick and went to bed and kept her bed a week after whereby she caused him this respondent to spend 40 s. in keeping of her in that her counterfeit sickness.

To the 4th he responds that the same day that he this respondent did so strike his said wife presently after one Mistress Cotes one of his said wife's acquaintance being there told him this respondent that if his wife did otherwise than well he this respondent should be hanged whereupon he this respondent said unto her that if she would not be quiet she might and it were well she were gone out at doors, but she went away none the sooner . . .

To the 8th and 9th he responds that such hath, been and was the wickedness of the articulate Ann his this respondent's said wife towards him this respondent as that she hath divers times when he this respondent hath gone out of doors she hath fallen down of her knees and prayed to God that he this respondent might never come in at the doors again whereby this respondent was in a desperate mind about the time articulate for which he is now heartily sorry and desireth almighty God to forgive him as that in the morning when he arose out of his bed (he lying alone as he had done long before and after his said wife refusing his company) he did stab himself with a knife which he carrieth to bed with him in the breast in two places.

To the 14th he responds that he this respondent is a tailor and getteth thereby 2s. 6d. a week and not above 3s. and is not worth forty shillings his debts paid but he saith that if his said wife would be quiet and live quietly with him in the face of God as he this respondent desireth to do he doubteth not but he should get much more and be better able to keep and maintain both himself and her than now he is to keep him self his mind is so unquiet by reason of this trouble.

Source: London Metropolitan Archives DL/C 218, pp. 50–2, 88.

Document 41   THE WEAVERS' GUILD

A series of ordinances set out the restrictions on women's participation in weaving.

Ratification by Sir Nicholas Bacon, Sir Christopher Wraye, and Sir James Dyer of the Ordinances for Regulating the Weavers' Guild, June 25th, 1577.

Item it is ordained and agreed that no manner of person or persons using or exercising the said art or mystery of weaving shall keep, teach, instruct or bring up in the use, exercising or knowledge of the same art or mystery of Weaving any maiden, damsel or other woman in or to the use or exercising of the said art or mystery, six shillings and eightpence of lawful money of England to the use of the said Guild.

Source: Frances Consitt, *The London Weavers' Company*, Oxford: Clarendon Press, 1933, p. 285.

THE LAWES RESOLUTIONS OF WOMENS RIGHTS   **Document 42**

The anonymous text of 1632, The Lawes Resolutions of Womens Rights, *outlined the property, marital and other legal positions of women, distinguishing carefully between the single and the married. These sections deal with property.*

SECTION VIII

That which the husband hath is his own
But the prerogative of the husband is best discerned in his dominion over all external things in which the wife by combination divesteth herself of propriety in some sort, and casteth it upon her governor, for here practice everywhere agrees with the theoricke of law, and forcing necessity submits women to the affection thereof, whatsoever the husband had before coverture either in goods or lands, it is absolutely his own, the wife hath therein no seisin at all. If anything when he is married be given him, he taketh it by himself distinctly to himself.

If a man have right and title to enter into lands, and the tenant enfeoff the baron and feme, the wife taketh nothing. Dyer fol. 10. The very goods which a man giveth to his wife, are still his own, her chain, her bracelets, her apparel are all the goodman's goods.

If a woman taketh more apparel when her husband dieth than is necessarily for her degree, it makes her executrix *de son tort demesne, 33.H6.* A wife how gallant soever she be, glistereth but in the riches of her husband, as the moon hath no light, but it is the sun's. Yea and her Phoebe borroweth sometime her own proper light from Phoebus.

SECTION IX

That which the wife hath is the husband's
For thus it is, if before marriage the woman were possessed of horses, meat, sheep, corn, wool, money, plate and jewels, all manner of moveable substance is presently by conjunction the husband's, to sell, keep or bequeath if he die; and though he bequeath them not, yet are they the husband's executor's and not the wife's which brought them to her husband.

Source: The Lawes Resolutions of Womens Rights, 1632, pp. 129–30.

A TREATISE OF TESTAMENTS   **Document 43**

Henry Swinburne's A Treatise of Testaments *(1590) became the authority on testamentary law and was reprinted and cited throughout the seventeenth century. Here he articulates the different provisions that applied for married men making wills in the two ecclesiastical provinces, the North and the South.*

The first case is, when the testator hath neither wife nor child, at the time of his death, for then he may dispose all the residue of his clear goods and chattels at his pleasure.

The second case is, when the testator at the time of his death hath a wife and no child, or else some child or children, but no wife. In which case by a custom observed, not only throughout the province of York, but in many other places besides, within this realm of England, the goods are to be divided into two parts, and the testator cannot bequeath any more than his part, that is to say, the one half, for the other half is due to the wife, or else to the children, by virtue of the said custom.

The third case is, where the testator leaveth behind him both a wife, and also a child or children: In which case the custom observed in diverse places of this realm of England, and namely within the province of York: the testator cannot bequeath any more of his goods, than the third part of the clear goods, for in this case the said clear goods are to be divided into three parts, whereof the wife ought to have one part, the child or children another part, and the third part (which is called the death's part) remaineth, to the testator, by him to be given or bequeathed to who he thinketh good.

. . .

The fourth case is, when there is no such custom, of dividing the goods of the testator into two parts, or into three parts, as is before mentioned, in which case albeit some were of this opinion, that even by the common laws of this realm, the clear moveable goods were to be divided into three parts or into two parts as before, whereof the wife and children were to have their parts, and consequently that the testator could not dispose any more thereof, than the half or third, being the death's part. Nevertheless others (whose opinion hath prevailed) do hold the contrary, to wit that there is no such division to be made by force of the common laws of this land, but only by force of custom, and consequently that it is lawful for the testator, by the laws of this realm, (except in those places where the custom is observed) to dispose all the whole residue of his goods (his funerals and debts deducted) at his liking, and that the wife or child can claim no more thereof, but according as the testator shall devise by his testament.

And in the opinion of some, the law of this land which leaveth all the residue to the disposition of the testator, funerals and debts deducted, seemeth to have better ground in reason, than the custom, whereby he is forced either to leave two parts of three, or at least the one half to his wife and children. For what if the son be an unthrifty, or naughty person, what if the wife be not only a sharp shrew, but perhaps of worse conditions? . . .

But the custom whereby the liberty of the testator is restrained is not without reason also. For where it is asked, what if the child be an unthrift, the wife worse than a shrew? So it may be demanded with like facility, what if the child be no unthrift, but frugal and virtuous? What if the wife be an honest and modest woman? Which thing is the rather to be presumed? But if it be not amiss to fear the worst, then on the contrary, what if the testator be an unnatural father or unkind husband? perhaps also greatly enriched by his wife. . . . ? Surely the custom hath as good ground in reason against lewd husbands and unkind fathers, as hath the law in meeting with disobedient wives and unthrifty children?

Source: Henry Swinburne, *A Treatise of Testaments and Last Wills*, 1590, pp. 105–6.

EDWARD BARLOW **Document 44**

Edward Barlow was born at Prestwich, near Manchester, in 1642. At fourteen he was apprenticed to a whitester (whitening yarn and fustians) but he left his service, dissatisfied with the conditions; these extracts from a long journal, written from memory in later life, tell of his perceptions of the household he worked in, and then of his decision to leave home to go to sea.

Moreover I perceived my master to be of a hasty nature, and my dame none of the best conditions as I judged by her looks; also they had a great many children, some of them grown to marriage estate, which made me think that ere long I should have more masters and dames than one. Likewise I considered their manner of keeping two tables of victuals. Though we all ate together, yet at the upper end of the table, where my master and dame and the children did sit, there was a great difference of victuals, namely a pudding with suet and plums; but at the lower end of the table one without both, though there might be a little strong butter to eat with it, melted and poured upon it: and at the upper end a piece of fat beef, but at the lower end a piece of sirloin next to the horns: there was always something or other which we had not. We also had meat broth two or three times heated, which would never have vexed me had I eaten and drunk of the same as they did, though I had not sat at table with them.

My fellow servant would also be telling me how many broils and com-bustions he had had with my master and dame about their beating of him. Some of the neighbours told him in my hearing that he deserved his master's daughter for a wife for his good services to him, which made me think he might take her in God's name, for I did not care for buying a wife at so dear a rate as to serve apprenticeship for her, which might not prove worth a man's labour at cost of marrying her.

. . . [He leaves the position and returns home, shortly to leave again for London].

So coming down the stairs, my mother and one of my sisters being in the house and not knowing my intent, marvelled to see me put on my clothes that day. Passing by them, not staring at all, I bid them farewell and came out of the house. They sat still awhile to see whither I would go, and by and by when I was gotten almost out of call, my mother came out, and seeing that I did intend to go, called to me in the manner you see here drawn, beckoning her hand to come again, and willing me not to go I could not tell whither, and if I would go, to stay till my father came home and see what he would say to it. Yet with all her persuasions she could not entreat me to stay; but away I came to my father. He, seeing me coming, asked me whither I intended to go. I told him to London to see if I could get me a place to live in; and I desired him to lend me the six shillings upon my part of the fowling piece, for I did hope to trouble him no more, and [told him] that he might take it upon my partner or else give him six shillings more and take the fowling piece to himself. So my father considering of it lent it me and said if I would I might go in God's name: and bid me have a care of myself that I did not come into a worse place than that which he had provided for me at the whitesters, where I would not stay; and so prayed God to bless me. And I came away with tears in my eyes and (in my pocket) that sum of six shillings and one or two shillings more that I had of my own, which I had gotten before I went to my master's of some of our neighbours by working by the day for twopence and threepence a day.

Considering with myself I decided I had as good to go seek my fortune abroad as live at home, always in want and working hard for very small gains. Likewise I had never any great mind to country work, as ploughing and sowing and making of hay and reaping, nor also of winter work, as hedging and ditching and thrashing and dunging amongst cattle, and suchlike drudgery. And I thought I had as good go see what I could, knowing that it could not be much worse wheresoever I came, and that any rate I should be out of the ill-will of some of our neighbours. Some of them would not venture a day's journey from out of the smoke of their chimneys or the taste of their mother's milk; not even upon the condition that they might eat and drink of as good cheer as the best nobleman in the land, but they would rather stay at home and eat a brown crust and drink a little whey.

Source: Edward Barlow, *Barlow's Journal of His Life at Sea in King's Ships, East and West Indiamen and Other Merchantmen from 1659 to 1703,* 2 vols, ed. Alfred Basil Lubbock, Hurst and Blackett, 1934, vol. 1, pp. 20–1.

THE STATUTE OF ARTIFICERS **Document 45**

Passed in 1563, the Statute of Artificers brought together a mass of legislation attempting to control wages and labour. These sections relate to the power it gave local authorities to compel the single into service.

7. And be it further enacted, by the authority aforesaid, That every person between the age of twelve years and the age of sixty years not being lawfully retained, nor apprentice with any fisherman or mariner haunting the seas: nor being in service with any kidder or carrier of any corn, grain, or meal for provision of the city of London; nor with any husbandman in husbandry; nor in any city, town corporate, or market-town, in any of the arts or sciences limited or appointed by this statute to have or take apprentices; nor being retained by the year, or half the year at the least, for the digging, seeking, finding, getting, melting, fining, working, trying, making of any silver, tin, lead, iron, copper, stone, sea-coal, stone-coal, moor-coal, or charcoal; nor being occupied in or about the making of any glass; nor being a gentleman born, nor being a student or scholar in any of the universities, or in any school; nor having lands, tenements, rents, or hereditaments, for term of life, or of one estate of inheritance of the clear yearly value of forty shillings; nor being worth in goods and chattels to the value of ten pound; nor having a father or mother then living, or other ancestor whose heir apparent he is, then having lands, tenements, or hereditaments of the yearly value of ten pound, or above, or goods or chattels of the value of forty pound; nor being a necessary or convenient officer or servant lawfully retained, as is aforesaid; nor having a convenient farm or holding, whereupon he may or shall imploy his labour; nor being otherwise lawfully retained, according to the true meaning of this estatute; shall, after the aforesaid last day of September now next ensuing, by virtue of this statute, be compelled to be retained to serve in husbandry by the year, with any person that keepeth husbandry, and will require any such person so to serve within the same shire where he shall be so required.

24. And be it further enacted, by the authority aforesaid, That two Justices of Peace, the mayor or other head officer of any city, borough or town corporate, and two aldermen, or two other discreet burgesses of the same city, borough or town corporate, if there be no aldermen, shall and may, by virtue hereof, appoint any such woman as is of the age of twelve years, and under the age of forty years, and unmarried, and forth of service, as they shall think meet, to serve, to be retained or serve by the year, or by the week or day, for such wages, and in such reasonable sort and manner as they shall think meet; and if any such woman refuse so to serve, then it shall be lawful for the said Justices of Peace, mayor or head

officers, to commit such woman to ward, until she shall be bounden to serve as aforesaid.

Source: An Act containing divers Orders for Artificers, Labourers, Servants of Husbandry, and Apprentices, 5 Eliz. c. 4.

Document 46   SEARCHERS OF THE DEAD

In the plague times of the late sixteenth and early seventeenth centuries, the City of London issued orders for coping with infection. These clauses prescribe the provision of women as searchers of bodies.

That the churchwardens and constable in every precinct, provide, and have in readiness, one, or more sober discreet women, as the case shall require to be providers and deliverers of necessaries for the infected houses, and to attend the persons sick and infected, at the charge of such householders of such houses, if they be able: and if not, then at the charge of the parish. And that such women once entering into charge of such provision and attendance, shall carry red wands, go by the channel[10] side, and forbear assemblies, as is aforesaid.

. . .

That in or for every parish there shall be appointed two sober ancient women, to be sworn to be viewers of the bodies of such as shall die in time of infection, and two other to be viewers of such as shall be sick, and suspected of infection, which women shall immediately upon such their views, by virtue of their oath, make true report to the Constable of that precinct, where such person shall die, or be infected, to the intent that true notice may be given both to the Alderman or his deputy, and to the Clerk of the Parish, and from him to the Clerk of the Parish Clerks, that true certificate may be made as hath been used. And that every of the said women, Constable, or Clerk, failing in the premises, shall suffer imprisonment as is aforesaid. And every woman so sworn, and for any corruption, or other respect falsely reporting, shall stand upon the pillory, and bear corporal pain by the judgement of the Lord Mayor and Court of Aldermen. They at their going abroad to bear red wands, go near the channel, and shun assemblies, as before.

That every woman, or other appointed to any service for the infected, and refusing, or failing to do that service, shall not have any pension out of the hospital or parish.

Source: Orders to be used in the time of the infection of the plague within the citie and liberties of London, 1625.

[10] Gutter.

NORWICH CENSUS OF THE POOR

Document 47

In 1570 the Norwich city authorities commissioned a survey of its poor. This extract from the resulting list records work, circumstances and housing. Several shared housing; others occupied a number of different houses owned by one landlord.

Alice Reade, the wife of Robert Coke, reeder,[11] by whom she hath had 2 sons, the eldest 9 years old, which she set to spinning; and Jone Reade of 14 years that spin middle warp. The same Alice is a 40 year old, & her husband hath left her with the 3 children aforesaid & a sucking child without help, & is run away, & had a wife before, & have dwelt here a 5 years, & she spin wool. *Heminge's house. No alms. Very poor.*

Robert Heminge of 60 year, keelman, & lieth miserably of a disease on his body, & Miriel, his wife, of 52 year; she spins white warp; & a daughter of 6 years. They have dwelt here 13 years. *John Heminge's house. No alms. Very poor.*

Margaret Palmer, widow, of 48 year, that spin white warp & wash, & keep wives, & hath dwelt here all her life. **Able** *Heminge's house. Very poor. No alms.*

Alyce Whitfyld, widow, of 60 years, that spin white warp, & have dwelt here ever. **Able** *Henry Mather. Very poor. No alms.*

Anne Kynge, widow, of 48 years, that spin & card webbing, & Helen, her daughter, of 17 years, that work, & have dwelt here 17 years. **Able** *Heminge's. 1d a week. Very poor.*

There is Dorothy Balles of 27 year, that pick chalk.

Anthony Smythe, mason, lieth miserably of the gout, of 50 years, & Elizabeth, his wife, of 50 years, that spin white warp, & their daughter of 11 years that knit hose, that hath dwelt here 40 years. **Able** *Widow Damme. No alms. Very poor.*

John Whayberde of 40 years, labourer, and Elizabeth, his wife, of 26 years, that spin webbing. They keep together, & hath dwelt here 5 years. **Able** *John Bende's house. Poor. No alms.*

~~Also they have taken in one Hele[n] of Wyndham, wedow, about 40 years, that do also spin webbing, that has dwelt here since 1 fortnight before Christmas last~~[She is gone to Trowse & Brakendal] *Indifferent. To depart.*

[11] Reeder: thatcher.

John Browne, vagrant, of 46 years & Jone, his wife, of 40 years, a woman's tailor; and 2 sons that sucketh & 2 daughters, the eldest 15 years that makes buttons & the youngest 4 years. They dwell together, & have dwelt here 20 years. *John Bende's house 1d. a week. Very poor.*

William Maxwell of 40 years, labourer, & Isbel, his wife, of 41 years, she spin linen; & 2 daughters, the eldest 6 year. They keep together, & he labour, and have dwelt here 12 year. **Able**
No alms. Very poor.

Elizabeth Leche, widow, of 60 years, that spin white warp, & hath dwelt here always. **She is in North Consford.** Also Margery Balles, a maid late diseased in her mouth, born here, that starch sheets & help to wash & scour etc. **Able**
Select. Edward Paulin's. No alms. Indifferent.

Agnes Cotton, widow, of 60 year, able, & dwelt here 20 year.

John Browne of 50 years, baker, & occupy to gather cony skins, & Cycely, his wife, of 52 years, that spin small[st]uff; & 2 sons, the eldest 9 year that go to school, the other sucketh, & his daughter, 10 years, that spin small[st]uff. They have dwelt here 20 years.
Thomas Knitte. No alms. Very poor.

Thomas Hayeward of 28 years, tailor that do occupy, and Katherine, his wife, of 30 years, that spin white warp; & 2 daughters, & the eldest 5 years. They keep together & have dwelt here 8 years. **Able**
Mr. Cullye's. No alms. Indifferent.

Jone Thornton of 80 years, widow, that do no work, & live very poorly.
Very poor. 1d a week.

Robert Polter of 30 year, a keelman that occupy,[12] & Agnes, his wife, Abel's daughter, of 30 year that spin webbing, & 2 sons, the eldest 4 year. They have dwelt here ever. **Able**
Select. Mr. Cullye. No almes. Indifferent.

Wyllam Harison of 60 years, reeder, not able to work for that his ribs be broken, & a daughter of 8 year & spin white warp, & have dwelt here ever. **Able**
Peter Coper's house. No alms. Indifferent.

Katheryn Bloker, not married ever, of 50 year, that spin white warp when she will, & go abroad.
2d. a week.

Source: John F. Pound, *The Norwich Census of the Poor 1570*, Norwich: Norfolk Record Society, 1972, pp. 25–6.

---

[12] Occupy: work.

PUNISHING BASTARD GETTERS

Document 48

A parliamentary diary recorded the discussion on 31 March 1593 over a pro-
viso to enable magistrates to have those responsible for begetting bastards
whipped. The original statute, 18 Eliz. Ic.3, simply referred to 'punishment of
the mother and reputed father'.

The bill for continuance of statutes passed. A proviso was engrossed in the
bill for giving larger power to Justices of Peace upon the statute of 18 Eliz: for
punishing of bastard getters. This day the proviso was again misliked, many
thought too liberal to leave it to the discretion of a Justice of Peace to have
power to whip one that should offend that law. The chief reasons against it
were, first the punishment thought slavish and not to be inflicted upon a
liberal man. Sir John Unton said, 'natura me mitem fecit respublica severum
neuter crudelem', but this he thought too cruel. 'Est et misericordia puniens et
iustitia parcens'.[13] Secondly the malice of a Justice of peace feared, that upon
ill will might give this correction to one not offending if he were accused by
a whore. Thirdly the case might chance upon gentlemen or men of quality,
whom it were not fit to put to such a shame. On the contrary side many good
reasons were yielded to enforce the punishment by whipping, and those
reasons answered as was easy to do. Upon many contradictory voices and
speeches the motion was made by the speaker to have a proviso added which
he drew then presently. The proviso was that no person offending in that
point of the law should be whipped by the discretion of the Justice, if the said
party who begat the bastard would keep and maintain it at his own charges
and not leave it to the charge and alms of the parish. This provision he added
because it was clearly delivered by Sergeant Harris to be the resolution of the
Judges, and their practice too, that a man offending that statute might by
the discretion of the Justice be whipped, but plainly he that would keep the
child could not be whipped. This proviso of Mr Speaker was not liked neither
but many would needs have the clause of whipping clean left out of our new
act, and that point in the statute of 18. to be explained not to extend to whipping.
Upon dissention it was agreed that a committee should go up presently to
the chamber and agree how to have it. They dissented likewise and could not
agree but some would now have the old law of 18 to stand wholly as it was
without addition or alteration. Mr Wroth shewed good cunning to reduce it
to this otherwise I fear the act would have passed shamefully. . . . The house
was divided on this question but we of the no got it 28 voices.

Source: Anonymous Journal, British Library Mss Cotton Titus F. ii, f. 80v–81v.

[13] Two Latin commonplaces from Cicero and Augustine: Nature made me mild, the
republic strict, but neither made me cruel; There is both a mercy in punishing, and
justice in sparing.

Document 49   ELIZABETH BROMLEY VS. EDITH GRIFFYN

A deposition from a defamation case sued between two women at the London consistory court in 1566. Sections in italics are translated from the Latin.

Repeated in front of the bishop's official on the 18 November 1566 in the presence of me William Blakwell notary

Marion Johnson, *wife of Francis Johnson, of the parish of St Giles in the Fields, where she has lived for 6 years and before that at Grindon Underwood, Bucks for 2 years, born at Simpson in the same county, aged about 40, and says she testifies freely. Examined first as to her knowledge of the parties she has known Elizabeth Bromley for 6 years and Edith Griffyn alias Mayne well since the time of quadragesima last.*

To the first she says that the contents of this one are true.

To the second by virtue of her oath she says and deposes that upon a certain day happening about midsummer last past before this her examination *as she remembers the time otherwise she does not remember* and in the afternoon of the same day the articulate Elizabeth Bromley came home to this deponent's house being situated by the Strand within the parish of St Giles in the Field where she this deponent and the articulate Elizabeth Bromley sitting at her door and talking together Edith Griffyn articulate being next neighbour unto this deponent and espying the said goodwife Bromley came to her and said unto her 'Thou burdenest me that I should steal a saw and a pair of shoes out of Mr Darbie's shop. But' quoth the said Edith 'thou art a whore and an arrant whore and if thou didst as I do thou wouldst not be so fat nor maintained by other women's husbands and the best in the town will say that thou art an arrant whore.' Then being present and hearing the premises this deponent Margaret Boothe and Elizabeth Reynoldes with divers of the neighbours there about whose names this deponent remembreth not *as she says and otherwise she knows nothing to depose.*

To the third she says that the good fame or credit of the said Elizabeth Bromley by the speaking of the said words in the eyes of good and honest men is diminished as she says.

Source: London Metropolitan Archives, DL/C/ 210 fos 6ᵛ–7ᵛ.

Document 50   DOD AND CLEAVER ON HONESTY

This extract is from the section entitled The duty of children towards their parents.

Maids and young women are to be put in mind, and always to remember, that the best portion, the greatest inheritance, and the most precious jewel that they can bring with them on the marriage day, is shamefastness: the want whereof is most hurtful in all women. And therefore they must carefully shun and avoid all idle and wanton talk, nice looks, dalliance, and light countenance, when they walk abroad or be in company. A man needeth many things: as wisdom, eloquence, knowledge of things, remembrance, skill in some trade or craft to live by, justice, courage and other things and qualities more, which were too long to rehearse: and though some of these be lacking, yet he is not to be disliked, so that he have many of them. But in a maid, no man will look for eloquence, great wit, ordering of the Commonwealth, prudence, etc.

Finally, no man will look for any other thing of a woman, but her honesty: the which only if it be lacking, she is like a man that wanteth all that he should have. For in a maid, the honesty and chastity is in stead of all. She verily may truly be said to be an evil keeper, that cannot keep one thing well, committed to her keeping, and put in trust to her, with much commendation of words: and especially which no man will take from her against her will, nor touch it, except she be willing her self. The which thing only, if a woman remember, it will cause her to great heed unto, and to be a more wary and careful keeper of her honesty, which alone being lost, though all other things be never so well and safe, yet they perish together therewith, because she that hath once lost her honesty, should think there is nothing left.

Source: John Dod and Robert Cleaver, *A godlie forme of householde government*, 1612, pp. 350–1.

ANTONY RATCLIFF   **Document 51**

Antony Ratcliff, a squire, was prosecuted at the Durham consistory court in 1560 for defamatory words.

Christopher Egleston, *of Hunstonworth, yeoman, aged 40 years*
He saith that about the time libellate the said Mr. Antony, coming out of the church of Hunstanworth, called for one Roger Doon, which at last came to him, to whom the said Antony said, 'Did not thou promise me that thou would tell me and the parson of Hunstonworth who stole George Whitfeld's sheep?' and Doon answered and said, 'I need not unless I will.' Mr. Ratcliff said then to Doon, 'Thou breaks promise.' And Doon answered that he would not. 'You will know it soon enough, for your man, Nicoll Dixson, stole them, that there stands, upon Thursday before Christmas then last past,' saying the words was spoke about Michaelmas last past betwixt the said Antony and Doon. And the said Doon said further, at that time, that the said Nicoll should

drive the said stolen sheep to one William Dixson of Hexhamshire, his brother, and there remained unto the Sunday next after, and then the said Nicoll rode to his said brother William Dixson's, and brought away the caise [carcase] of one of the said sheep to his own house at Newton, and did his use therewith. Then Mr. Ratclif called upon Robson, and said to him, 'Did not thou tell me that Doon had the 40s. to sell the said 4 sheep of Dixson, my man?' And the said Robson said that Doon bad him bide it; and Doon, yet then present, said, 'What made matter of that? for the poor man that aught [owned] the said sheep, then also present, had 40s. to have. . . . other things than it.' And Doon said that he should never be able to prove him a thief, 'for although ye be a gent., and I a poor man, my honesty shall be as good as yours.' 'What saith thou?' said Mr. Ratcliff then, 'likens thou thy honesty to mine?' And then Mr. Ratcliff, being then in the church yard after service, lifted up his hand at Doon, which gave back; but to this examinant's knowledge the said Mr. Anthony did not then touch the said Doon, neither with his hand nor with any kind of weapon, nor no weapon was then drawn, by virtue of his oath.

Source: Depositions and Other Ecclesiastical Proceedings from the Courts of Durham, ed. James Raine, Surtees Society 21, J.B. Nichols and Son, 1845, pp. 62–3.

Document 52   WILLIAM STOUT

William Stout (1665–1752), a Lancaster shopkeeper and Quaker, wrote his autobiography in later life from memory. He never married and, following the principles of his religion, maintained a lifetime reputation for honest trading, evidenced by his frequent appointment as executor for wills. This section describes his master, to whom he was apprenticed in 1685.

1698

The 10th day of the second month this year my master, Henry Coward, died being about 50 years of age. He had been an active and affable man, and very much respected by people of all ranks and professions, and particularly by his friends called Quakers, to whom he was assistant in their sufferings and other ways. But at the same time [he] affected popularity and to be drawn into some gentlemen's company, and to pretend [to] skill in horses; which drew him from his necessary business, which, whilst I was with him, was very good, and his credit so good that if any had money to dispose of, if they got it into his disposal, they concluded it was safe. But this large credit, and his freedom in conversation in company, and in some houses of no good character, hurt his esteem of his best friends. He also dealt in merchandise with loose partners, and became concerned much with persons of declining circumstances, where neither profit nor credit could be got; and he gave uneasiness to his wife by his frequenting some houses of no good character. And she was a very indolent woman, and drew money privately from him, and his circumstances became so burdensome to him, that he daily expected to be made a prisoner; which, with the shame of forfeiting his former reputation, it drew him into despair, and broke his heart, so that he kept to his house for some time, and died for grief or shame. He made a will and made his wife executor, to pay his debts as far as his personal estate extended, and invested his real estate in Robert Lawson and me, to sell towards the payment of the rest of his debts which proved more than all would disburse. The widow, although she had a brother and other rich relations in the town, yet none of them would be bound with her in the bishop's court for the due performance of her husband's will here; so she got a poor man well dressed, and went to Kirby Lonsdale and got legal administration; and the poor man was accepted as her bondsman. She made a sale of the shop goods, mostly to Elijah Salthouse; I then having no intention to the retail trade. She paid part of his debts, to whom and where she pleased, but not regularly not subject to take good advice, in order to discharge her trust in manner.

Source: Autobiography of William Stout, of Lancaster, wholesale and retail grocer and ironmonger, a member of the Society of Friends. A.D. 1665–1752, ed. J. Harland, Simpkin & Marshall, 1851, p. 47.

NEHEMIAH WALLINGTON **Document 53**

Nehemiah Wallington (1598–1658) was a London woodturner. In the numerous notebooks he left recording his reflections on life, his conduct and sense of self is driven by his Puritan beliefs. In this extract from a notebook entitled 'The Growth of a Christian' he expresses his helplessness in the face of the wrong 'done unto religion', but also to his standing in the community, by a dishonest apprentice.

On the second of May [1641] I went to the sacrament and found some comfort. But this month I had as sad a thing befallen me as ever I had in my life for it pierced me to my soul. For my man William had sold some trenchers and told the customer they were maple when they were aspe[n] which was a lie and I did sharply reprove him for it. And when the customer was gone my neighbour's man called the customer and told her that we had cozened her. And a day after the gentlewoman came to me and told me my man had cozened her and had sold her aspes trenchers for maple and that his sin was mine and that I ought to make good what wrong my man doth. And they say you are a religious man but you will lie and cozen so that you bring a slander on Religion and I partly know you for an honest man and that you have lived under a faithful minister a long time which makes your sin so much the greater. Then I answered all this I know and for the wrong he hath done to you it shall be no loss to you for I will return all your money to you again but as for the wrong he hath done unto Religion I can no way help it.

Source: *The Notebooks of Nehemiah Wallington, 1618–1654: A Selection*, ed. David Booy, Aldershot: Ashgate, 2007, p. 151.

Document 54   NICHOLAS MARDEN AND FRIENDS

Nicholas Marden of Corringham in Essex was presented at the Archdeaconry Court on 2 May, 1599, for a drinking game. He was sentenced to acknowledge the offence.

Nicholas Marden of Curringham. – Detected, that he and one John Smith of the parish of Curringham and one Richard Cottes of Orsett and George Landishe of Barking, after greate abuse in drinking, did at their parting, take with them into the field, at the town's end where they meant to part, four or six pots of beer; and there setting them down, did themselves upon theire bare knees humbly kneel down, and kissing the pots and drinking one to the other, and prayed for the health of all true and faithful drunkards; and especially for Mr. Andrew Browghton, as they said the maintainer and upholder of all true and faithful drunkards; and having done they kissed each other and for a memory of their worthy act did every man make his mark or name, upon an ashen tree, that stood there by them.

Source: William Hale Hale, *A Series of Precedents and Proceedings in Criminal Causes: Extending from The Year 1475 to 1640, Extracted from the Act-Books of Ecclesiastical Courts in the Diocese of London*, F. and J. Rivington, 1847, p. 219.

Document 55   MERCURIUS DEMOCRITUS

An extract from one of the royalist tracts of the 1650s. John Crouch's Mercurius Democritus *appeared weekly, featuring streams of scurrilous fantasy, lewd stories and prophecies; this section imagines a prophecy from William Lilly, the parliamentary-sympathising astrologer.*

He [Lilly] moreover prophesied of strange events to happen next Shrove Tuesday to excise-men and committee-men, which rose from the effects of the great eclipse happening the last Black Monday in Friday Street, right against the maypole in the Strand, at which instance the Star in Bread Street was in conjunction with the Star in Old Fish Street, the sign being in Aries opposite to Pisces foretells the great esteem of ramshorns in the year 1653, when all citizens shall have them made into seal rings, with their arms graven on them; maids shall that year be very rare, and fresh-cod much coveted by females of the city; that merchants' wives will not be content unless they have London Measure in all the commodities they are to deal withall; they will also be very rantipoll, proud, and imperious over their husbands, ambitious of bringing them under their commands, and giving them rules and laws to observe; which they may not infringe or break without the danger of being labelled over the coxcombs, which shall make their husbands rave, horn-mad . . .

That this year 1650 women will be troubled with agues in their tongues, insomuch that they will never leave shaking till about December following, about which time they are subject to break out at their lips, and then it is good for their husbands to let them blood in a great black vein under their tongues to make them silent creatures a whole day after.

Source: *Mercurius democritus, or, A true and perfect nocturnall*, 1652–54, Nov. 10– Nov. 17 1652, no. 32, pp. 251–2.

SIR THOMAS SMITH   **Document 56**

The classic statement of the division of political roles in the commonwealth.

Chapter 16: The division of the parts and persons of the commonwealth.
To make all things yet clear before, as we shall go, there ariseth another division of the parts of the commonwealth. For it is not enough to say that it consisteth of a multitude of houses and families which make streets and villages, and the multitude of the streets and villages make towns, and the multitude of towns the realm, and that freeman be considered only in this behalf, as subjects and citizens of the commonwealth, and not bondmen who can bear no rule nor jurisdiction over freemen, as they who be taken but as instruments and the goods and possesssions of others. In which consideration also we do reject women, as those whom nature hath made to keep home and to nourish their family and children, and not to meddle with matters abroad, nor to bear office in a city or common wealth no more than children and infants: except it be in such cases as the authority is annexed to the

blood and progeny, as the crown, a duchy, or an earldom for there the blood is respected, not the age nor the sex. Whereby an absolute Queen, an absolute Duchess or Countess, those I call absolute, which have the name, not by being married to a king, duke, or earl, but by being the true, right and next successors in the dignity, and upon whom by right of the blood that title is descended: These I say have the same authority although they be women or children in that kingdom, duchy or earldom, as they should have had if they had been men of full age. For the right and honour of the blood, and the quietness and surety of the realm, is more to be considered, than either the tender age as yet impotent to rule, or the sex not accustomed (otherwise) to intermeddle with public affairs, being by common intendment understood, that such personages never do lack the counsel of such grave and discreet men as be able to supply all other defects.

Source: Thomas Smith, *De Republica Anglorum: The Manner of Government or Policy of the Realm of England*, 1583, pp. 18–19.

Document 57   LUCY HUTCHINSON

Lucy Hutchinson's memoir of the life of her husband John, one of the parliamentary leaders in the Civil War, recorded their opinions of Charles I.

But above all these the king had another instigator of his own violent purpose, more powerful than all the rest, and that was the queen, who, grown out of her childhood, began to turn her mind from those vain extravagancies she lived in at first, to that which did less become her, and was more fatal to the kingdom; which is never in any place happy where the hands which were made only for distaffs affect the management of sceptres. – If any one object the fresh example of Queen Elizabeth, let them remember that the felicity of her reign was the effect of her submission to her masculine and wise counsellors; but wherever male princes are so effeminate as to suffer women of foreign birth and different religions to intermeddle with the affairs of state, it is always found to produce sad desolations; and it hath been observed that a French queen never brought any happiness to England. Some kind of fatality, too, the English imagined to be in her name of Marie, which, it is said, the king rather chose to have her called by than her other, Henrietta, because the land should find a blessing in that name, which had been more unfortunate; but it was not in his power, though a great prince, to control destiny. This lady being by her priests affected with the meritoriousness of advancing her own religion, whose principle it is to subvert all other, applied that way her great wit and parts, and the power her haughty spirit kept over her husband, who was enslaved in his affection only to her, though she had no more passion for him than what served to promote her designs.

Source: Lucy Hutchinson, *Memoirs of the life of Colonel Hutchinson, governor of Nottingham*, John C. Nimmo, 1885, vol. I, pp. 125–6.

REINFORCING QUEENLY POWER   **Document 58**

The second year of Mary I's reign saw the passing of an act insisting that the powers laid down for kings applied also to queens, despite the errors of 'malicious and ignorant' persons.

An act declaring that the Regal power of this realm is in the Queen's Majesty as fully and absolutely, as ever it was in any of her most noble progenitors kings of this realm.

. . . Be it declared and enacted by the authority of this present Parliament, that the law of this realm is, and ever hath been, and ought to be understand, that the kingly or regal office of the realm, and all dignities, prerogative, royal power, pre-eminences, privileges, authorities, and jurisdictions thereunto annexed, united, or belonging, being invested either in male or female, are, and be, and ought to be, as fully, wholly, absolutely, and entirely deemed, judged, accepted, invested and taken in thone as in thother, so that what, or whensoever statute or law doth limit and appoint, that the King of this realm may . . . do anything, as King. The same the Queen (being supreme governor, possessor, & inheritor to the imperial crown of this realm, as our said sovereign lady, the Queen most justly presently is) may by the same authority & power likewise have, exercise, execute, punish, correct, and do, to all intents, constructions, and purposes, without doubt, ambiguity, scruple, or question.

Source: *Anno Mariae primo Actes made in the parliamente*, 1554, April 1554, fo. iiv (STC 9443).

REASONS FOR CROWNING THE PRINCE AND PRINCESS OF ORANGE JOINTLY   **Document 59**

This broadside of 1689 explained the rationale for crowning William and Mary jointly. Mary's father, James II, had fled during the Revolution of 1688; the executive power was given not to Mary, but to her husband.

III. The making the Prince and Princess of Orange King and Queen jointly, is the Nation's gratitude and generosity: And by re-continuing the line in remainder, is manifested the inesteemable value the people have for the two Princesses, notwithstanding the maladministration of their unhappy father.

IV. The present state of Europe in general, and of these kingdoms in particular, require a vigorous and masculine administration. To recover what's lost, rescue what's in danger, and rectify what's amiss, cannot be effected but by a prince that is consummate in the art both of peace and war. Though the Prince and Princess be King and Queen jointly, and will equally share the glory of a crown, and we the happiness of their auspicious reign: yet the wisdom of the grand convention is manifested, (1st) in placing the executive power in one of them, and not in both; for two persons, equal in authority, may differ in opinion, and consequently in command; and it is evident no man can serve two masters. (2ndly) it's highly necessary and prudent, rather to vest the administration in the husband than in the wife: (1.) Because a man, by nature, education and experience, is generally rendered more capable to govern than the woman. Therefore, (2.) The husband ought rather to rule the wife, than the wife the husband, especially considering the vow in matrimony. (3.) The Prince of Orange is not more proper to govern as he's man, and husband only, but as he is a man, a husband, and a prince of known honour, profound wisdom, undaunted courage, and incomparable merit; as he's a person that's naturally inclin'd to be just, merciful and peaceable, and to do all public acts of generosity for the advancement of the interest and happiness of human societies, and therefore most fit under heaven, to have the sole executive power.

Source: Reasons for crowning the Prince and Princess of Orange king and queen joyntly, and for placing the executive power in the Prince alone, Edinburgh, 1689.

Document 60   EDWARD COKE ON ELECTIONS

This single sentence from Edward Coke's four-volume treatise on the common laws of England mentions, in passing, the categories of people bound to obey Parliament without participating in elections. The sentence is an incidental point in a discussion of the role of proctors of the clergy in summoning bishops to Parliament, but it provided a touchstone for the block to women voting for centuries.

. . . and in many cases multitudes are bound by Acts of Parliament which are not parties to the elections of Knights, Citizens, and Burgesses, as all they that have no freehold, or have freehold in ancient Demesne, and all Women having freehold or no freehold, and men within the age of one and twenty years, andc.

Source: Edward Coke, The fourth part of the Institutes of the laws of England concerning the jurisdiction of courts, 1644, pp. 4–5.

THE ELECTION AT IPSWICH 1640

Document 61

Amongst the disputed elections for the Long Parliament in 1640 was one at Ipswich where women's votes, originally taken, were subsequently disallowed. The account is by Simonds D'Ewes, the High Sheriff for Suffolk, who had been criticised for partisanship for the Puritan candidates.

The next morning October 22 the said High Sheriff made open publication of the said Notes and pronounced the said Sir Nathaniel Barnardiston and Sir Philip Parker the due elected knights for the said counties of Suffolk. And then caused the Indentures witnessing the same election to be there ensealed and legally executed.

'Tis true that by the ignorance of some of the clerks at the other two tables the oaths of some single women that were freeholders were taken without the knowledge of the said High Sheriffe who as soon as he had noticed thereof instantly sent to forbid the same, conceiving it a matter very unworthy of any gentleman and most dishonourable in such an election to make use of their voices although they might in law have been allowed nor did the said High Sheriff allow of the said votes upon his numbering the said Poll, but with the allowance and consent of the said two Knights themselves discount them and cast them out.

Source: 'A short and true relation of the carriage of the election of the Knights for the countie of Suffolke at Ipswich which beganne there upon Monday morning October 19 this present yeare 1640 and ended upon the Thursday morning then next ensueing', British Library Mss Harl 158, f. 285v.

LAMBARD ON THE ASSEMBLY OF WOMEN

Document 62

This passage from William Lambard's handbook for magistrates describes the rationale for treating women as unaccountable for riot, and recalls recent cases that undermine it. 'Mar.' refers to Marowe's De Pace, one of Lambard's main sources.

And if a number of women, or infants (under the age of discretion) do assemble themselves for their own cause, this is no unlawful assembly punishable by these Statutes: But if a man of discretion cause them to assemble to commit an unlawful act, then it is otherwise saith Mar. And I remember, that not many years since women were punished in the Star Chamber, and worthily, for that (having put off their seemly shamefastness, and apparelling themselves in the attire of men) they assembled in great number, and in riotous manner pulled down an enclosure.

Source: William Lambard, *EIRENARCHA: Or of the office of the Justices of Peace, in two Bookes*, 1581, p. 179.

Document 63   ALICE BAINE AND DOROTHY DAWSON

These extracts are from a Star Chamber suit about a protest against the enclosure of fifty acres of ground on Grewelthorpe Moor in Yorkshire by the Puritan gentleman Sir Stephen Proctor. While Proctor elsewhere alleged the women's behaviour was masterminded by their husbands, the bill of complaint noted that Dawson was known as 'Captain Dorothy' for her rude and riotous behaviour. Many of those involved were middle-aged married women. The witnesses are answering interrogatories posed by Proctor, the plaintiff.

Alice Baine, wife of Roger Baine of Grewelthorpe in the county of Yorkshire, about the age of 44 years, sworn and examined, deposeth as followeth.

To the first she saith that Dorothy Dawson, Jane Walton, Luce Walker, Dorothy Lie, Ellen Walker, Isabel Baines, Francis Dunne, Jennett Adamson, Jane Burniston and this examinant with others whom she cannot remember about the time mentioned in this interrogatory did assemble themselves on Grewelthorpe moor, and did cast down a piece of a fence begun by the complainants to be enclosed near the coal pits, and the quantity so thrown down at that time exceeded not to her thinking a yard and a half in measure, and there was a man on the said ground, whose name she knoweth not, neither to whom he did belong, neither was he working at that time to her remembrance.

To the second she saith that she knoweth not who did move or procure the said women first to throw down the said ditch or to go to the said moor at that time when the ditch was so cast down, but saith it was a matter of general grievance to them, and did not know, one more willing than another, but the persons aforenamed did all go together to pull down some little part of the said ditch, that they might thereby have their commons as before; And saith for her own part she did not make her husband privy to the intention, neither was she willed or moved by her said husband to do the same, neither knoweth any other thing mentioned in this Interrogatory.

Dorothy Dawson wife of Richard Dawson of Grewelthorpe aforesaid, about the age of 44, sworn and examined, deposeth as followeth . . .

To the third she saith that about the time mentioned in this interrogatory this examinant and Alice Baines went at one time to the said moor where the fifty acres mentioned in this interrogatory was in hand to be enclosed to have made a hap for their cattle into the said ground and there put down a sod or two with their hands not carrying any weapons nor drawing any knives and the workman being there present did interrupt this examinant and the other at that time to pull down any more of the said ditch, and so they went quietly home at that time. And shortly after within a day or two, the said Elizabeth Branston a very poor woman being great with child came to this deponent, and said that she had but one cow and if she might not go on the moor she were beggared, for she had no money to set her with at grass, and requested this deponent to go with her to pull down a gap to let her cow go into the said enclosure. At whose intreaty she this examinant went and there finding nobody to resist they two with their hands did pull down a gap, which when they had done and returning home again six of the complainants' servants or workfolks came forth of a house near to the enclosure, and running after them overtook them and drew them back again to the place which they had thrown in, and offering to throw the said Elizabeth Branston into a ditch being full of water, and three quarters in depth this examinant offered to help the said woman and being holden by one John Branley this examinant got hold of the said Elizabeth Branston with one hand, and of him that would have thrown her in the ditch with the other hand, and pulled out a piece of his coat that so held the said woman, and the same fellow did rive the said Elizabeth Branston's coats which if it had not riven he had thrown her into the ditch, and she verily thinketh that the said Elizabeth Branston got her death by that struggling, for she then told this examinant that they had given her that which she could never cast, and shortly after the said Elizabeth died. But this examinant or any other to her knowledge did not strike with knives the said Branley nor pulled him by the hair of the head but only touched him when he held her and she further saith that this examinant's husband was privy to her going when they went but two together for the pulling of the said ditches in such manner as is beforehand only for passing of their cattle.

Source: Proctor v Dawson *et al.*, 1608, The National Archives, Stac8/227/3.

JOHN PEATCH

Document 64

This case of seditious words was heard by the Northern Assizes on 31 January, 1687. It seems to refer to James Scott, duke of Monmouth and illegitimate son of Charles II, who had been executed for his part in the Monmouth Rebellion against James II in 1685, but rumours persisted that he was alive. The Queen, Mary of Modena, had had a series of miscarriages and five children who died in infancy; the eventual birth of an heir in 1688 led to a popular outcry that the child was an impostor (the Warming Pan Scandal). A body-maker makes bodices.

Assizes: Periodic criminal courts for the most serious offences.

Before Sir Jonathan Jenings, Knight.
John Peatch, of Ripon, body-maker, saith that yesterday morning, being Sunday and in the time of divine service, this informant being churchwarden, together with William Walker and James Suttrice, alias Clarkeson, his fellow churchwardens, entering into the house of James Foxton to see what order was therein kept, one Stephen Duffield of Ripon came in, and entering into discourse with them, told them that the Queen told the King that she could

not conceive unless she drank Charles Monmouth's blood; upon which the King told her that he would send for him and that he should be let blood, that she might drink it; upon which she replied, that unless she might drink his heart's blood it would do her no good.

Source: Depositions from the Castle of York, ed. James Raine, Surtees Society 40, Durham, 1861, p. 283.

Document 65   SARAH WALKER

Another, earlier, outbreak of sedition, from Newcastle against Charles II.

July 28, 1663
Newcastle-upon-Tyne

Before Robert Shaftoe, Esq. and Mark Milbank, Esq.
Sarah, wife of Oswald Walker, yeoman, did say on the 13th of July these words (to wit) 'There was never a King in England that was a chimney sweeper but this', meaning his Majesty that now is, and that she would petition and endeavour to get and raise an army to fight against his Majesty and all his officers that came to demand any such thing as the hearth money.

Source: Depositions from the Castle of York, ed. James Raine, Surtees Society 40, Durham, 1861, p. 99.

Document 66   BRILLIANA HARLEY TO HER HUSBAND

Lady Brilliana Harley, the third wife of Lord Robert Harley, wrote to him in 1643 when he was in London and she was in Herefordshire with one of their sons, Ned, defending their castle, Brampton Bryan, against royalist forces. She died a month later of a cold.

24 Sept 1643
My Dear Sir

I hope before this you have heard by Proser that the Lord has been gracious to us, and has sent our enemies away from before Brampton: for which great goodness of our God to us his poor despised servants, I hope you and the rest who prayed for us will now help us to praise our God for his great mercy to us never to be forgotten.

    On Saturday last the 23 of this month I received your letter by Fischer in which you advise me to come away from Brampton.

Dear Sir, hitherto God has made me (though an unworthy one) an instrument to keep possession of your house that it has not fallen into the hands of spoilers, and to keep together a handful of those such as feared the Lord together so that his word has yet had an abiding in these parts, which if the Lord remove Herefordshire is miserable. In this work I have not thought my life dear, neither shall I.

Sir could Ned Harley come down I should think myself to have much comfort, and I think he would do his country service and himself good in helping to keep what I hope shall be his, and in maintaining the Gospel in this place, Oh let me beg of you to take poor Herefordshire into consideration and commiseration, if the faithful ministry be removed and carried up to London so as they are, what shall become of the country, I think it had been a thousand times better if Mr Yarts had stayed in the Country for upon his going away there is a popish minister crowded in here I have still disavowed his being there and as far as I can I suffer him not to have the benefit of the place neither dare he abide there, if please you to send Mr Banyte a commission from the parliament to take possession of it he would and I believe the people would be glad of him.

To my sorrow I hear Mr Gower has accepted of another place at London. If so let me desire you to place another in Brampton by the mystery of the Parliament or else there will some wicked one get in.

Sir my Lord of Essex is gone from Gloucester so that I cannot expect a convoy from him and by this enclosure you may see what I may expect from Gloucester.

If my son could come down I should hope we might comfortably keep what we have left, if that can not be then I pray you think how some commission may be granted that some strength may be raised.

Sir the man you write of to entrust your house with if I should have followed his counsel it had been gone. Therefore I do not think he would keep it. Mr Banyte is of an opinion that if please God I go away, it will not be long kept not that I do any great matter but I have something more authority and should have more care than any other.

My dear Sir I pray you consider all things and do not look upon me as if I were afraid but what you would have me do in that which may be best for you, and that I shall most gladly do, all my pleasures are in you and then I must be most pleased when you are pleased. And therefore dear Sir think what you would have me do and let me know it and I shall be best pleased to do that.

This bearer can relate all passages to you and I hope you will hasten him out of town.

I might begin a new letter in letting you know how good God has been to me in all things he has exceedingly blessed the provisions of my house so that it has held out beyond expectation.

I thank God the children are all well and all in my house

Dear Sir when you write to Colonel Massy give him thanks for the kindness he shows to me

I beseech the Lord to preserve you and to give you a happy meeting with her that begs your love and prays for [you]

Your most affectionate wife
Brilliana Harley

Sir I sent to you a great while ago for a gown I pray you will you send me one I desire it may be silk cheap made up plain I believe my [torn]s measure will serve me and my cousin Davis's men may bring it down

Sept 24 1643
Brampton Castle

Source: British Library Ms Add 70110.

Document 67   1 CORINTHIANS 1:27–29

These phrases from Paul's letter to the Corinthians were a touchstone for prophets and sectarians.

27. But God hath chosen the foolish things of the world to confound the wise; and God hath chosen the weak things of the world to confound the things which are mighty;
28. And base things of the world, and things which are despised, hath God chosen, yea, and things which are not, to bring to nought things that are:
29. That no flesh should glory in his presence.

Source: 1 Corinthians 1:27–29, King James Version.

Document 68   ABIEZER COPPE

Abiezer Coppe (1619–1672), Ranter and prophet, published this exchange between himself and a female follower in a collection of epistles in 1649. The first is from 'Mrs. T. P.', and goes on to describe a vision of beasts and fish; the second is Coppe's reply.

Dear Brother,
My true love in the spirit of one-ness, presented to your self – with all that call on the name of the Lord; both yours and ours. It hath pleased The Father

of late, so sweetly to manifest his love to my soul, that I cannot but return it to you, who are the image of my Father.

I should rejoice, if the Father pleased also, to see you, and to have some spiritual communion with you, that I might impart those soul-ravishing consolations, which have flown from the bosoms of the Father, to our mutual comfort. What though we are weaker vessels, women etc. yet strength shall abound, and we shall mount up with wings as eagles; we shall walk, and not be weary, run and not faint, when the man-child Jesus is brought forth in us. Oh what a tedious, faint way have we been led about to find out our rest, and yet when all was done, we were twice more the sons of slavery then – But blessed be our God, who hath brought us by a way that we know not, and we are quickly arrived at our rest.

. . .

Dear Sister, in the best fellowship, mine entire love, etc. presupposed –

I have received your letter, and the Father's voice in it, but it came not into our coast till the 12 of November, which was the Fathers time, since which time, I have scarce been one whole day at home, but abroad, at my Meat and Drink – so (that if I durst, yet) I could not so much as plunder an opportunity, – but now it is freely given me to write. –

I know you are a vessel of the Lord's house, filled with heavenly liquor, and I see your love, – The Father's love, in the sweet returns of your (I mean) his sweets to me. I love the vessel well, but the wine better, even that wine, which we are drinking new, in the Kingdom.

And it is the voice of my Beloved, that saith, drink oh friends! yea, drink abundantly oh Beloved!

Dear friend, why dost in thy letter say, [what though we are weaker vessels, women? etc] I know that Male and Female are all one in Christ, and they are all one to me. I had as lief hear a daughter, as a son prophesy. And I know, that women, who stay at home, divide the spoil – whilst our younger brethren, who are (as we were) abroad, and not yet arrived at our Father's house, or are at home, are spending their substance in riotous living, and would fain fill their bellies with husks; the outside of the grain.

Source: Abiezer Coppe, *Some sweet sips, of some spirituall wine* (1649), Epistles IV and V, pp. 39–40, 45–6.

PETITION OF THE GENTLEWOMEN AND TRADESMEN'S WIVES **Document 69**

This petition, presented to Parliament in early 1642 by a group of women led by Mrs Anne Stagg, a brewer's wife, and printed shortly afterwards, spoke in the voice of working women to urge Parliament to press the King to purge the

kingdom of Catholicism. Earlier on, it details the alleged atrocities in Ireland,
including rape and murder; this section concludes the seven-page document
with a discussion of the rights of petitioning.

To the Honourable Knights, Citizens and Burgesses, of the House of Commons
assembled in Parliament. The most humble Petition of the Gentlewomen, Tradesmen's
wives, and many others of the Female Sex, all Inhabitants of the City of London,
and the Suburbs thereof.

With lowest submission shewing,

That we also with all thankful humility acknowledging the unwearied
pains, care and great charge, besides hazard of health and life, which you the
noble worthies of this honourable and renowned assembly have undergone,
for the safety both of church and commonwealth, for a long time already past;
for which not only we your humble petitioners, and all well affected in this
kingdom, but also all other good Christians are bound now and at all times to
acknowledge; yet not withstanding that many worthy deeds have been done
by you, great danger and fear do still attend us, & will, as long as popish
lords and superstitious bishops are suffered to have their voice in the House
of Peers, and that accursed and abominable idol of the mass suffered in the
kingdom, and that arch-enemy of our prosperity and Reformation lyeth in
the Tower, yet not receiving his deserved punishment.

All these under correction, gives us great cause to suspect, that God is angry
with us, and to be the chief causes why your pious endeavours for a further
Reformation proceedeth not with that success as you desire, and is most
earnestly prayed for of all that wish well to true religion, and the flourishing
estate both of King and kingdom; the insolencies of the papists and their
abettors, raiseth a just fear and suspicion of sowing sedition, and breaking
out into bloody persecution in this kingdom, as they have done in Ireland,
the thoughts of which sad and barbarous events, maketh our tender hearts to
melt within us, forcing us humbly to petition to this honourable Assembly,
to make safe provision for your selves and us, before it be too late.

And whereas we, whose hearts have joined cheerfully with all those
Petitions which have been exhibited unto you in the behalf of the purity of
religion, and the liberty of our husbands' persons and estates, recounting our
selves to have an interest in the common privileges with them, do with the
same confidence assure our selves to find the same gracious acceptance with
you, for easing of those grievances, which in regard of our frail condition,
do more nearly concern us, and do deeply terrify our souls: our domesticall
dangers with which this kingdom is so much distracted, especially growing
on us from those treacherous and wicked attempts already are such, as we
find ourselves to have as deepen a share as any other.

We cannot but tremble at the very thoughts of the horrid and hideous
facts which modesty forbids us now to name, occasioned by the bloody wars

in Germany, his Majesty's late northern army, how often did it affright our hearts, whilst their violence began to break out so furiously upon the persons of those, whose husbands or parents were not able to rescue: we wish we had no cause to speak of those insolencies, and savage usage and unheard of rapes, exercised upon our sex in Ireland, and have we not just cause to fear they will prove the forerunners of our ruin, except Almighty God by the wisdom and care of this Parliament be pleased to succour us, our husbands and children, which are as dear and tender unto us, as the lives and blood of our hearts, to see them murthered and mangled and cut in pieces before our eyes, to see our children dashed against the stones, and the mothers' milk mingled with the infants' blood, running down the streets; to see our houses on flaming fire over our heads: oh how dreadful would this be! We thought it misery enough (though nothing to that we have just cause to fear) but few years since for some of our sex, by unjust divisions from their bosom comforts, to be rendered in a manner widows, and the children fatherless, husbands were imprisoned from the society of their wives, even against the laws of God and Nature; and little infants suffered in their fathers' banishments: thousands of our dearest friends have been compelled to fly from episcopal persecutions into desert places amongst wild beasts, there finding more favour than in their native soil, and in the midst of all their sorrows, such hath the pity of the prelates been, that our cries could never enter into their ears or hearts, nor yet through multitudes of obstructions could never have access or come nigh to those royal mercies of our most gracious Sovereign, which we confidently hope, would have relieved us: but after all these pressures ended, we humbly signify, that our present fears are, that unless the blood-thirsty faction of the papists and prelates be hindered in their designs, our selves here in England as well as they in Ireland, shall be exposed to that misery which is more intolerable than that which is already past, as namely to the rage not of men alone, but of devils incarnate, (as we may so say) besides the thraldom of our souls and consciences in matters concerning God, which of all things are most dear unto us.

Now the remembrance of all these fearful accidents aforementioned, do strongly move us from the example of the woman of Tekoa to fall submissively at the feet of his Majesty, our dread Sovereign, and cry Help O King, help o ye the noble worthies now sitting in Parliament: And we humbly beseech you, that you will be a means to his Majesty and the House of Peers, that they will be pleased to take our heart breaking grievances into timely consideration, and to add strength and encouragement to your noble endeavours, and further that you would move his Majesty with our humble requests, that he would be graciously pleased according to the example of the good King Asa, to purge both the court and kingdom of that great idolatrous service of the Mass, which is tolerated in the Queen's court, this sin (as we conceive) is able to draw down a greater curse upon the whole kingdom, then all your noble and pious endeavours can prevent, which was the cause that the good and pious King Asa would not suffer idolatry in his own mother, whose example if it shall please his Majesty's gracious goodness to follow, in putting down popery and idolatry both in great and small, in court and in the kingdom throughout, to subdue the papists and their abetters, and by taking away the power of the prelates, whose government by long and woeful experience we have found to be against the liberty of our conscience and the freedom of the Gospel, and the sincere profession and practice thereof, then shall our fears be removed, and we may expect that God will power down his blessings in abundance both upon his Majesty, and upon this Honourable Assembly, and upon the whole land.

For which your new petitioners shall pray affectionately.

The Reasons follow.

It may be thought strange, and unbeseeming our sex to shew our selves by way of Petition to this Honourable Assembly: but the matter being rightly considered, of the right and interest we have in the common and public cause of the Church, it will, as we conceive (under correction) be found a duty commanded and required.

First, because Christ hath purchased us at as dear a rate as he hath done Men, and therefore requireth the like obedience for the same mercy as of men.

Secondly, because in the free enjoying of Christ in his own Laws, and a flourishing estate of the Church and Common-wealth, consisteth the happiness of Women as well as Men.

Thirdly, because Women are sharers in the common Calamities that accompany both Church and Common-Wealth, when oppression is exercised over the Church or Kingdom wherein they live; and an unlimited power have been given to Prelats to exercise authority over the Consciences of Women, as well as Men; witness Newgate, Smithfield, and other places of persecution, wherein Women as well as Men have felt the smart of their fury.

Neither are we left without example in Scripture, for when the state of the Church, in the time of King Ahasuerus was by the bloody enemies thereof sought to be utterly destroyed, we find that Esther the Queen and her maids fasted and prayed, and that Esther petitioned to the King in the behalf of the Church: and though she enterprised this duty with the hazard of her own life, being contrary to the Law to appear before the King before she were sent for, yet her love to the Church carried her through all difficulties, to the performance of that duty.

On which grounds we are emboldened to present our humble Petition unto this Honourable Assembly, not weighing the reproaches which may and are by many cast upon us, who (not well weighing the premises) scoff and deride our good intent. We do it not out of any self-conceit, or pride of heart, as seeking to equal ourselves with men, either in authority or wisdom: But according to our places to discharge that duty we owe to God and the cause of the Church, as far as lieth in us, following herein the example of the men, which have gone in this duty before us.

A relation of the manner how it was delivered, with their answer, sent by Mr. *Pym*.

This Petition, with their Reasons, was delivered the 4th of Feb. 1641. by Mrs Anne Stagg, a Gentlewoman and Brewers Wife, and many others with her of like rank and quality, which when they had delivered it, after some time spent in reading of it, the Honourable Assembly sent them an Answer by Mr Pym, which was performed in this manner.

Mr Pym came to the Commons door, and called for the Women, and spake unto them in these words: Good Women, your Petition and the reasons have been read in the House; and is very thankfully accepted of, and is come in a seasonable time. You shall (God willing) receive from us all the satisfaction which we can possibly give to your just and lawful desires. We intreat you to repair to your houses, and turn your Petition which you have delivered here, into Prayers at home for us, for we have been, are, and shall be (to our utmost power) ready to relive you, your husbands, and children, and to perform the trust committed unto us, towards God, our King and Country, as becometh faithful Christians and loyal subjects.

Source: A True copie of the petition of the gentlewomen and tradesmens-wives, in and about the city of London delivered to the honourable, the knights, citizens, and burgesses of the House of Commons in Parliament, the 4th of February, 1641, 1642, pp. 5–6.

THE PARLIAMENT SCOUT **Document 70**

A parliamentary newsletter reports on women's petitions in August 1643, while parliament was considering the Lords' peace proposals.

There hath been several appearances or apparitions at Westminster, from the City and parts about: one appearance was of Common Counsel; not against peace, but such a peace as might destroy: there were diverse appeared among these, that did speak unadvised words to the Lords, had that been true that was spoke, truth is not to be spoken at all times, and in all manners; there is no question but people may appear in multitudes to petition for redress in case injustice be done: yet that rarely, and in desperate cases, but for multitudes to appear to extort or fright a judicature to do justice is questionable: There appeared since many hundreds of women who cry for peace and swear by the blood of Christ, and God confound them they will have peace, or somebody shall smart for it: these were very numerous, on Wednesday many conceived them five or six thousand, some say 500 of them were whores they are all of the poorer sort, and most have their husbands in one or other Army, who fall upon all that have short hair and pull them, both Ministers, Soldiers and others, this grew so high, and the multitude pressed so hard, that from words they fell to blows; there were diverse hurt, two men and a woman killed, at last a troop of horse came with canes and drove them all away; thus we see, to permit absurdities, is the way to increase them; tumults are dangerous, swords in women's hands do desperate things; this is begotten in the distractions of Civil War.

Source: John Dillingham, *The Parliament Scout communicating his intelligence to the kingdome*, 1643, 3–10 August 1643, p. 55.

Document 71   A PARLIAMENT OF WOMEN

This satirical text, one of a series produced in the 1640s, the 1650s, and later the 1680s, used Aristophanes's plot of rule by women in response to the failure of men, typically proposing sexual property in common. In satire, it asserts rights for women which would later be taken up more seriously.

It is not unknown to all the world, how we have been, and still are deprived of our liberties, living in the bonds of servitude, and in the apprenticeship of slavery, (not for term of years, but during life) therefore we held it not amiss to assemble ourselves together in counsel, whereby we may find out a way to rid ourselves, and our posterity after us, from those Egyptian task-masters (men) who by their subtle policy still insult and domineer over us, by making us their drudges their wills being a law, we forced are to obey: Our grievances being intolerable, and so likewise are the whole body of our sex, finding men only to act for themselves, doing nothing for us, unless to curb and diminish that little which we have: We do and shall disclaim that tyrannical government, which men have over us, and to the utmost of our powers abolish, abrogate, and destroy it, by being not subject and subordinate to it. Therefore we do invite all women who have any spark of valour, or a desire of freedom, to be aiding and assisting us in this great work: as also it is, and shall be lawful for all women, widows, and maids, to make their grievances known, whereby they may have redress; that so hereafter they and we may all enjoy such privileges, as are fit for free-born women.

Source: Now or never: or, A new Parliament of women assembled and met together neer the Popes-Head in Moor-Fields, on the Back-side of Allsuch, 1656, sig. A4.

Guide to further reading

There is now a wide range of primary sources available in print and online. Printed collections of sources on women's history include Patricia Crawford and Laura Gowing (eds) *Women's Worlds in Seventeenth-Century England* (London: Routledge, 2000); Valerie Frith, *Women & History: Voices of Early Modern England* (Toronto: Coach House Press, 1995); Helen Ostovich and Elizabeth Sauer (eds), *Reading Early Modern Women: An Anthology of Texts in Manuscript and Print, 1550–1700* (London: Taylor & Francis, 2004). A number of local record societies' publications of legal records have been reprinted in paperback: for example James Raine (ed.) *Depositions from the Castle of York, relating to offences committed in the Northern Counties in the seventeenth century*, Surtees Society 40 (Durham: 1861, reprinted Elibron, 2007); James Raine (ed.) *Depositions and Other Ecclesiastical Proceedings from the Courts of Durham*, Surtees Society 21 (Durham: 1845, reprinted Elibron, 2007). Autobiographies provide another source: good starting points are Elspeth Graham, *et al.* (eds) *Her Own Life: Autobiographical Writings By Seventeenth-Century Englishwomen* (London: Routledge, 1989); Ralph Josselin, *The Diary of Ralph Josselin, 1616–1683*, Alan Macfarlane (ed.) (Oxford: Oxford University Press, 1976); and of course Samuel Pepys, *The Diary of Samuel Pepys*, Robert Latham (ed.) (London: HarperCollins, 1970). (*The Diary of Elizabeth Pepys*, ed. Dale Spender (1991) has befuddled generations of students, but is a literary fiction.) Printed primary sources are now most easily accessed online via *Early English Books Online* (http://eebo.chadwyck.com/home) and the *English Broadside Ballad Archive* (http://ebba.english.ucsb.edu/). The *Old Bailey Online* (http://www.oldbaileyonline.org/) provides a marvellous searchable resource for London's legal records from the late seventeenth century.

There are several general books on early modern women, of which the outstanding is Sara Mendelson and Patricia Crawford, *Women in Early Modern England 1550–1720* (Oxford: Oxford University Press, 2000). Amanda Capern, *The Historical Study of Women: England 1500–1700* (Basingstoke: Palgrave Macmillan, 2008) provides an excellent guide to the field. Anthony Fletcher,

Gender, Sex, and Subordination in England, 1500–1800 (New Haven, CT and London: Yale University Press, 1995) is the only one to take gender rather than women as its category of analysis. Manhood is explored by Alexandra Shepard, *Meanings of Manhood in Early Modern England* (Oxford: Oxford University Press, 2006) and 'From Anxious Patriarchs to Refined Gentlemen? Manhood in Britain, circa 1500–1700', *The Journal of British Studies*, 44 (2005), 281–295; see also Elizabeth Foyster, *Manhood in Early Modern England: Honour, Sex and Marriage* (Harlow: Longman, 1999). A more cultural approach is taken by works covering the later period, notably Tim Hitchcock and Michele Cohen (eds) *English Masculinities, 1660–1800* (Harlow: Longman, 1999).

On bodies, Thomas Laqueur, *Making Sex: Body and Gender from the Greeks to Freud* (Cambridge, MA: Harvard University Press, 1992) has been influential in presenting the transformation in models of sexual difference; for another narrative of change see Mary Fissell, *Vernacular Bodies: The Politics of Reproduction in Early Modern England* (Oxford: Oxford University Press, 2006). Other aspects of body and gender are explored in Gail Kern Paster, *The Body Embarrassed: Drama and the Disciplines of Shame in Early Modern England* (Ithaca, NY: Cornell University Press, 1993); Laura Gowing, *Common Bodies: Women, Touch and Power in Seventeenth-Century England* (New Haven, CT and London: Yale University Press, 2003); Ruth Gilbert, *Early Modern Hermaphrodites: Sex and Other Stories* (Basingstoke: Palgrave Macmillan, 2002); Patricia Crawford, 'Attitudes To Menstruation in Seventeenth-Century England', *Past & Present*, 91 (1981), 47–73. Ageing is a growing field: see the essays in Lynn Botelho and Pat Thane (eds) *Women and Ageing in British Society Since 1500* (Harlow: Longman, 2001), and discussions of age in Shepard, *Meanings of Manhood*. Margaret Sommerville, *Sex and Subjection: Attitudes To Women in Early-Modern Society* (London: Hodder Arnold, 1995) is a thorough account of rationales for female subordination.

The literature of manners and civility is oddly short on reflections on gender, but there are brief discussions in Anna Bryson, *From Courtesy To Civility: Changing Codes of Conduct in Early Modern England* (Oxford: Oxford University Press, 1998) and a fuller analysis in Sara Mendelson, 'The Civility of Women', in Peter Burke *et al.* (eds) *Civil Histories: Essays presented to Sir Keith Thomas* (Oxford: Oxford University Press, 2000). Philip Carter analyses the forms of manly politeness in the later period in *Men and the Emergence of Polite Society: Britain 1660–1800* (Harlow: Longman, 2001). On gesture, see John Walter, 'Gesturing at Authority: Deciphering the Gestural Code of Early Modern England' in Michael Braddick (ed.) *The Politics of Gesture: Historical Perspectives* (Oxford: Oxford University Press, 2009).

While the history of ethnic minorities in this period remains scanty, there are excellent recent works on ideas of race: Jonathan Burton and Ania Loomba (eds) *Race in Early Modern England: A Documentary Companion*

(Basingstoke: Palgrave, 2007) and Kim Hall, *Things of Darkness: Economies of Race and Gender in Early Modern England* (Ithaca, NY: Cornell University Press, 1995). Some interesting fragments are recorded in the Guildhall Library's list of Black and Asian people in City of London records, at http://www.history.ac.uk/gh/baentries.htm.

On clothes, there is now a rich analysis attentive to gender: see Susan Vincent' *Dressing the Elite: Clothes in Early Modern England* (London: Berg, 2003); Ann Rosalind Jones and Peter Stallybrass, *Renaissance Clothing and the Materials of Memory* (Cambridge: Cambridge University Press, 2000); David Kuchta, 'The Semiotics of Masculinity in Renaissance England', in James Turner (ed.) *Sexuality and Gender in Early Modern Europe* (Cambridge: Cambridge University Press, 1993); Jean Howard, 'Crossdressing, The Theatre, and Gender Struggle in Early Modern England' *Shakespeare Quarterly* 39 (1988), 418–40.

Two useful introductions to sexualities in the period are Katherine Crawford, *European Sexualities, 1400–1800* (Cambridge: Cambridge University Press, 2007) and Barry Reay, *Popular Cultures in England 1550–1750* (Harlow: Longman, 1998). More specifically two articles in *Gender and History* raise important issues: Miranda Chaytor, 'Husband(ry): Narratives of Rape in the Seventeenth Century', *Gender & History*, 73 (1995), 378–407 and Garthine Walker, 'Rereading Rape and Sexual Violence in Early Modern England', *Gender & History*, 10/1 (1998), 1–25. On the later seventeenth century, James Grantham Turner's *Libertines and Radicals in Early Modern London* (Cambridge: Cambridge University Press, 2002) surveys a huge range of erotic texts and activities; David Turner's *Fashioning Adultery: Gender, Sex and Civility in England, 1660–1740* (Cambridge: Cambridge University Press, 2002) illuminates the changing meanings of adultery and cuckoldry; Faramerz Dabhoiwala, 'Lust and Liberty', *Past & Present* 207 (2010), 89–179, describes an arc of moral change. On the demographic ground, illegitimacy rates are examined by Richard Adair, *Courtship, Illegitimacy, and Marriage in Early Modern England* (Manchester: Manchester University Press, 1996), which also reviews earlier literature. On masturbation see Thomas Laqueur, *Solitary Sex: A Cultural History of Masturbation* (New York: MIT Press, 2003). Little critical history exists on prostitution in this period, but see Paul Griffiths, 'The Structure of Prostitution in Elizabethan London', *Continuity and Change*, 8/1 (1993), 39–63, and references in his *Lost Londons: Change, Crime, and Control in the Capital City, 1550–1660* (Cambridge: Cambridge University Press, 2008).

On male homosexuality, the work of Alan Bray remains central, beginning with *Homosexuality in Renaissance England* (New York: Columbia University Press, 1982), and his later work on friendship, including 'Homosexuality and the Signs of Male Friendship in Elizabethan England', *History Workshop Journal*, 29 (1990), 1–19. Randolph Trumbach's argument on the changing configurations of sexuality in the late seventeenth century is summed up in his 'Sex, Gender and Sexual Identity in Modern Culture: Male Sodomy and Female Prostitution in Enlightenment England', *Journal of the History of Sexuality*, 2 (1991), 186–203. On lesbianism see Valerie Traub, *The Renaissance of Lesbianism in Early Modern England* (Cambridge: Cambridge University Press, 2002), and on the Pulter case, Patricia Crawford and Sara Heller Mendelson, 'Sexual Identities in Early Modern England: The Marriage of Two Women in 1680', *Gender & History*, 7/3 (1995), 362–77.

Reproduction is covered from a number of angles, mostly focusing on women. Two edited collections offer a range of perspectives on motherhood: Valerie Fildes (eds) *Women as Mothers in Pre-industrial England* (London: Routledge, 1990), and Naomi J. Miller (eds) *Maternal Measures: Figuring Caregiving in the Early Modern Period* (Aldershot: Ashgate, 2000). David Cressy's *Birth, Marriage, and Death: Ritual, Religion, and the Life-Cycle in Tudor and Stuart England* (Oxford: Oxford University Press, 1997) explains the early modern approach to life stages, including discussions of baptism and churching, which has been the subject of extensive other articles.

Gendered mental worlds are most likely to be discussed in relation to dreams and madness: see Michael MacDonald, *Mystical Bedlam: Madness, Anxiety and Healing in Seventeenth-Century England* (Cambridge: Cambridge University Press, 1983); Katharine Hodgkin, *Madness in Seventeenth-Century Autobiography* (Basingstoke: Palgrave, 2007); Patricia Crawford, 'Women's Dreams in Early Modern England', *History Workshop Journal*, 49 (2000), 129–42. The notion of self-mastery in relation to masculinity is explored by Katharine Hodgkin, 'Thomas Whythorne and the Problems of Mastery', *History Workshop Journal*, 29 (1990), 20–41.

On reading and writing, see David Cressy, *Literacy and the Social Order: Reading and Writing in Tudor and Stuart England* (Cambridge: Cambridge University Press, 1980) and Heidi Brayman Hackel, *Reading Material in Early Modern England: Print, Gender, and Literacy* (Cambridge: Cambridge University Press, 2005). The impact of gender on constructions of the self for women is examined in much recent work on autobiography: see for example Helen Wilcox (ed.) *Women and Literature in Britain, 1500–1700* (Cambridge: Cambridge University Press, 1996). There is an extensive critical literature on women's writing of the period: one starting point is Laura Lunger Knoppers, *The Cambridge Companion To Early Modern Women's Writing* (Cambridge: Cambridge University Press, 2009). On letters, James Daybell, *Women Letter-Writers in Tudor England* (Oxford: Oxford University Press, 2006) and Susan Whyman, *Sociability and Power in Late-Stuart England: The Cultural Worlds of the Verneys, 1660–1720* (Oxford: Oxford University Press, 1999) cover each end of the period.

For other forms of print culture, see Pamela Allen Brown, *Better a Shrew Than a Sheep: Women, Drama, and the Culture of Jest in Early Modern England*

(Ithaca, NY: Cornell University Press, 2002); Tim Reinke-Williams, 'Misogyny, Jest-Books and Male Youth Culture in Seventeenth-Century England', *Gender & History*, 21/2 (2009), 324–39; Elizabeth Foyster, 'A Laughing Matter?: Marital Discord and Gender Control in Seventeenth-Century England', *Rural History*, 4 (1993), 5–21; Joy Wiltenburg, *Disorderly Women and Female Power in the Street Literature of Early Modern England and Germany* (Charlottesville, VA: University of Virginia Press, 1992); Helen Berry, *Gender, Society and Print Culture in Late Stuart England: The Cultural World of the Athenian Mercury* (Aldershot: Ashgate, 2003). On the gender debates, see Diane Purkiss, 'Material Girls: The Seventeenth-century Woman Debate', in Clare Brant and Diane Purkiss (eds) *Women, Texts and Histories, 1575–1760* (London: Routledge, 1992), and Cristina Malcolmson and Mihoko Suzuki (eds) *Debating Gender in Early Modern England, 1500–1700* (Basingstoke: Palgrave, 2002). Much has been published recently on Mary Astell, between Ruth Perry, *The Celebrated Mary Astell: An Early English Feminist* (Chicago, IL: University of Chicago Press, 1986) and William Kolbrener and Michal Michelson (eds) *Mary Astell: Reason, Gender, Faith* (Aldershot: Ashgate, 2007). On the Enlightenment, see the essays in Sarah Knott and Barbara Taylor (eds) *Women, Gender, and Enlightenment* (Basingstoke: Palgrave, 2005).

The intersection of religion and gender has been explored mainly in relation to women. Patricia Crawford, *Women and Religion in England 1500–1720* (London: Routledge, 1993), and later Christine Peters, *Patterns of Piety: Women, Gender and Religion in Late Medieval and Reformation England* (Cambridge: Cambridge University Press, 2003), consider the distinctiveness of women's spiritual experiences. Megan Hickerson, 'Gospelling Sisters "goinge Up and Downe": John Foxe and Disorderly Women', *Sixteenth Century Journal*, 35/4 (2005), 1035–51, examines Foxe's women. Frances Dolan, *Whores of Babylon: Catholicism, Gender, and Seventeenth-Century Print Culture* (Ithaca, NY: Cornell University Press, 1999) analyses gender in both Catholicism and anti-Catholicism.

Households and families have a huge bibliography, and marriage in particular is at the heart of most of the general works on women and manhood mentioned elsewhere, especially Fletcher, Capp, and Foyster. In addition see Will Coster's Seminar Study, *Family and Kinship in England, 1450–1800* (Harlow: Longman, 2001); some new perspectives are represented in Helen Berry and Elizabeth Foyster (eds) *The Family in Early Modern England* (Cambridge: Cambridge University Press, 2007). Several books use legal records to examine violence, adultery and courtship cases; Susan Dwyer Amussen, *An Ordered Society: Gender and Class in Early Modern England* (Oxford: Oxford University Press, 1988); Martin Ingram, *Church Courts, Sex and Marriage in England, 1570–1640* (Cambridge: Cambridge University Press, 1990); Laura Gowing, *Domestic Dangers: Women, Words, and Sex in Early Modern London* (Oxford:

Oxford University Press, 1996); Joanne Bailey, *Unquiet Lives: Marriage and Marriage Breakdown in England, 1660–1800* (Cambridge: Cambridge University Press, 2003).

On household advice, see Anthony Fletcher, 'The Protestant Idea of Marriage in Early Modern England', in Anthony Fletcher and Peter Roberts (eds) *Religion, Culture and Society in Early Modern Britain* (Cambridge: Cambridge University Press, 1994), and Patricia Crawford, 'Katharine and Philip Henry and their Children: A Case Study in Family Ideology', in her *Blood, Bodies and Families in Early Modern England* (Harlow: Longman, 2004). On space and building, recent works of interest include Amanda Flather, *Gender and Space in Early Modern England* (Woodbridge: Boydell Press, 2007) and Anne Laurence, 'Women Using Building in Seventeenth-Century England: A Question of Sources?', *Transactions of the Royal Historical Society, 6th Ser.,* 13 (2003), 293–303.

The relationship of gender to work, as well as the history of women's work, is still understudied: case studies are better than general works, for example Judith Bennett, *Ale, Beer and Brewsters in England: Women's Work in a Changing World, 1300–1600* (Oxford and New York: Oxford University Press, 1996); Penelope Lane *et al.* (eds), *Women, Work and Wages in England, 1600–1850* (Woodbridge: Boydell Press, 2004); and the essays on women's medical work in Margaret Pelling, *The Common Lot: Sickness, Medical Occupations and the Urban Poor in Early Modern England* (Harlow: Longman, 1998). On the earlier period, see Margerie McIntosh, *Working Women in English Society 1300–1620* (Cambridge: Cambridge University Press, 2005). The fullest work on property is Amy Erickson's *Women and Property In Early Modern England* (London: Routledge, 1993); on lending and investment, see Craig Muldrew, ' "A Mutual Assent of Her Mind"? Women, Debt, Litigation and Contract in Early Modern England', *History Workshop Journal*, 55 (2003), 47–71, and Judith Spicksley, 'Usury Legislation, Cash and Credit: the Development of the Female Investor in the Late Tudor and Stuart Periods', *Economic History Review*, 61: 2 (2008), 277–301. An innovative comparative perspective on marital economy is provided in Maria Ågren and Amy Erickson (eds) *The Marital Economy in Scandinavia and Britain, 1400–1900* (Aldershot: Ashgate, 2005), and Erickson's article, 'Coverture and Capitalism' in *History Workshop Journal* 59 (2005), 1–16, lays out the thesis of the relationship between the restrictions of property law and the development of financial markets.

Single women have attracted more attention than men. Amy Froide's *Never Married: Singlewomen in Early Modern England* (Oxford: Oxford University Press, 2005) offers a comprehensive examination of spinster opportunities; see also Pamela Sharpe, 'Dealing With Love: The Ambiguous Independence of the Single Woman in Early Modern England', *Gender & History*, 11/2 (1999), 209–32, and Judith Spicksley, ' "Fly with a Duck in Thy Mouth": Single Women as Sources of Credit in Seventeenth-Century England', *Social History* 32 (2007), 187–207. Other relevant essays on women, work and other roles feature in a special issue of *Women's History Review*, 19 (2010). On widows, Barbara Todd's, 'Demographic Determinism and Female Agency: The Remarrying Widow Reconsidered . . . Again', *Continuity and Change*, 9/3 (1994), 421–50, sums up and continues a debate on demographic assumptions, and more generally see Sandra Cavallo and Lyndan Warner (eds) *Widowhood in Medieval and Early Modern Europe* (Harlow: Longman, 1999).

Servants and apprentices are examined in Paul Griffiths, *Youth and Authority: Formative Experiences in England 1560–1640* (Oxford: Oxford University Press, 1996); Ilana K. Ben-Amos, *Adolescence and Youth in Early Modern England* (New Haven, CT and London: Yale University Press, 1994); Laura Gowing, 'The Haunting of Susan Lay: Servants and Mistresses in Seventeenth-century England', *Gender & History*, 14/2 (2002), 183–201; Ann Kussmaul, *Servants in Husbandry in Early Modern England* (Cambridge: Cambridge University Press, 1981); Tim Meldrum, *Domestic Service and Gender, 1660–1750: Life and Work in the London Household* (Harlow: Longman, 2000).

The gender dynamics of communities are discussed in Keith Wrightson, 'The Politics of the Parish in Early Modern England', in Adam Fox *et al.* (eds) *The Experience of Authority in Early Modern England* (Basingstoke: Palgrave, 1996), and Bernard Capp, *When Gossips Meet: Women, Family and Neighbourhood in Early Modern England* (Oxford: Oxford University Press, 2003). Michael Braddick, *State Formation in Early Modern England, c.1550–1700* (Cambridge: Cambridge University Press, 2000), considers the patriarchal dimensions of state formation, and his edited collection, *Negotiating Power in Early Modern Society: Order, Hierarchy, and Subordination in Britain and Ireland* (Cambridge: Cambridge University Press, 2001) contains several relevant pieces. On the roles of women in parochial government and work, see Diane Willen, 'Women in the Public Sphere in Early Modern England: The Case of the Urban Working Poor', *The Sixteenth Century Journal*, 19 (1988), 559–75; Richelle Munkhoff, 'Searchers of the Dead: Authority, Marginality, and the Interpretation of Plague in England, 1574–1665', *Gender & History*, 11/1 (1999), 1–29. Much of the historiography of poverty says little explicit about gender, but see Tim Wales, 'Poverty, Poor Relief and the Life-Cycle: Some Evidence From Seventeenth-Century Norfolk', in Richard Smith, ed., *Land, Kinship and Life-cycle* (Cambridge: Cambridge University Press, 1984); Patricia Crawford, *Parents of Poor Children in England, 1580–1800* (Oxford: Oxford University Press, 2010).

On communal regulation of gender relations, see David Underdown, 'The Taming of the Scold: The Enforcement of Patriarchal Authority in Early Modern England', in Anthony Fletcher and John Stevenson (eds) *Order and Disorder in Early Modern England* (Cambridge: Cambridge University Press,

1985) and Martin Ingram, 'Ridings, Rough Music, and Mocking Rhymes in Early Modern England', in Barry Reay, ed., *Popular Culture in Seventeenth-Century England* (London: Routledge, 1985). Reputation is examined in a special issue of *Transactions of the Royal Historical Society*, 1995; see also Steve Hindle, 'The Shaming of Margaret Knowsley: Gossip, Gender and the Experience of Authority in Early Modern England', *Continuity and Change*, 9/3 (1994), 391–419, the works by Amussen, Gowing and Ingram referenced under marriage above, and Bernard Capp, 'The Double Standard Revisited: Plebeian Women and Male Sexual Reputation In Early Modern England', *Past & Present*, 162 (1999), 70–100. Non-sexual aspects of reputation are discussed in Alexandra Shepard, 'Honesty, Worth and Gender in Early Modern England, 1560–1640', in Jonathan Barry (ed.) *Identity and Agency in England, 1500–1800* (Basingstoke: Palgrave, 2004).

On crime, law and gender, Jenny Kermode and Garthine Walker's collection of essays contains some key articles: *Women, Crime and the Courts in Early Modern England* (London: Routledge, 1994); more specific studies include Garthine Walker, *Crime, Gender and Social Order in Early Modern England* (Cambridge: Cambridge University Press, 2003); Tim Stretton, *Women Waging Law in Elizabethan England* (Cambridge: Cambridge University Press, 1998). On witchcraft, begin with Diane Purkiss, 'Women's Stories of Witchcraft in Early Modern England: The House, the Body, the Child', *Gender & History*, 7/3 (1995), 408–32; Malcolm Gaskill, 'Masculinity and Witchcraft in Seventeenth-Century England', in Alison Rowlands (eds) *Witchcraft and Masculinities in Early Modern Europe* (Basingstoke: Palgrave, 2009); Deborah Willis, *Malevolent Nurture: Witch-Hunting and Maternal Power In Early Modern England* (Ithaca, NY: Cornell University Press, 1995); James Sharpe, *Instruments of Darkness: Witchcraft in Early Modern England* (Harmondsworth: Penguin, 1997).

The history of friendship has largely focused on men: see for example Alan Bray and Michel Rey, 'The Body of the Friend: Continuity and Change in Masculine Friendship in the Seventeenth Century', in Tim Hitchcock and Michele Cohen (eds) *English Masculinities, 1660–1800* (Harlow: Longman, 1999). A variety of friendship bonds are discussed in Laura Gowing, Michael Hunter and Miri Rubin (eds) *Love, Friendship, and Faith in Europe, 1300–1800* (Basingstoke: Palgrave, 2005). Relationships between women are discussed in the essays, mostly with a literary focus, in Susan Frye and Karen Robertson (eds) *Maids and Mistresses, Cousins and Queens: Women's Alliances in Early Modern England* (New York: Oxford University Press, 1999).

On politics, Hilda L. Smith (ed.) *Women Writers and the Early Modern British Political Tradition* (Cambridge: Cambridge University Press, 1998) provides a wide-ranging set of relevant essays; see also James Daybell (ed.) *Women and Politics In Early Modern England, 1450–1700* (Aldershot: Ashgate, 2004). Hilda Smith's *All Men and Both Sexes: Gender, Politics, and the False Universal* in *England, 1640–1832* (University Park, PA: Pennsylvania State University Press, 2002) provides a powerful narrative of the exclusion of the feminine from the political sphere. On citizenship and participation, see two suggestive articles by Patricia Crawford, 'Public Duty, Conscience and Women in Early Modern England', in John Morrill *et al.* (eds) *Public Duty and Private Conscience in Seventeenth-Century England* (Oxford: Oxford University Press, 1992) and '"The Poorest She": Women and Citizenship in Early Modern England', in Michael Mendle (ed.) *The Putney Debates of 1647: The Army, the Levellers and the English State* (Cambridge: Cambridge University Press, 2001).

All works on protest have something to say on women's role; a fine starting point is Andy Wood, *Riot, Rebellion and Popular Politics in Early Modern England* (Basingstoke: Palgrave, 2001). More specifically see Wood, '"Poore Men Woll Speke One Daye": Plebeian Languages of Deference and Defiance in England, c.1520–1640', in Tim Harris (ed.) *The Politics of the Excluded., c.1500–1850* (Basingstoke: Palgrave, 2001); on Ann Carter see John Walter, 'Grain Riots and Popular Attitudes to the Law: Maldon and the Crisis of 1629', in his *Crowds and Popular Politics in Early Modern England* (Manchester: Manchester University Press, 2006), and on Dorothy Dawson see Andy Wood, 'Subordination, Solidarity and the Limits of Popular Agency in a Yorkshire Valley c.1596–1615', *Past & Present*, 193 (2006), 41–72. The gender politics of sedition are analysed in Andy Wood, 'The Queen is "a Goggyll Eyed Hoore": Gender and Seditious Speech in Early Modern England', in Nicholas Tyacke (ed.) *The English Revolution c.1590–1720: Politics, Religion and Communities* (Manchester: Manchester University Press, 2007) and Dagmar Freist, 'The King's Crown is the Whore of Babylon: Politics, Gender and Communication in Mid-Seventeenth-Century England', *Gender & History*, 7/3 (1995), 457–81; for an extensive survey of seditious words, see David Cressy's *Dangerous Talk: Scandalous, Seditious, and Treasonable Speech in Pre-Modern England* (Oxford: Oxford University Press, 2010). Discussions of gender and monarchy have focused on Elizabeth I, on which see Carole Levin *'The Heart and Stomach of a King': Elizabeth I and the Politics of Sex and Power* (Philadelphia, PA: Pennsylvania State University Press, 1994). Broadening the perspective are the articles by Judith Richards, including 'Mary Tudor as "Sole Quene"?: Gendering Tudor Monarchy', *Historical Journal*, 40 (1997), 895–924, and 'The English Accession of James VI : "National" Identity, Gender and the Personal Monarchy of England', *English Historical Review*, 117/472 (2002), 513–35, and Anne McLaren, 'Gender, Religion, and Early Modern Nationalism: Elizabeth I, Mary Queen of Scots, and the Genesis of English Anti-Catholicism', *The American Historical Review*, 107/3 (2002), 739–67. Cynthia Herrup unpicks the gendering of monarchy in 'The King's Two Genders', *Journal of British Studies*, 45/3 (2006), 493–510, and the masculinity of monarchs is analysed in Rachel Weil, 'Sometimes a Sceptre is Only a Sceptre: Pornography and Politics in Restoration England', in Lynn Hunt (ed.) *The Invention of Pornography* (New York: Zone Books 1996), and Diane Purkiss, *Literature, Gender and Politics During the English Civil War* (Cambridge: Cambridge University Press, 2005).

Gender in the Civil War now has a rich historiography. Ann Hughes's work has laid out new terrain for gender and politics: see Ann Hughes, 'Gender and Politics in Leveller Literature', in Susan Amussen and Mark Kishlansky (eds) *Political Culture and Cultural Politics in Early Modern England* (Manchester: Manchester University Press, 1995); 'Men, the "public" and the "private" in the English Revolution', in Peter Lake and Steven Pincus (eds) *The Politics of the Public Sphere in Early Modern England*, (Manchester: Manchester University Press, 2007); and Ann Hughes's latest book *Gender and the English Revolution* (London: Routledge, 2011). The essential work on women petitioners remains Patricia Higgins, 'The Reactions of Women, with Special Reference to Women Petitioners', in Brian Manning (ed.) *Politics, Religion and the English Civil War* (London: Hodder & Stoughton, 1973). On the pamphlet literature, see Sharon Achinstein, 'Women on Top in the Pamphlet Literature of the English Revolution', *Women's Studies*, 24 (1994), 131–63; Susan Wiseman, ' "Adam, the Father of all Flesh," Porno-political Rhetoric and Political Theory in and after the English Civil War', *Prose Studies: History, Theory, Criticism*, 14 (1991), 134–57; and most recently, Marcus Nevitt, *Women and the Pamphlet Culture of Revolutionary England, 1640–1660* (Aldershot: Ashgate, 2006). Phyllis Mack's definitive work on female prophets, *Visionary Women: Ecstatic Prophecy in Seventeenth-Century England* (Berkeley: University of California Press, 1995), is also relevant to many other aspects of gender relations. Useful approaches to women's writing in the civil war are articulated in Hilary Hinds, *God's Englishwomen: Seventeenth-Century Radical Sectarian Writing and Feminist Criticism* (Manchester: Manchester University Press, 1996), and Susan Wiseman, *Conspiracy and Virtue: Women, Writing, and Politics in Seventeenth-Century England* (Oxford: Oxford University Press, 2006).

On the configurations of family in Stuart politics, see Rachel Weil, *Political Passions: Gender, the Family, and Political Argument in England, 1680–1714* (Manchester: Manchester University Press, 1999); for another perspective on the same period see Melissa Mowry, *The Bawdy Politic in Stuart England, 1660–1714: Political Pornography and Prostitution* (Aldershot: Ashgate, 2004).

References

Beauvoir, Simone de (1972) *The Second Sex*, transl. Howard Parshley. Harmondsworth: Penguin.

Bennett, Judith M. (1996) *Ale, Beer and Brewsters in England: Women's Work in a Changing World, 1300–1600*. Oxford & New York: Oxford University Press.

Bennett, Judith M. (2006) *History Matters: Patriarchy and the Challenge of Feminism*. Philadelphia, PA: University of Pennsylvania Press.

Bray, Alan (2003) *The Friend*. Chicago: Chicago University Press.

Breitenberg, Mark (1996) *Anxious Masculinity in Early Modern England*. Cambridge: Cambridge University Press.

Bryson, Anna (1998) *From Courtesy to Civility: Changing Codes of Conduct in Early Modern England*. Oxford: Clarendon Press.

Capp, Bernard (2007) 'Republican Reformation: Family, Community and the State in Interregnum Middlesex, 1649–1660', in Helen Berry and Elizabeth Foyster (eds) *The Family in Early Modern England*. Cambridge: Cambridge University Press.

Carlton, Charles (1992) *Going to the Wars: The Experience of the British Civil Wars, 1638–1651*. London: Taylor & Francis.

Connell, Raewyn (2009) *Gender*. Cambridge: Polity.

Consitt, Frances (1933) *The London Weavers' Company*. Oxford: Clarendon Press.

Cowan, Brian (2001) 'What Was Masculine About the Public Sphere? Gender and the Coffeehouse Milieu in Post-Restoration England', *History Workshop Journal*, 51: 127–57.

Crawford, Patricia (2001) '"The Poorest She": Women and Citizenship in Early Modern England', in Michael Mendle (ed.) *The Putney Debates of 1647: The Army, the Levellers and the English State*. Cambridge: Cambridge University Press.

Earle, Peter (1989) 'The Female Labour Market in London in the Late Seventeenth and Early Eighteenth Centuries', *Economic History Review*, 42/3: 328–53.

Elias, Norbert (1969) *The Civilizing Process*, transl. Edmund Jephcott. Oxford: Blackwell.

Erickson, Amy Louise (2005) 'Coverture and Capitalism', *History Workshop Journal*, 59: 1–16.

Froide, Amy M. (2005) *Never Married: Singlewomen in Early Modern England*. Oxford: Oxford University Press.

Harris, Frances (2003) *Transformations of Love: The Friendship of Margaret Evelyn and John Godolphin*. Oxford: Oxford University Press.

Harvey, Karen and Alexandra Shepard (2005) 'What Have Historians Done with Masculinity? Reflections on Five Centuries of British History, circa 1500–1950', *Journal of British Studies*, 44/2: 274–80.

Herrup, Cynthia (2006) 'The King's Two Genders', *Journal of British Studies*, 45/3: 493–510.

Hitchcock, Tim (1996) 'Sex and Gender: Redefining Sex in Eighteenth-Century England', *History Workshop Journal*, 41: 72–90.

Hughes, Ann (2011) *Gender and the English Revolution*. London: Routledge.

Ingram, Martin (1994) ' "Scolding Women Cucked or Washed": A Crisis in Gender Relations in Early Modern England?', in Garthine Walker and Jenny Kermode (eds) *Women, Crime and the Courts in Early Modern England*. London: Routledge.

Kelly-Gadol, Joan (1977) 'Did Women Have a Renaissance?' in Renate Blumenthal and Claudia Koonz (eds) *Becoming Visible: Women in European History*. Boston, MA: Houghton Mifflin.

Laqueur, Thomas (1990) *Making Sex: Body and Gender From the Greeks To Freud*. Cambridge, MA: Harvard University Press.

Loomba, Ania and Jonathan Burton (eds) (2007) *Race in Early Modern England: A Documentary Companion*. Basingstoke: Palgrave.

Mendelson, Sara Heller and Patricia Crawford (1995) 'Sexual Identities in Early Modern England: The Marriage of Two Women in 1680', *Gender & History*, 7/3: 362–77.

Morrill, John (1999) *Revolt in the Provinces: The People of England and the Tragedies of War, 1630–48*, 2nd edn. Harlow: Longman.

Pateman, Carole (1988) *The Sexual Contract*. Stanford, CA: Stanford University Press.

Peters, Christine (2003) *Patterns of Piety: Women, Gender and Religion in Late Medieval and Reformation England*. Cambridge: Cambridge University Press.

Richards, Judith (1999) 'Love and a Female Monarch: The Case of Elizabeth Tudor', *Journal of British Studies*, 38/2: 133–60.

Richards, Judith (1997) 'Mary Tudor as "Sole Quene"?: Gendering Tudor Monarchy', *Historical Journal*, 40/4: 895–924.

St Botolph Bishopsgate Parish Register 1558–1628, London Metropolitan Archives MS 04515/1.

Sharpe, Pamela (1999) 'Dealing with Love: The Ambiguous Independence of the Single Woman in Early Modern England', *Gender & History*, 11/3: 209–32.

Stone, Lawrence (1977) *The Family, Sex and Marriage in England, 1500–1800*. London: Weidenfeld and Nicholson.

Thomas, Keith (1958) 'Women and the Civil War Sects', *Past & Present*, 13: 42–62.

Thomas, Keith (1959): 'The Double Standard', *Journal of the History of Ideas*, 20: 195–216.

Thomas, Keith (1978) 'The Puritans and Adultery: The Act of 1650', in D. H. Pennington and Keith Thomas (eds) *Puritans and Revolutionaries: Essays in Seventeenth-Century History presented to Christopher Hill*. Oxford: Oxford University Press.

Tittler, Robert (1994) 'Money-Lending in the West Midlands: The Activities of Joyce Jefferies, 1638–1649', *Historical Research*, 67: 249–63.

Underdown, David (1985) 'The Taming of the Scold: The Enforcement of Patriarchal Authority in Early Modern England', in Anthony Fletcher and John Stevenson (eds) *Order and Disorder in Early Modern England*. Cambridge: Cambridge University Press.

Walby, Sylvia (1989) 'Theorising Patriarchy', *Sociology*, 23: 213–234.

Walker, Garthine (2003) *Crime, Gender and Social Order in Early Modern England*. Cambridge: Cambridge University Press.

Weil, Rachel (1999) *Political Passions: Gender, the Family, and Political Argument in England, 1680–1714*. Manchester: Manchester University Press.

Wiesner-Hanks, Merry E. (2008) 'Do Women Need the Renaissance?', *Gender & History*, 20/3: 539–57.

Wrightson, Keith (1980) 'Two Concepts of Order: Justices, Constables and Jurymen in Seventeenth-Century England', in John Brewer and John Styles (eds) *An Ungovernable People: The English and their Law in the Seventeenth and Eighteenth Centuries*. London: Hutchinson, pp. 21–46.

Wrigley, Edward Anthony and Roger Schofield (1981) *The Population History of England, 1541–1871: A Reconstruction*. Cambridge: Cambridge University Press.

Index